ON DISMANTLING SETTLER COLONIALISM

UTP insights

UTP Insights is an innovative collection of brief books offering accessible introductions to the ideas that shape our world. Each volume in the series focuses on a contemporary issue, offering a fresh perspective anchored in scholarship. Spanning a broad range of disciplines in the social sciences and humanities, the books in the UTP Insights series contribute to public discourse and debate and provide a valuable resource for instructors and students.

For a list of the books published in this series, see page 249.

On Dismantling Settler Colonialism

An Insider's Perspective on Reconciliation with *Indigenous Peoples*

JOHN A. OLTHUIS

UNIVERSITY OF TORONTO PRESS
Toronto Buffalo London

© University of Toronto Press 2025
Toronto Buffalo London
utppublishing.com
Printed and bound by CPI Group (UK) Ltd, Croydon, CR0 4YY

All rights reserved. No part of this publication may be reproduced, stored in or introduced into a retrieval system, or transmitted in any form or by any means (electronic, mechanical, photocopying, recording, or otherwise) without the prior written permission of both the copyright owner and the above publisher of this book.

ISBN 978-1-4875-6922-8 (cloth)   ISBN 978-1-4875-6925-9 (EPUB)
                                    ISBN 978-1-4875-6924-2 (PDF)

___

Library and Archives Canada Cataloguing in Publication

Title: On dismantling settler colonialism : an insider's perspective on reconciliation with Indigenous peoples / John A. Olthuis.
Names: Olthuis, John A., 1940- author
Series: UTP insights.
Description: Series statement: UTP insights | Includes bibliographical references and index.
Identifiers: Canadiana (print) 2025028913X | Canadiana (ebook) 20250289164 | ISBN 9781487569228 (cloth) | ISBN 9781487569242 (PDF) | ISBN 9781487569259 (EPUB)
Subjects: LCSH: Indigenous peoples—Canada—Social conditions. | LCSH: Reconciliation—Canada. | LCSH: Settler colonialism—Canada.
Classification: LCC E78.C2 O486 2025 | DDC 971.004/97—dc23

___

Cover design: Heng Wee Tan
Cover image: George Littlechild, "Heartbeat Mother Earth," 24 × 24, Mixed Media, 2014

We wish to acknowledge the land on which the University of Toronto Press operates. This land is the traditional territory of the Wendat, the Anishnaabeg, the Haudenosaunee, the Métis, and the Mississaugas of the Credit First Nation.

University of Toronto Press acknowledges the financial support of the Government of Canada, the Canada Council for the Arts, and the Ontario Arts Council, an agency of the Government of Ontario, for its publishing activities.

  Canada Council   Conseil des Arts
        for the Arts   du Canada

ONTARIO ARTS COUNCIL
CONSEIL DES ARTS DE L'ONTARIO
an Ontario government agency
un organisme du gouvernement de l'Ontario

Funded by the   Financé par le
Government   gouvernement
of Canada   du Canada

For Lois, my Rock and Soft Place

With deep gratitude to self-determining Indigenous Peoples

With deep hope that Settler Colonialism will be Dismantled

Contents

Foreword, Bob Rae   ix

Foreword, Stan McKay   xiv

Foreword, Aaron Mills   xv

Acknowledgments   xvi

Preface: Fifty Years of Walking Alongside First Nations   xviii

1 The Dene Nation and the Mackenzie Valley Pipeline   1
2 Mercury Pollution and the Grassy Narrows Fight for Justice   36
3 The Aboriginal Peoples Constitutional Conferences   65
4 Paradise Threatened: The Innu of Labrador Fight for Their Homeland – Nitassinan   88
5 The Struggle of the Teme-Augama Anishnabai for Old-Growth Trees and Their Land   130

6 The Struggle for Healing Among Mushuau
Innu of Labrador   151

7 The Road Home: The Innu of Labrador and Modern
Treaty Negotiations   168

8 Groundbreaking Blueprints for Reconciliation with
Indigenous Peoples and Nations   184

9 Doing Our Part for Reconciliation with HEART   198

Notes   227

Index   235

Foreword

BOB RAE

John Olthuis has done us that great favour of writing an invaluable memoir, and, like all things about him, he downplays his own central role in the events and turbulence he has described so well. I have had the pleasure of knowing John for almost half a century and was his law partner and close collaborator from 2014 to 2020 at the law firm he founded with Nancy Kleer and Roger Townshend.

In this brief introduction I want to say something about John as a person, because he would never say it about himself, and also about the extraordinary times in which he has lived and worked. He is a man of deep faith, which he does not so much talk about as simply practice. As the hymn says, "he who would valour see, let him come hither."

John's life has indeed been a pilgrimage. When he began his career after law school at the University of Alberta, there were few who joined him – most lawyers knew or cared little about Indigenous rights, and the idea of building a practice with that as the focus seemed far-fetched. But the social gospel which has been such a key part of his life would not let him take the path of conformity. Instead, he chose one of joy as well as struggle.

As with many a non-conformist, there is nothing holier than thou about John. He is funny, passionate, deeply knowledgeable about the law, and shrewd in its practice. He has embraced the wisdom and determination of his clients, and together they have faced, with great success, what the great American civil rights leader John Lewis described as "good trouble."

When John began his life role as an advisor to Indigenous communities across the country, there was no Charter of Rights and Freedoms and no section 35. There were few good precedents and even fewer judges willing to listen to arguments about the fundamental injustices of the ways in which Indigenous people were being treated.

Deeply influenced by the traditions of dissent, just thinking, and right actions, John was inspired by the clients whose causes he took up in the 1960s and 1970s. The Indigenous leadership of those years – a remarkable generation who led the way to profound social, political, and legal changes – were ironically forced to take a firm stand because Pierre Trudeau's White Paper put forward the propositions that Treaties themselves were outdated, that there were no separate Indigenous rights, and that the end of "paternalism" meant that Indigenous people would have no more "separate status." This was the brave new world Trudeau Sr. tried to usher in at the beginning of his first term.

But John's early clients were having none of it. Nor were they having anything to do with pipeline developments being proposed for the Yukon and Northwest Territories. Their fierce and trenchant protests forced the Trudeau government to withdraw the White Paper as the basis for public policy (although the arguments in it have been taken up by a great many on the political right since). Shortly afterwards, the *Calder* case led Pierre

Trudeau to admit ruefully that "maybe indigenous people have more rights than we thought they had."

It was around this time that I was initiated into this milieu, as part of the federal New Democratic Party caucus. We played a role in getting the language of section 35 into the patriated constitution, and it was during those discussions, and in the Meech and Charlottetown debates that followed, that I came to know John in his role as advisor to the Assembly of First Nations. By that time he had moved to Toronto and had also become counsel to the Innu Nation in Labrador, a relationship that has been a defining element of both his legal practice and his legal and moral commitment ever since.

I went on to serve as leader of the provincial NDP and premier of Ontario during those years, and when I became his law partner two decades later, we would talk often about them: about the steps taken, the opportunities missed, and the challenges ahead. These chats were always full of good humour and I recall them fondly, because it was in conversation that John's character really shone through: calm, reasoned, learned, wise, and deeply passionate about the great divides still to be crossed.

In his later years, John has received the Law Society Medal and the Order of Canada – recognition, at long last, of the enormous importance of the work he has been doing for over a half century. He is richly deserving of these and the many other honours he has received, particularly those from Indigenous communities and nations across the country. More than any other lawyer practising in Canada in the past fifty years, John Olthuis has played a central part in the country's ongoing transformation, both in public policy and in the changes to federal and provincial legislation, which he describes so well in this remarkable memoir.

John is generous about the role of others and modest about himself. We all know that he vastly underrates his own influence.

But he would be the first to tell us that he did not do any of this alone: he took enormous inspiration from the courage of his clients and great strength from the friendship they offered him. He was proud to stand with them. The leaders of the Innu Nation single-handedly stopped NATO planes from flying low over their territory, something which others might have said could never be done.

Through it all, John never forgot that the lawyer's fundamental obligations are to both their clients and to the law. John helped his clients fight, and he helped them negotiate too. His skills at the bargaining table have helped to free up hundreds of millions of dollars for his clients, led to important breakthroughs in self-government agreements, and fostered much broader recognition among non-Indigenous political leaders of their ongoing obligations to make good on the deeper meaning of truth and reconciliation.

John has had the vision and strength to build a transformative law practice, entirely dedicated to advancing the interests of Indigenous people across the country. He started out nearly on his own and led us all by the power of his example. He is now content to let others lead, but he continues to mentor, negotiate, and guide every day. That is all to the good.

I started by referring to one hymn, "To Be a Pilgrim." Let me close by quoting from a verse of "Amazing Grace":

> Through many dangers, toils and snares
> We have already come
> 'Twas grace that brought us safe thus far
> And grace will lead us home.

John is leading a life that is full of grace, a quality that is often devalued in the world of power politics, where success is worshipped above all else. On the long pilgrimage, it is people like John Olthuis that are leading us home. I am grateful for his guidance, and very proud to have spent time with him along the way.

Bob Rae, former premier of Ontario and former partner and counsel at Olthuis Kleer Townshend LLP, currently serves as Canadian Ambassador and Permanent Representative to the United Nations in New York.

Foreword

STAN McKAY

As a child on the prairies, John Olthuis was not aware of the history of his Indigenous neighbours whom he had not met. Then he learned about the exclusion and marginalization of the First Nations. After spending time with the Dene in the 1970s, he was given a teaching about his role, which was that he was to work to dismantle the oppressive settler institutions and the ways of non-Indigenous people. *On Dismantling Settler Colonialism* is a detailed account of how John Olthuis gave more than five decades of his life to this calling.

I first learned of John's work when the call for a moratorium on the plans for the Mackenzie Valley Pipeline was put before the Berger Inquiry, which then recommended the moratorium to Prime Minister Trudeau, who declared it.

The Very Reverend Stan McKay, the first Indigenous moderator of the United Church of Canada, lives on the Fisher River Cree First Nation in northern Manitoba and serves as an Elder as his community continues to self-determine.

Foreword

AARON MILLS

This book is John Olthuis's clarion call for robust Indigenous self-determination. A fifty-year legal career spent carefully listening to his Indigenous clients and battling settler colonialism has taught him that the fundamental problem Indigenous peoples face is the expectation that they reconcile themselves to, not with, Canadian legal and political authority. John shows that decades of careful reports already offer a path of structural change to genuine power-sharing. He aims to light a fire in settler Canadians to take up the great work of reconciliation – *with* their Indigenous partners. Presented in both institutional and grass-roots registers, this is a work of careful listening, collective integrity, and personal responsibility. Like all Elders, John shows the way.

Aaron Mills, Canada Research Chair in Indigenous Constitutionalism and Philosophy, and assistant professor of law, McGill University.

Acknowledgments

Over the years, in casual discussion with people at airports, cafes, and other places, I sometimes mentioned that I worked with Indigenous people. The frequent response was along the lines of "I am so glad they are doing so much better," to which I often responded, "well, that's really not the case." I would give some examples to back this up, like Canada's ongoing failure to positively respond to the hundreds of systemic change recommendations of the Truth and Reconciliation Commission (TRC), and other inquiries, and that a growing number of Indigenous people are in jail, experience poverty, live in mouldy houses, and suffer intergenerational trauma as a result of residential schools and ongoing settler colonialism.

My wife, Lois, and friends often said, "you should write about what is really happening," and so I did. I am thankful that the University of Toronto Press decided to publish the book.

The book would not have emerged without the exceptional writing and editing skill and encouragement of Patricia Pearson. I cannot thank her enough.

Acknowledgments | xvii

There are so many other dear people to thank:

Cathy Ball, my amazing Olthuis Kleer Townshend LLP assistant, with skill and endless patience, turned my unvarnished thoughts into typed drafts.

Stephanie Kearns's research was stellar. Jane Warren made good suggestions, and Murray MacAdam worked on a few early chapters.

My wife Lois Kunkel, my son Matthew Kunkel, and family members Jim Olthuis, Bill Olthuis, Doug Olthuis, and Shelley Fenton offered insightful comments and encouragement on draft chapters, as did friends Barbara Flagler, Bob Fugere, Bob Haverluck, Barbara Henderson, Hallett Llewellyn, Karen MacKay Llewellyn, Jeanne Moffat, David Reid, Roger Townshend, and Gerry Wolfram. My spirit group companions Lynne Brennan, Gabrielle Earnshaw, and Paula Nieuwstraten, encouraged me along the way.

I continue to be inspired by the "dismantling of colonialism" work of Nancy Kleer and Roger Townshend, my co-founding partners at Olthuis Kleer Townshend LLP, and all the lawyers and exceptional support staff who have joined us since. OKT is especially blessed to have a number of lawyers who are Indigenous.

Indigenous artists George Littlechild (my cousin) and Mary Ann Penashue (my friend) contributed the amazing art that I treasure and that so enriches the text.

John Andrew Olthuis

Preface
Fifty Years of Walking Alongside First Nations

When I first met the leaders of the Dene Nation in Yellowknife during the early 1970s, offering my assistance as an activist and lawyer, Dene Nation president Georges Erasmus told me: "We know who we are. We don't need your help. We were self-determining for hundreds of years before your people took our land and children and set up institutions and enacted policies that tried to destroy our way of life. Your job is to work to dismantle the oppressive institutions and ways of your people so that we, the Dene, can again have the cultural, social, economic, and political room to be fully self-determining, to pass our own laws and steward our land and resources."

I have never forgotten those words of rebuke and *challenge*.

Fast forward to the mid-1980s on the other side of the country. Innu Nation president Greg Penashue met me one day at the Happy Valley-Goose Bay, Labrador airport. The Innu of Labrador were looking for a lawyer and had asked to meet with me. Greg shook my hand, smiled, glanced down and said, "Every time I shake hands with a white man, I count my fingers afterwards."

We got in his truck and drove to the post office in Northwest River, near the Innu community of Sheshatshiu. He went into the building and came out with a few letters and stuck them behind his truck seat – his filing cabinet, he told me – and said, "I'm not sure what these are about but, if they are important, they will write back."

Over the fifty years that I've been serving as advisor and legal counsel to First Nations across Canada, I have come to understand how deeply instructive those introductions were – both for my understanding of colonialism and of political self-determination – and how the Dene, the Innu, and so many First Nations march to their own drummers, not to the tunes of settler colonial governments.

In my walk with Indigenous peoples, I continue to learn and deepen my understanding of the de-humanization of settler colonialism. A settler colonial country is one where the invaders (to soften the impact, they are often called "settlers") never leave and their present-day laws, institutions, and governance systems continue to oppress the first peoples of the invaded land. Canada, the United States, and Australia stand out as settler colonial countries.

Unlike predatory countries (for example, like the many that invaded, pillaged, and left Africa), settler colonists stay and continue the systematic oppression of the original peoples. Sadly, such is the case in Canada. In these pages I share my experiences, thoughts, and feelings about the over fifty years I have worked to dismantle settler colonialism and how constructive and healing that dismantling can be.

In essence, dismantling settler colonialism means the collective abandonment of pursuing reconciliation as a softer process of assimilating Indigenous people to the mainstream values and institutions of settler colonialism. It means embracing reconciliation with Indigenous people, a reconciliation to create the political, economic, social, and cultural public space in which Indigenous peoples and nations can govern themselves, care for their traditional lands, and live in harmony with the Earth according to their beliefs and values. Reconciliation *to* is oppressive and harmful. Reconciliation *with* can be respectful and healing.

In my wildest childhood dreams, I never imagined that I would be blessed with the opportunity to walk with so many incredible Indigenous people and First Nations in my career. Growing up in Edmonton in the 1940s and 1950s, the only knowledge I had about the Cree, Chipewyan, and Stoney Nations whose homeland I inhabited was that they had some reserves near the city. Whatever that meant; I couldn't quite picture it. My uncle and aunt fostered a child named George Littlechild Price, who was largely being raised as a white boy. George is now a celebrated Cree artist and advocate for residential school survivors. In 2021, he staged a moving exhibit at the Art Gallery of Alberta, featuring his tribute to the victims. I am deeply grateful that George agreed to offer his painting, "Heart Beat – Mother Earth and Dancer" (which hangs in my living room) as this book's cover image.

I lived near the Charles Camsell Hospital in Edmonton and occasionally played on its grounds. If I thought about it at all, I assumed it was a good institution that treated Inuit and other Indigenous children from Northern Alberta and the Northwest Territories suffering from tuberculosis. I knew nothing of the deplorable living conditions at the hospital, or that many of the patients arrived coughing and shivering straight from residential schools. No one told me anything about the abuse, suspicious deaths, and unmarked burials. Regrettably, like many Canadians, I lived in a bubble of blissful ignorance.

On 19 September 2024, the Canadian Medical Association (CMA) formally apologized for the role of physicians in causing harm to Indigenous people.¹ Dr. Joss Reimer, president of the association, said they are "deeply ashamed" of their racist actions and *in*actions throughout Canadian history that caused so much neglect and abuse of First Nations, Inuit, and Métis community members. The apology quoted what CMA called a "haunting message from beyond the grave." Métis Elder Sonny James Mac-Donald, who was incarcerated at that very same Charles Camsell Hospital in the 1940s whose grounds I played in spoke of his devastating treatment, including sexual abuse and isolation, at the tuberculous hospital.

The CMA, according to its statement of apology, had undertaken "a multiyear review of its archives and other documented interactions with Indigenous communities, finding a long history of harm caused by Canadian doctors." This review, according to Dr. Paula Cashin, showed that physicians contributed to "systematically embedding and upholding anti-Indigenous racism into Canada's health-care system and policies, creating an unsafe environment for patients from Indigenous communities." Cashin also said that some children were subjected to experiments at residential schools testing the effect on humans of malnourishment and the withholding of necessary care. The full extent of that experimentation remains unknown.

It continues to shock me every time I hear or read about how systemic anti-Indigenous racism *even extends* to healthcare. My heart raced as I recalled looking up at that hospital while I was playing on its grounds as a happy but ignorant white boy.

My ancestors came to Canada from the Netherlands in the early 1900s. They homesteaded near Barrhead in northern Alberta, unaware that they'd been offered traditional First Nations land surrendered, in the eyes of Ottawa and Alberta, by the 1876 signing of Treaty 6. Governments across Canada continue to reject the Indigenous understanding that the original Treaties were about *sharing* land and resources with the newcomers, not surrendering everything to a faraway British monarch in return for tiny, unproductive reserves. Even to construe land as a commodity to trade away was looking through a colonialist lens, not an Indigenous one.

My Edmonton childhood was somewhat typical for a conservative Christian family on the Prairies, except that my father adamantly believed in a crucial part of the gospel message: to love one's neighbour. He taught us to care for the marginalized. So, I went to the University of Alberta Law School in the early 1960s, naively believing that becoming a lawyer was a good way to work for justice and equality. There were no Indigenous law courses then, which, on reflection, made colonialist sense since the Indian Act prohibited Indigenous people from gathering politically or hiring lawyers to advance their collective interests until 1951. In my first years of practice in Edmonton, I was shocked to discover close up how the legal system is largely set up to protect vested interests and advance capitalist aspirations, with only passing nods to social justice. I decided to see if there were better ways to pursue my goals.

Early in the 1970s, I moved to Ontario and became research director for what was then somewhat inaptly called the Committee for Justice and Liberty (CJL) Foundation, a membership-based group that evolved, in part, out of a fledgling organization I co-founded in law school to focus on public justice issues. Some years later, the CJL foundation changed its name to Citizens for Public Justice (CPJ) and is now a national membership organization based in Ottawa, advocating, often in coalition with like-minded organizations, for justice for the poor, undocumented refugees, and Indigenous peoples and nations.

In 1986, I analysed the federal government's budget priorities to see how well Canada was caring for its most vulnerable citizens. It was clear we were failing to provide housing, adequate incomes, childcare, job counselling, and retraining, or to meet other social needs. I scrutinized the federal budget to see the best way to divert 10 per cent to these causes. My proposal, which CPJ advocated for publicly, was an $11-billion Social Development and Job Creation Fund for people living on social assistance and unemployment insurance, to provide low-cost housing, community projects such as energy conservation, and childcare programs. The funds would be raised by a range of fair tax measures, including reduced tax exemptions for corporations and surtaxes on the wealthiest Canadians and corporations. I consulted several economists as I developed the plan, including prominent economist Abraham Rothstein from the University of Toronto. The *Toronto Star* put a mainstream media spotlight on our proposal. A chain reaction followed, with coverage in the *Hamilton Spectator*, *London Free Press*, and CBC's *As It Happens*. These outlets, and many others, trumpeted CPJ's call for a bold new direction.

Meanwhile, New Democratic Party MPs Margaret Mitchell and David Orlikow raised our proposal in the House of Commons. Mitchell urged Minister of National Health and Welfare Jake Epp to include it in the next federal budget. Not surprisingly, this never happened, but our work did raise public awareness that political measures *could* express love for less fortunate neighbours.

The following year, 1987, I was admitted to the Ontario bar. By this time, as you will see in the following chapters, I had begun advising First Nations as they fought to reclaim their identities and protect their lands. I had renewed hope that, with the recognition of the rights of Aboriginal peoples in Canada's patriated 1982 Constitution, a path had been opened to advance their rights legally. I committed myself full time to the Indigenous quest for justice and to building a law firm that expanded that work.

I am now a senior counsel at Olthuis Kleer Townshend LLP (OKT Law) – a firm I co-founded in 2000. OKT has offices in Toronto and Yellowknife and does legal work with First Nations and Inuit in every province and territory. With over fifty lawyers, OKT is the largest law firm in the country working exclusively with First Nations and has consistently been named Canada's Best Indigenous Law Firm. OKT has many lawyers who are Indigenous themselves, fulfilling one of my dreams. I have flown over four million miles in countless trips to Indigenous communities in every part of Canada. But my real journey has been one of learning: a spiritual, emotional, and intellectual awakening to the amazing history, resilience, creativity, and generosity of First Nations people. In tents, boats, ceremonies, strategy sessions, in courts and at innumerable negotiation tables across Canada, Elders and young Aboriginal leaders continue to teach me about the richness of their cultures, spiritualities, histories, and philosophies, and the extent to which Canada remains stubbornly colonialist in its relationship with them.

Former prime minister Justin Trudeau said that reconciliation with Indigenous people was the most important matter on his government's agenda. These words were encouraging insofar as Indigenous issues are federal concerns. But so many pressing matters for Indigenous people are land- and resource-based, falling within provincial jurisdictions. And truth be told, the provinces pay scant, if *any*, attention to reconciliation. Moreover, my experience is that the former prime minister's actions did not match his words. Nor did the actions of his father, Pierre Trudeau, nor any of the prime ministers or, consistently, any premiers in between.

Prime Minister Carney was elected as this book was going to press. Regrettably, his Building Canada Act, passed in June 2025, falls far short of requiring Indigenous consent to fast tracked projects earmarked for their lands. At the provincial level, Ontario and British Columbia have passed similar legislation to authorize project go-aheads without Indigenous consent. These alarming developments are compelling evidence that Canadian public policy continues to be firmly grounded in the settler colonial view that reconciliation is about forcing Indigenous people to bow to the sovereignty of the colonial Crown rather than establishing an equitable partnership WITH Indigenous peoples and nations.

Some say that government apologies and steps of redress like the residential schools' settlement or the more recent child welfare settlement are reconciling steps. In reality, they are just long overdue *reparations* for horrendous wrongs done in the past and secured only by the patient, creative, and tenacious efforts of Indigenous people. Authentic reconciliation demands *structural* change. In our personal, community, and work relationships, all Canadians understand how distressful it is to be coerced to reconcile oneself *to* the desires, whims, and plans of another. There is no equality in relationships in which, at the end of the day, one of the parties has all the agency and calls all the shots. We need to recognize First Nations as co-partners, not as inferiors to treat more nicely at our own discretion, if we are to journey with them towards a nation-to-nation reconciliation. Otherwise, why even deploy the word?

Canada's policy of forced impoverishment and assimilation has effectively been in place since the days of Christopher Columbus and the Doctrine of Discovery, which provided a framework of justification. That doctrine was set out in a papal bull by Pope Alexander VI in 1493 to support Spain's right to exclusively claim the lands visited by Columbus. It declared North America to be *terra nullius*, or unclaimed land, because it was inhabited by "savages" who were not civilized enough to assert ownership or governance over the world they inhabited. *Why, that would be like saying the wolves and bears ruled the land!* This utterly racist doctrine legitimized the theft of land for all European "discoverers." It rationalized genocidal attacks and paternalistic policies. In March of 2023, Pope Francis renounced the doctrine but – significantly – did not rescind it. His statement was symbolically important but in itself would not lead to any systemic change unless Canada actually committed to dismantling the institutions, policies, and practices that were built on the foundation of that doctrine.

I was urged to write this book by many, and I decided I wanted to share what I'd learned about the foundational shame that haunts Canada. But, even more so, I wanted to discuss how those of us who are not Indigenous might respond to Indigenous peoples' justice-based desire to reclaim self-determination, by reflecting on our perceptions of reconciliation. How can we advocate for and participate in systemic change, so that Canada becomes a place where First Peoples have the cultural, political, spiritual, and economic space necessary to both self-determine and to live in balance with the earth and with other Canadians?

I have worked with the Dene in the NWT, the Lubicon in Alberta, the Innu in Labrador, as well as with Grassy Narrows, the Teme-Augama, and the Nishnawbe Aski Nation, which represents forty-nine First Nations in northern Ontario. I have, at various times, been angered, surprised, puzzled, and saddened by the refusal of Canada and the provinces to embrace the integration of their rights and jurisdictional powers with those of Indigenous peoples and nations, to build a modern and strong pluralistic society. What a magnificent country we could build together!

For there to be authentic reconciliation, all federal and provincial political parties must work together with the support of

Canadians to chart a new course – one that would properly align the respective decision-making rights of Canada, the provinces, and Indigenous peoples. I will show you the deeply considered and, indeed, bipartisan road maps that have *already been drawn* for this to happen, in the work of the 1983 Penner Report, the 1996 Royal Commission on Aboriginal Peoples (RCAP), the 2015 report of the TRC, and the 2019 report of the Missing and Murdered Indigenous Women and Girls Inquiry (MMIWGI). Millions of dollars, countless hours, exhaustive research, and – most importantly – hours of grass-roots testimony have gone into drawing up an authentic reconciliation roadmap. What has been lacking is not concrete plans for a nation-to-nation reset. What's been absent for so long is political will.

The good news is that Indigenous self-respect, confidence, and strategic vision is thriving. A prime example is that in recent years First Nations have signed over 600 Impact Benefit Agreements (IBAs) directly with resource companies, in which they have consented to developments on their traditional lands in return for environmental and cultural protection, a share of project profits, and the right of first refusal for jobs and contracts. This recent and growing economic power ultimately confers more political potency. Non-Indigenous peoples and governments are listening to Indigenous voices with new interest. Meanwhile, Canadians are beginning to respect Indigenous knowledge about stewarding the land and all its creatures. Thankfully, many of us are starting to sense our incredible arrogance in assuming that our values, which are so rooted in the concepts of settler colonialism, are, by definition, *more evolved* and more *just*.

I think it eminently reasonable that I choose to measure Canada's commitment to reconciliation by using equitable considerations. It is dawning on more and more Canadians that there is a huge gap between what politicians say they are doing for reconciliation and what is actually happening when judged equitably. Canada talks reconciliation but practises assimilation. We offer land acknowledgments but evince scant intention of sharing stewardship of that land. We invite Indigenous people to join Western institutions but refuse to allow them to educate their children in their traditional ways. We hand out grants to beef up "Indigenous content" in films and television, but then strictly regulate their capacity to pursue an Indigenous lifestyle through hunting, trapping, and fishing. What we are engaging in is a blend of fawning apology and assimilation. That is *not* what the Dene, the Innu, and the other First Nations ever asked for or are willing to accept from us.

Now that I am in the twilight of my life's vocation, I continue to work with my OKT colleagues Nancy Kleer and Larry Innes as legal counsel for the Innu of Labrador in their efforts to conclude a modern Treaty. I marvel at the brilliance of OKT's contingent of younger lawyers, and the many others who work with First Nations in leading the way to reconciliation *with* Canada, by resisting Canada's ongoing efforts to get them to reconcile *to* the sovereignty of the colonial Crown and the "innate superiority" of Western culture. My plea and invitation to non-Indigenous Canadians is that we work together for equitable reconciliation. We have the blueprints. We just need the awareness, the will, and the non-partisan commitment of all federal and provincial parties to embrace authentic reconciliation *with* Indigenous peoples and nations.

CHAPTER ONE

The Dene Nation and the Mackenzie Valley Pipeline

At first, it looked like resistance was futile. It was 1974, and the world's energy conglomerates and Western governments were declaring a global fuel crisis. The Canadian Arctic Gas consortium had just launched a bid to build a $10-billion, 2,625-mile, 48-inch-diameter high-pressure gas pipeline from Prudhoe Bay, Alaska, across the northern Yukon to the delta of the Mackenzie River and south through Denendeh, the homeland of the Dene people, to the markets of southern Canada and the United States. It would be the largest engineering project in Canadian history. What could stop it? Public anxiety about running out of fossil fuels ran high. Few people worried about the environment. This was an era when people still tossed soda cans out of car windows. Nobody thought about the "Indians." What could they know about societal progress? And the corporate forces seemed virtually unstoppable. Arctic Gas represented twenty-seven companies, including the so-called Seven Sisters: British Petroleum, Chevron, Gulf, Texaco, Exxon, Mobil, and Shell. Powerful interests wanted this pipeline built. Key members of Pierre

Trudeau's cabinet, including Jean Chrétien, actively promoted it. Only thus, Canadians were told, would we be able to avoid "freezing in the dark."

Nevertheless, thanks to the growing strength of the Dene Nation of the Northwest Territories, a slow awakening about our fragile natural world, and the commitment to social justice among Canada's faith and volunteer communities in the 1970s, resistance emerged with surprising results.

On the first day of spring, 1974, the federal government appointed BC Judge Thomas Berger to lead an inquiry into the Mackenzie Valley Pipeline, to explore the impact of such a massive construction project on our largely untouched "frontier" North. The government wanted to avoid – or at least mitigate – conflict between the gas companies and the newly assertive Aboriginal communities, who had won recognition of their legal right to make land claims for the very first time in the previous year. Justice Berger would hold hearings throughout the North and then travel across southern Canada. More than 1,000 individuals and 183 organizations ultimately contributed to the discussion. Owing to the zeitgeist of the era, a relatively obscure set of hearings into pipeline construction became, in the words of one observer, "more like an inquiry into the future of a great nation and its people." The hearings were broadcast by the CBC, garnering intense interest from Canadians who had never listened to the voices or seen the faces of the Dene, Métis, and Inuit peoples who lived thousands of miles to their north. Jim Sittichinli, a Dene Elder who acted as the CBC's Gwich'in language reporter, was an early participant.

"The other day I was taking a walk," he told Judge Berger. "I passed a house there with a dog tied outside. I didn't notice it, and all of a sudden this dog jumped up and gave me a big bark. I was saying to myself: 'Well, that dog taught me a lesson. The

Native people, they are tied down too much by the government. We never go and bark, therefore nobody takes notice of us. It is about time that we, the people of this north land, should get up and bark."[1] At the time, the Seven Sisters essentially drove energy policy in the country because nobody questioned our national appetite for fuel. Canada and the United States together made up about 8 per cent of the global population and yet were guzzling almost 50 per cent of the world's energy.[2] The only hoop that oil and gas projects had to jump through was a National Energy Board (NEB) hearing, which would grant what is misleadingly called a "Certificate of Public Convenience and Necessity." The Calgary-based NEB had been established by Prime Minister John Diefenbaker in 1959 and just rubber-stamped any economically feasible project. You could ask the NEB, "What about the environment? What about Aboriginal rights? What about the overconsumption of energy?" But these matters were dismissed as minor stumbling blocks. The decision-making framework was economic, pure and simple. Jobs and profits. Money makes the world go round.

As a young lawyer working for what was then a small nonprofit, the CJL (then based in Toronto, now in Ottawa), I viewed the Mackenzie Valley Pipeline proposal – both during Berger's inquiry and at the NEB hearings – as a chance to fight for a different perspective, one that respected Dene teachings about how to revere and safeguard the natural world. This was a time when the Club of Rome had expressed grave concern about the carrying capacity of the environment. People were reading books like E.F. Schumacher's *Small Is Beautiful*, and Barry Commoner's *Poverty of Power*, which convincingly argued that the economic system drives production which then devastates the ecosystem – when it should be the other way around: the ecosystem should come first, then a production system based upon its capacity, with conservation considerations top of mind, and then an economy reflecting those realities. So, the CJL advocated for what we called a Just Energy Policy, meant to promote a different set of objectives.

I remember my first discussions with Dene representatives after our team at CJL reached out to them and offered legal support. I explained that we wanted to participate in the public debate; to call for a moratorium on the construction of any pipeline until the Dene had reached a Comprehensive Land Claims Agreement (modern Treaty), which would put them in a better position to deny or grant consent to large-scale economic development on land they had inhabited for thousands of years. Georges Erasmus told us that they were feeling the pipeline pressure because of the consumerist values of Canadian society. He welcomed any help in challenging that mindset.

As a strategy, we decided that calling for the moratorium – instead of outright opposing a pipeline – would enable public discussion about energy policy, about its goals, its impacts, and its decision-making framework. I saw the pipeline issue as, in many ways, a struggle for liberation – a call to liberate resource management from a framework dominated by the addiction to unfettered economic growth. It continues to surprise me how many people, including so many thoughtful ones, believe in the theory of trickle-down economics in the face of so much damage and suffering. A moratorium, we believed, would allow for more serious consideration of Aboriginal rights and environmental protection, a deeper dive into the Seven Sisters' rationale, and some exploration of fossil fuel alternatives. Ultimately, to discuss what *really* constitutes "public convenience and necessity." With this aim in mind, the CJL and the Dene Nation became intervenors in the NEB's Mackenzie Valley hearings.

In the fall of 1976, I travelled to Yellowknife to meet with Georges Erasmus and other Dene leaders, including George

Barnaby. The two young men had been elected as president and vice president, respectively, of the Dene Nation that summer. They were known locally as "the two Georges." Erasmus was in his late twenties and had grown up in Yellowknife where he'd lost much of his native language in school. Barnaby was in his mid-thirties and still lived on the land as a trapper. He was more fluent in his mother tongue than in English, a soft-spoken man with a fierce commitment to his traditional culture. Both men were adamant that the Dene had a right to their own governance and decision-making.

Flying into Yellowknife for the first time, I studied the beautiful landscape below me. I was excited to be going to Denendeh and hoped I would get to stand on the banks of the Dehcho River, the mighty waterway known to non-Dene as the Mackenzie River. Second only to the Mississippi in length, and sometimes called Canada's cold Amazon, it flows for nearly 2,000 kilometres from Great Slave Lake through the Mackenzie Delta to the Arctic Ocean. Many Dene communities – whose original names had been replaced with colonial monikers like Fort Simpson, Wrigley, Fort Norman, Norman Wells, Fort Good Hope, Fort Providence, and Fort McPherson – are located along the Dehcho. These colonial settlement names give you a sense of the defensive, frontier mentality of Westerners exploring these northlands, whereas the Dene and the Inuit had long occupied this vast region alongside a large herd of caribou, grizzlies, and wolverines, while moose wandered the boreal forest's northernmost edge. The ecology, fragile and finely balanced amidst permafrost, had been expertly safeguarded by Dene and Inuit, who never took more than they needed, mindful of cycles and seasons.

I wondered about how building a pipeline might change the Dene way of life. I had read a lot about the social impacts of huge development projects in other parts of the world, including rising prices, housing costs, the sexual harassment of women, and pollution. I feared how these impacts would accompany a pipeline built in Denendeh. Above all, I thought that this land had been inhabited by the Dene since most Canadians' ancestors lived in Europe and that neither Canada nor the oil companies had any right to do *anything* on this land without Dene counsel and consent.

Europeans began slowly eroding the culture and health of the Dene people in the late eighteenth and nineteenth centuries, first bringing smallpox, influenza, white supremacist assumptions, and innocent-seeming trading posts. For some decades, the Dene participated in the fur trade while maintaining their wary independence. Then, the discovery of gold glimmering in the frosty streams dramatically altered their interaction with settlers. As prospectors scrambled north to participate in the Yukon Gold Rush carrying picks and sieves and dreams, the government of Canada drew up what became known as Treaty No. 8, covering parts of northern British Columbia and Alberta, and the NWT up to Great Slave Lake. That was in 1896. A couple of decades later, oil was discovered and "Indian agents" presented another pre-written Treaty, No. 11, to the Aboriginal villages and communities, meant to cover a huge swath of land north of Great Slave Lake. Often priests or other missionaries, in many cases purposely, misinterpreted English words of those pre-written documents to Native peoples.

Although the Dene remained a majority of the residents in their territory, they swiftly lost all semblance of self-determination. There was to be no majority will. White minority rule via Ottawa, in the guise of police officers, teachers, nurses, business representatives, and administrators came to resemble the colonial rule in nations like India and South Africa. While the Dene had had their own way of choosing leaders and educating children and pursuing sustenance on the land, that was all summarily tossed aside. "Usually," one former administrator told the Berger Inquiry, "it would be tacitly agreed that the role of the Native person would be to remain silent throughout [a] meeting except for nodding or providing a one-word approval if the meeting needed to know 'if the Eskimos would agree.'"[3]

After a period of shock and disorientation, not least due to being forced to surrender their children to residential schools, the desire of the Dene to reassert their culture and protect their lands began animating young leaders. They founded the Indian Brotherhood of the NWT in 1970, one year after Ottawa had officially declared a strategy of assimilating Aboriginal people "for their own good." Georges Erasmus would become the Brotherhood's president and continue in that role when the organization evolved, in 1978, into the Dene Nation. The Brotherhood's slogan was "Land and Unity." They did not, however, view land as commodifiable property, as something to *own*. They did not want "ownership" of their land back, because they rejected that very concept. Land cannot be separated from cosmos, from relationship, from survival. The caribou may carry the souls of one's ancestors. The winds and rivers are sentient. A nourishing heart beats in the depths of Great Bear Lake. The Earth is sacred, not something to gouge and burn for profit. To assert ownership would be like vandalizing a temple or murdering in a cathedral.

To understand the rising determination of the Dene and other Aboriginal peoples to fight back against Canada's dishonourable conduct, I want to touch briefly on the years following the Second World War. Over 4,000 Indigenous soldiers served in that theatre of conflict, and many others, both men and women, contributed directly to the war effort on the home front. Yet, to become eligible for veterans' services in the aftermath, they had to renounce their status as Indians and move out of their own communities.

Reward for their service and their allyship was conditional upon their self-erasure. As Canadians became aware of this wartime contribution, they also took note of the lack of services and dire circumstances faced by Indigenous people across the country. This led, in 1951, to some amendments to the draconian Indian Act, which had first been passed in 1876 under section 91.24 of the British North America Act.[4] The Indian Act's clear intent was to corral and dominate Aboriginal communities, to explicitly empower the Canadian government to make decisions about their lives and lands. The extent of control was wide-ranging. As constitutional expert Peter Hogg has noted, "the federal Parliament has taken the broad view that it may legislate for Indians on matters which otherwise lie outside its legislative competence and on which it could not legislate for non-Indians."[5] And as legal scholar Joshua Nichols notes, this "broad view" has never been qualified or restricted by our courts, despite the fact that there is *no* explicit language in s.91.24 that authorizes such sweeping domination.[6]

An amendment to the Indian Act in 1927 prohibited First Nations from seeking legal advice or gathering for political purposes.[7] This followed on the heels of a 1921 decision of the Privy Council (the British Court that then acted as Canada's last Court of Appeal for civil cases until 1949) in a case involving Southern Nigeria. "Aboriginal title," the Council ruled, "pre-existed British authority and remains in place unless explicitly extinguished."[8] This, in turn, was based on an 1888 decision of the Privy Council in the *St. Catherine's Milling* case, a case of a dispute over logging rights in Treaty 3 territory in northwestern Ontario. Canada argued that they had acquired the logging rights from the Anishinaabe in Treaty 3. But the court said Ontario had acquired those rights. In the Southern Nigeria case in 1921 the Privy Council found that Aboriginal title remains in place unless explicitly extinguished. Because of the Privy Council decision that explicit extinguishment of Aboriginal title is required, Canada was concerned that the Canadian courts might find that Canada had not explicitly extinguished those rights. So, it is logical to conclude that the 1927 Indian Act amendment was meant to forestall First Nations from bringing to the courts any cases based on the claim that their Aboriginal rights had not been extinguished in their Treaties. It was not until 1951 that public pressure forced the federal government to amend the Indian Act to permit First Nations to hire lawyers to argue for their Aboriginal rights and titles.

In 1964, again due to mounting public concern, Ottawa appointed a commission to study the social, educational, and economic status of Indigenous peoples. Overseen by University of British Columbia anthropologist Harry Hawthorn, who had close ties with both Māori and West Coast First Nations, the commission issued its "Survey of the Contemporary Indians of Canada" two years later.[9] Among other things, the report attempted to address assimilationist policy by arguing that "Indians should be treated as 'Citizens Plus'" – which, the report explained, meant that, in addition to the normal rights and duties of citizenship, Indigenous people possess certain additional rights, as they were charter members of the Canadian community, "who once occupied and used a country to which others came to gain enormous wealth, in which Indians shared little." Although Hawthorn and his colleagues were sympathetic to the plight of Aboriginal peoples, their recommendations were mostly assimilationist, with a focus on using charity to help Aboriginal folks move into the Western economy. In any event, the entire 400-page report might as well have been used to wrap fish because the government ignored it, being far more preoccupied with the political demands of Quebec.

In 1969, ostensibly in response to the 1966 Hawthorn Report but not really, Prime Minister Pierre Elliott Trudeau and his minister of Indian affairs, Jean Chrétien, tabled a "White Paper," which proposed to rip up the Indian Act and, in effect, transform Aboriginal peoples into "Citizens Minus." The declared aim was to "end the legal distinction between Indians and other Canadians," because "Canada cannot seek [a] just society and keep discriminatory legislation on its books."[10] Abruptly revoking the Indian Act, pursuant to which Canada's Indian Affairs bureaucrats had literally controlled every aspect of Aboriginal lives for a century, would have cast Indigenous people into the rapids without life jackets. Make no mistake, they *despised* the Indian Act, but they wanted it revoked only after their rights were entrenched in Canada's Constitution and their Treaties were honoured. Otherwise, there would be no ground beneath their feet. They would be forcibly assimilated on the spot. This, less than two decades after they'd even won back the right to hire lawyers.

The White Paper proposed that Canada transfer responsibility to the provinces for providing services on reserve. It also said that historic Treaties should be "equitably ended" based on the fact that the terms and effects of the Treaties between Indigenous peoples and the government were widely misunderstood: "a plain reading of the words used in the Treaties reveals the limited and minimal promises which are included in them." *They were just vague promises anyway, so let's get rid of them!* With respect to reserve lands, which are held by Canada in trust for First Nations, Canada proposed that they be transferred to the First Nations to become provincial municipalities, with fee simple ownership of land. (That is the legal term for how Canadians own the ground on which their houses stand.) As such, Indigenous people would be subject to property taxes. Finally, Canada disingenuously claimed that the White Paper was merely responsive to what First Nations had said in consultation meetings.

Indigenous leaders across the country responded to this White Paper with so much outrage that the prime minister had to withdraw it, reportedly saying with sarcasm and anger, "We'll keep them in the ghetto as long as they want."[11] How big a political mistake the White Paper was, and how lingering its aftermath, can be demonstrated by a resolution passed at the 2014 Biennial Convention of the Liberal Party of Canada to "openly and with regret acknowledge that the White Paper of 1969 was a serious mistake for the Party to consider and officially remove what it stands for." What was the serious mistake? It had many facets, and all of them were addressed in a June 1970 paper entitled "Citizens Plus" – that came to be known as the rejoindering "Red Paper."

This powerful rejection of the White Paper was led by the Indian Chiefs of Alberta and headed by charismatic twenty-four-year-old Cree leader Harold Cardinal, with unreserved support from the National Indian Brotherhood (now known as the Assembly of First Nations). Cardinal was a prodigious political fighter in a beaded buckskin jacket whose fierceness was belied by his soft, round face and thick, dark glasses. He published *The Unjust Society*, a bestselling and riveting book in which he laid out the injustices his people had suffered and what needed to be fixed. (Arguably, it was this book that opened many Canadian eyes and made citizens so curious about the Mackenzie Valley Pipeline hearings and Berger Inquiry a few years later.) "Citizens Plus," presented directly to Trudeau, was just as blistering as *The Unjust Society*. Mocking Canada's claim that the White Paper merely reflected what government heard from Indigenous people, Cardinal said that if Indians met with Canada without a pen to write things down, and simply talked about the weather, Canada's representatives would turn around and tell Parliament they had accepted the White Paper. While Indigenous people had asked for major reforms to the Indian Act, they did *not* ask that it be immediately revoked. Nor did they ask that their Treaties be ripped up.

Cardinal denounced the White Paper as "a thinly disguised programme of extermination through assimilation," and "a form of cultural genocide."[12] He agreed that it was essential to review the hated Indian Act, with some sections altered and others deleted, but *not before Canada honoured the Treaties*. Indigenous people, the Red Paper contended, were indeed Citizens Plus because they had signed agreements to share their land and resources, and "nothing is more important than our Treaties, our lands and the well-being of future generations." Canada must accept the Treaties as binding and pledge to modernize and incorporate them into the Canadian Constitution.

Only then, Cardinal argued, would Indigenous rights be assured "as long as the sun rises, and the river runs." He proposed that the Indian Affairs branch (as it was then called) be reduced and act as "the keeper of the Queen's promises." The branch should stop being racist and authoritarian, he added, and instead actually serve people. Cardinal wanted to "open the eyes of the Canadian public to its shame," as "generations of Indians have grown up behind a buckskin curtain of indifference, ignorance, and all too often, plain bigotry."[13] He added, in a way both amusing and poignant, that, "It sometimes seems that Canada shows more interest in preserving its rare whooping cranes than its Indians. And Canada does not ask the cranes to become Canada Geese."[14]

"Citizens Plus" made it very clear that Aboriginal peoples did not consider themselves to be whites with an extra layer of neediness. They are Canada's First Peoples with many different beliefs, languages, histories, and social, political, and economic structures. What they were confronting were academics and policymakers whose paternalism had been shaped by over a century of British imperial prejudice, imbued in Canada's educational system, which portrayed Indigenous people as incompetent savages, unable to make decisions for themselves. Residential schools were set up to civilize them. The mainstream school systems glorified explorers like Samuel de Champlain and Alexander Mackenzie while stereotyping Indigenous people as belonging to a heathen, inferior race. No more evidence than the Indian Act itself need be presented to make the case that the very same mentality permeated the federal and provincial governments.

Canada's withdrawal of its White Paper in the face of the powerful pushback did nothing, however, to alter its assimilationist agenda. Calls for justice by honouring the Treaties went ignored. But this time, Aboriginal leaders were undaunted and simply intensified their demands. Finally, a 1973 decision of the Supreme Court of Canada in a case brought by the Nisga'a Nation of BC (known as the *Calder* case, for Nisga'a Chief Frank Calder) forced Canada's attention. There were *no* Treaties in BC, so the Nisga'a sought a declaration that they had Aboriginal title to their traditional lands. Justice Emmett Hall's forceful and compelling dissent in that case argued that the Nisga'a's Aboriginal title had not been extinguished. Although Hall's opinion was a dissent (that is, the majority of the judges did not agree), it led Canada, apparently out of an abundance of caution, to decide to negotiate modern Treaties in areas of British Columbia, Yukon, Labrador, NWT, and Quebec where First Nations had never surrendered the land beneath their feet.

In Denendeh (otherwise known as the Northwest Territories) the Indian Brotherhood decided to express their outrage about Canada's interpretation of Treaties 8 and 11 as acts of surrendered title. So they went to court, challenging the view that their ancestors had sold off 450,000 square miles of the Mackenzie

Valley for $5 per person, per year. This was a profound cultural insult to a people who did not sell land, to suggest they had done any such thing, and further the Brotherhood pointed out that Elders who had been alive when the Treaties were signed remembered the clear intent of the Dene, which was to arrange peace and friendship Treaties, in which they agreed to share their bounty with the newcomers. These were not real estate transactions in which they ceded their expansive, beloved territory for pennies. Canada's interpretation was seen as nothing but a cynical swindle. In 1973, Justice William Morrow ruled – for the first time – that Aboriginal peoples had a right to file a caveat on the title of the land claimed by Canada, warning would-be purchasers or lessees that the Dene continued to have "what is known as aboriginal rights," and that they "are prima facie owners of the lands covered by the caveat."[15] (This was known as the Paulette Caveat Case.)

In 1976, the Dene boldly exercised their self-determination by issuing the Dene Declaration, passed in 1975 by an Assembly of 300 delegates from their communities in Denendeh.[16] As I was travelling to Yellowknife for my first meeting with the two Georges, I re-read the declaration. It was an exciting assertion of values and principles.

"The Dene find themselves as part of a country. That country is Canada. But the government of Canada is not the government of the Dene," they declared. "The government of the NWT is not the government of the Dene. These governments were not the choice of the Dene, they were imposed upon the Dene ... What we Dene are struggling for is the recognition of the Dene Nation by the government and the peoples of the world."[17]

The Declaration concluded, "What we seek then is independence and self-determination within the country of Canada. This is what we mean when we call for a just land settlement for the

Dene Nation." This declaration, drafted by such brilliant men as Georges Erasmus – later recipient of multiple honorary degrees and the Order of Canada – was scoffed at by then-Indian affairs minister Judd Buchanan as "gobbledygook."[18] That was the kind of dismissive racism that Canada brought to the negotiating table. More of this would come in the arrogant conduct of Pierre Trudeau and Canada's premiers during the Constitutional Conferences of the 1980s.

When I entered the office of the Indian Brotherhood on the second floor of a low-rise building in downtown Yellowknife, I was immediately impressed by the high level of activity, the charged atmosphere of a group on a mission. Georges Erasmus, with his calm posture, struck me as self-assured, with a strong sense of his place and the place of the Dene in the world. He was articulate and charming in an unassuming and welcoming way. That first impression was reinforced when I was invited to his home and enjoyed the hospitality of him and his wife, Sandra. Georges also had a good sense of humour; he did not take himself more seriously than he took others, which served him well. In our conversations, it became obvious to me how deeply Georges was invested in the Dene Declaration and how well thought out his practical agenda was for getting recognition for his people – and for stopping the pipeline. He was bold and fearless when it came to confronting mainstream politicians. Georges went on to be National Chief of the Assembly of First Nations and, in 1991, co-chair of RCAP. As I had come to know Georges, none of this surprised me. He had immense leadership capacities, deep intellectual strengths, compassion, and a pragmatic willingness to work in partnership with people who did not necessarily share his vision. He recognized that the Dene needed partners if their self-determination was to be recognized and respected.

What Georges told me in our early meetings about the need to dismantle Canada's oppressive institutions and create room for Dene self-determination was a defining moment for my understanding of what decolonization meant. It also helped build my relationship with Georges and other Dene leaders, including Herb Norwegian, a Dene Nation vice-president who would go on to be Grand Chief of the group of Dene First Nations in the Dehcho region of Denendeh, and Steve Kakfwi, a Dene Nation president who later became premier of the NWT.

The immediate dismantling job we discussed in those meetings was how to stop the Mackenzie Valley Pipeline. We talked about the importance of participating in the NEB hearings. We discussed the southern Canadian hearings of the Berger Commission and the need for a sympathetic public to urge Justice Berger to recommend a ten-year moratorium on any developments, which would give the Dene and Canada time to negotiate a modern Treaty. We thought about how CJL could use its role as intervenor in the NEB hearings to present our own proposed Just Energy Policy, meant to address conservation and a new framework for understanding what "public convenience and necessity" actually meant. We planned for my daily presence at the NEB hearings to cross-examine the panels of witnesses who would appear for the Arctic Gas Consortium and what evidence CJL witnesses could counter with, via technical experts like Peter Russell and Mel Watkins, and the social justice reflections of church leaders whose presence the Dene requested. (It should be noted that few, if any, faith communities were yet fully aware of what had transpired in the residential schools. A national public inquiry was only talked about in the early 1990s, around the time that Catholic sexual abuse of non-Indigenous parish children around North America began coming to light.)

For the first time, a regulatory board like the NEB would hear the testimony of spiritual leaders who spoke to the human and environmental impacts of large energy projects. I will never forget the day that Archbishop Ted Scott, primate of the Anglican Church of Canada, arrived in his full regalia to proffer his testimony. The NEB heard that unfettered economic growth and careless capitalism were not, in fact, endorsed by all Christians. Inspired by the Dene, the participation of Canadian faith communities in both the NEB hearings and the Berger Inquiry was significant. For some time, Aboriginal leaders had been urging the churches to do more than simply pass resolutions and issue pious statements about colonialism. The Anglican and United Churches and the Canadian Conference of Catholic Bishops responded by setting up the "Inter-Church Project on Northern Development," which came to be known as "Project North." On Labour Day of 1975, the Catholic bishops released a pastoral letter questioning the pipeline projects, called "Northern Development: At What Cost?" It was time for the Christian community to do its own reflection on what shared gospel values had to say about Aboriginal rights, economic growth, and environmentalism.

The focus of many church basement discussions was on what the gospel pointed to – and it wasn't greed. That really mattered for our neighbours, the Dene, and for their natural world. This, in turn, created an opportunity to discuss the extent to which capitalism's values are institutionalized, not just in Parliament and the legislative assemblies, but also in Canadian boards and agencies. Many people who worked for the oil and gas industry belonged to churches that sponsored Project North. I was told that less money flowed into collection plates because of that sponsorship. But, in retrospect, the call for a moratorium rather than outright opposition was helpful, in that it provided a somewhat less confrontational forum for discussion.

In 1976, the Lutheran Church, the Mennonite Central Committee, and the Presbyterian Church joined in sponsoring Project North, and eventually the Jesuits, the Council of Christian Reformed Churches in Canada, the Quakers, and the Oblate Conference of Canada became partners too. The key staffers at Project North were Hugh and Karmel McCullum, an extremely passionate, articulate couple. They had travelled across the north and written a book about the Dene, *This Land Is Not for Sale*. Hugh was raised in the Yukon and worked as a journalist for several newspapers before becoming editor of the *Canadian Churchman*, and later the United Church *Observer*. Karmel was a nurse and community organizer. They were supported by a Project North Board of Church reps and key people, including Anglican primate Ted Scott. (Those were the days when it was possible to call Primate Scott directly and ask him to come to Ottawa for a press conference, and he would be there the next day, cutting such a dramatic figure that his comments received wide press coverage.) I served as the technical legal advisor to Project North while continuing my work at CJL. During this period, CJL tried hard to be courageous and often threw caution to the wind. But we did our homework and used our very limited resources as wisely as possible. In 1977, I co-wrote a book, *Moratorium Justice: Energy, the North, and the Native People*, with Hugh and Karmel McCullum, about all the issues we felt that a just energy policy needed to address.

As the NEB hearing date drew closer, it became clear that Marshall Crowe, the head of the NEB who would chair the hearings, had a conflict of interest. He had participated in putting the Arctic Gas proposal together in the first place. Now he was to decide whether that proposal should be approved. So, together with some other intervenors, in the majestic ballroom of the Chateau Laurier hotel in Ottawa where the hearings officially opened, CJL challenged Mr. Crowe's role. Mr. Crowe's work with the pipeline consortium raised a reasonable apprehension that he would be biased in favour of the application, we pointed out. When he declined to step down, we took the matter to court. Other public interest groups joined the court action.

Once, before the matter was resolved, Crowe and I were alone in an elevator going down from a hearing session to the main lobby of the Trebla building on Albert Street in Ottawa. It was an awkward moment for both of us. I think we were both at a loss for words. He was a product of the "rotating chair" system between industry and government that is still very much a problem today. I had no personal issues with him; it was this real apprehension that because he was part of the Arctic Gas Consortium he would be inclined to favour it. I also frequently rode the elevator with oil and gas company lawyers; they in their fancy suits and I, more often than not, in my work boots and plaid shirt. They called CJL and other activist organizations "special interest groups" while referring to themselves as "public interest representatives." What constitutes the public interest? Who decides? I don't think the men in the elevator had ever remotely considered this question.

The Federal Court of Appeal in 1978 ruled that there was no apprehension of bias, but on appeal, the Supreme Court of Canada disagreed. Mr. Crowe was removed as chair of the hearings. This was quite a shocking outcome for Ottawa politicians and the energy lobby, who were used to their cozy arrangements. At the NEB hearings and around the court proceedings we, at first, took a lot of "David versus Goliath" kidding and some derision from the oil and gas company folks – but that turned to anger when we won.

CJL had first proposed the pipeline moratorium to the Standing Committee on Natural Resources of the House of Commons in 1976. They had heard a lot from the fossil fuel industry about the need for this pipeline, even though the natural gas flowing through it was mostly destined for the US market. Joe Greene, Canada's minister of energy, mines and resources from 1968 to 1972, had projected that Canada had 372 years of natural gas left. Now, suddenly, the message coming from Ottawa was that Canada was running out of gas. The numbers didn't make sense. They were based on different price projections. Lower price scenarios showed fewer proven resources, and higher price scenarios indicated higher reserves, as some were more costly to bring to market than others. So, with some expert advice, we showed how the oil and gas industry misused numbers to make their case for more pipelines when, in fact, current supplies were more than adequate.

The CJL's Just Energy Policy called for royalty and tax provisions to ensure that private companies develop public resources for *public*, rather than private, benefit. Also, a portion of Canada's resources should be exported at below-market prices to struggling countries. These continue to be very important priorities. We also called for a new National Energy Policy based on human growth, not simply economic expansion; giving priority to developing alternative sources of energy based on renewable resources; for adopting a less energy-intensive lifestyle; and beginning the transition from high capital, energy-intensive production systems to more labour-intensive systems. We proposed a public inquiry that would study how the NEB could be structured to be more independent from its corporate and economic growth biases.

Alexander Campbell, premier of Prince Edward Island, put the underlying issues well at the 1975 Federal-Provincial Conference of First Ministers:

> We must face reality. Unless we are prepared within the next 8 to 10 years to change our way of life, to develop new sets of values,

to create a less materialistically oriented society, and to find new ways of growing as a people other than by an ever-increasing consumption of our natural resources, we will have missed perhaps the last chance open to us. Have we the wisdom – have we the courage?[19]

The answer, regrettably, was no. And to some degree, that was reflected in the rejection of Aboriginal proposals for self-government based on their values.

While the Berger Inquiry continued, the Dene began to consider how to bring their declaration of principles forward to the negotiating table. (Canada first set a deadline of 1 November 1976, by which Indian affairs minister Judd Buchanan told them they must have the settlement proposal together – or else what? It was never spelled out, and Buchanan left his post before the deadline.) The Dene did not want a modern Treaty in which they had to cede their rights of stewardship. The Elders said, "How can you extinguish what the Creator gave you? We were given our land and our right to control that land." The Elders and leaders decided that there must be a guarantee in any agreement that their rights would be recognized in Canadian law. So, they put together an Agreement in Principle (AIP), which was an attempt to express – in the language of other Canadians – their concept that land is the essence of life. ("Being Indian means being able to understand and live with this world in a very special way," Dene witness Richard Nerysoo told the Berger Inquiry. "It means living with the land, with the animals and the birds and the fish as though they were your sisters and brothers. It means saying the land is an old friend, and an old friend your father knew, your grandfather knew. We see our land as much, much more than the white people see it ... If the land is destroyed, we too are destroyed.")[20]

The AIP was modern in tone, realistic in demands, and faithful to the Dene Declaration. The Dene didn't have the money to hold a large assembly in which all representatives could consider the proposed AIP, so several Canadian churches assisted. The Roman Catholic Development and Peace Fund and the Anglican Primate's World Fund loaned them $100,000 to pay for this crucial assembly, which the Dene later repaid.

In October of 1976, Indian Brotherhood president Georges Erasmus, accompanied by thirty delegates, went to Ottawa to present the AIP to Warren Allmand, the new minister of Indian affairs. Discussions took place for a year. Former minister Judd Buchanan had said that "two Nations in the Northwest Territories is no more acceptable [there] than two nations in any other part of Canada."[21] By contrast, Peter H. Russell, professor of political economy and Canada's leading constitutional scholar, had told the NEB hearings that – far from violating Canada's Constitution – the Dene Declaration called for the *extension of the fundamental principles underlying Confederation.* "The working out of the institutional solutions required to accomplish the purpose," he said, "would be a major challenge to Canadian statecraft. In a sense the task entails the completion of Confederation by applying for the first time, the liberal philosophy of ethnic partnership, to our Native people. There are no *a priori* constitutional reasons for not attempting the task. On the contrary, if the Government understands the ideals upon which our constitutional system is based and wishes all of our citizens to participate in those ideals, it is imperative that it not refuse to negotiate a land settlement of the kind envisaged in the Dene Declaration."[22]

Nevertheless, refuse – or stall – they did.

Meanwhile, the Supreme Court decision regarding Mr. Crowe's apprehended bias proved fatal for Arctic Gas's

Mackenzie Valley proposal. The delay caused by the need to recruit a new chairperson and begin a new NEB hearing bought time for Justice Berger to table his Inquiry report, in June of 1977, calling for a moratorium on the pipeline. Justice Berger warned that any gas pipeline would be followed by an oil pipeline and that the infrastructure supporting the energy corridor would be enormous, including roads, airports, maintenance bases, and new towns. He said that the impact on the people, animals, and land would be equivalent to the building of railways across Canada. Those who wanted the pipeline tended to dismiss the impact, saying it would be like a thread stretched across a football field, while those closer to the land said the impact would be more like a razor slash across the *Mona Lisa*.

Project North's staff and support network proved key to the success of the Berger Commission's southern hearings. Interest intensified across the country. In the end, 183 organizations supported CJL's call for a moratorium, people from all segments of society – from Marxists through to groups focused on local economies. NDP leader Tommy Douglas got very engaged. He bought several hundred copies of our book *Moratorium* to distribute to NDP members and other folks. (We don't have many visionary social gospel politicians like Tommy Douglas around these days; they are sorely missed.)

Given the elevated public interest – Berger's report literally became a national bestseller – Prime Minister Pierre Trudeau accepted the Justice's recommendation and declared a ten-year pipeline moratorium. The NEB did approve the Foothills Alaska Highway pipeline, but that never got built, in part because of the moratorium, and due to public awareness of the impacts of such projects. The Mackenzie Valley Pipeline battle is an example of what can be done when folks set out in good faith to make principled change. And it doesn't have to be planned at the beginning.

There is a lot to be said for organic unfolding when like-minded people put their hearts into a quest for justice.

The Norman Wells Pipeline – Breaching the Moratorium

Shockingly, for those who thought the energy industry might have learned something from the Berger Inquiry, in 1980 a consortium called the Interprovincial Pipe Line Company applied to the NEB for permits to build an 860-kilometre crude oil pipeline from the town of Norman Wells in the heart of Dene territory to northern Alberta. Distraught by this application, and after discussion with the Dene Nation, the Métis Association of the NWT, and the Canadian Arctic Resources Committee (CARC), we went to bat again. At the opening of the NEB hearings on this new pipeline, held in Edmonton in October 1980, CJL challenged the jurisdiction of the NEB to consider the application at all. We had two grounds. The first was that the Dene and Métis were in the middle of negotiating their modern Treaty with Canada and the moratorium had to be respected. The second was that Canada possessed one-third ownership of the Norman Wells oilfield via the Department of Indian and Northern Affairs, and since the NEB was a government board, there was a reasonable apprehension that it would be biased in favour of licensing a pipeline on behalf of another branch of government.

Georges Erasmus asked for the hearings to be moved from Edmonton to the NWT, with sessions in Yellowknife and in the Dene communities most affected by the project. That motion was supported by the government of the Northwest Territories, and the bulk of the hearings were shifted. However, the NEB dismissed the CJL, Dene-Métis, and CARC submissions about lacking jurisdiction to consider the pipeline.

CJL presented evidence to make two points. One, the existence of the moratorium should be central to NEB's analysis of whether a project be approved on the basis of "public convenience and necessity," as the moratorium was put in place by the *government who represented the public*. We also argued that conserver values, Aboriginal rights, environmental concerns, and other such considerations should be included in assessing whether a project meets the test for licensing. We pointed out that, with the NEB's narrow definition of what constitutes "public convenience and necessity," every project proposal deemed economically and technically feasible got approved. That approach had to change to take into account the new realities of Indigenous rights and environmental sensitivities. In support of our submissions, CJL arranged two panels of witnesses, including economist Mel Watkins, University of Alberta anthropologist Michael Asch, and Meyer Brownstone, national chairman of Oxfam Canada.

Watkins, who was a research advisor to the Dene Nation, reminded the NEB that they cared for the lands and the valley along the route of the proposed pipeline, and that "it is not enough to say you will offer them jobs."[23] The Dene were not interested in being hired for industrial development and having wage labour imposed on them by others; they wanted money to modernize their communities and to develop renewable resources. This money would be forthcoming if the Dene claims were settled by Canada, and the Dene were recognized as the owners of the sub-surface rights from which royalties from resource production would flow. The Dene would then be entitled to tax existing operations in the Northwest Territories, including two goldmines in the Yellowknife area, a lead zinc mine at Pinepoint, gas production at Pointed Mountain, and the existing oil production at Norman Wells.

The Dene were as much opposed to the Norman Wells pipeline as they had been to the much larger Mackenzie Valley proposal, because, as Watkins put it, "if someone is trespassing on my land, I don't care what size of shoe he is wearing." Watkins added that Norman Wells would only provide 1 per cent of Canada's oil needs, which could be better served by promoting conservation. "It would appear," he said, "that the rights of the Dene would be prejudiced and violated for no better reason than a slight increase in the supply of oil that further puts off the day when we learn to use energy wisely."[24]

Meyer Brownstone told the hearing that Oxfam supported the struggle for self-determination and social justice worldwide and was concerned with the plight of the people in northern Canada. If this pipeline application were approved against their will, Brownstone argued, it would jeopardize their right to self-determination.[25]

Dr. Asch testified that Interprovincial Pipe Line didn't consult the people of Mackenzie Valley, that no interviews were held with locals, nor, it would seem, was any attempt made to contact them. The company's researchers "failed to pick up the most important factor in the assessment of the project: the fact that the local people, Dene and non-Dene alike, are strongly opposed to the project going ahead at this time."[26]

At the Yellowknife hearings in October 1980, CJL Foundation presented a panel of representatives from Canada's three largest churches: Dr. Tony Clarke of the Canadian Conference of Catholic Bishops, Father Clark Raymond of the Anglican Church, and Ms. Bonnie Green of the United Church. Dr. Clarke saw emerging in Canada's north forms of exploitation which are often assumed to only happen abroad. Ms. Green, the staff officer for human rights and international affairs, spoke on behalf of United Church Moderator Lois Wilson to argue that the pipeline posed a threat to all Canadians. "If the rights of Native people can be swept away like this, then so can the rights of everybody else." The United Church, she said, had long been concerned about global Aboriginal rights, and this concern had sensitized them to the violation of the human rights of Native people in Canada. The Norman Wells pipeline, if approved by the NEB and the federal cabinet, would constitute just such a violation. "Having heard the tragic histories of some of our partner churches around the world, having re-examined the Biblical record which we cherish, we are forced to speak up in support of the protests of the Native people of this country."[27]

Anglican Reverend Raymond said that the Anglican Church wasn't against northern development per se, but Aboriginal peoples should be able to develop political and economic institutions sufficient to engage the rest of us at least as equals before any development went ahead.[28]

Despite these calls, and in the face of the moratorium, on 22 April 1981, the NEB granted Interprovincial Pipe Line Company a Certificate of Public Convenience and Necessity to construct and operate a pipeline from Norman Wells in the Dene Territory to Zama City in Alberta. The CJL and other groups applied to the Federal Court of Canada for leave to appeal the decision. The Court denied us. It said there was ample evidence before the NEB upon which the board was entitled to make the findings of fact and to draw the conclusions it did. The court declined to comment on whether the NEB had properly examined the larger context of the moratorium, and the land claims negotiations underway between Canada and the Dene-Métis as important matters of public convenience and necessity.[29]

In a *Globe and Mail* op-ed in June 1981, Mel Watkins and I addressed this striking omission. The NEB had listened to the testimony of the Dene and supporting experts, and to argument and counter-argument. Yet, at the end of it, the members demonstrated incredible cowardice with its findings. "Although the Federal Government may be currently considering Treaty rights, ownership, territorial jurisdiction and other related questions," the NEB report said, "these are not matters with which the Board is involved." But, of course, the board couldn't actually refuse to say anything about the most contentious issue before it. So, it then added, with stunning dismissiveness, "the Board recognizes the importance of Native land claims. However, on the basis of the evidence before it, the Board is not convinced that approval of the proposed pipeline would in fact jeopardize the settlement of Native claims." Even though its finding was *fundamentally contrary* to the evidence, the Board made no attempt to even justify this conclusion.

What Watkins and I said about the NEB decision was also true about the Federal Court of Appeal's refusal to review it. I, along with the Dene, Métis, and many other Canadians, fully expected Canada to honour that moratorium, reject the NEB recommendation, and say no to any development until the Dene and Métis claims were settled. But in a stark betrayal of the Dene and Métis, who had so passionately and eloquently participated in the Berger Inquiry, Canada breached its own moratorium with six years still to go.

Dene-Métis Proposal for Public Government for the People of the North

On 1 January 1982, as negotiations to recognize and affirm Aboriginal rights in a patriated Canadian Constitution went on across Canada, Georges Erasmus and Jim Bourque, president of the Métis Association of the Northwest Territories, released a document called "Public Government for the People of the North." In the introduction, Erasmus and Bourque noted that the uppermost issue in reaching an agreement on Aboriginal rights would be creating political jurisdictions that could enhance the ability of all northerners to govern their lives, as well as to enable Native people to actually achieve the things agreed to in negotiations with the federal government. They noted that, for the descendants of the Dene, an agreement must include a transfer of power from the federal government to a new jurisdiction, which they suggested be called Denendeh. The word means "Land of the people," and the proposal included all people – not just Dene and Métis – who chose to make Denendeh their home. "We advocate that the government of Denendeh be a public government rather than a government designated only to protect our rights. We see no reason why a public government could not be designed by all northerners ... while at the same time having special features required to protect and enhance the rights of Native people."

The Dene and Métis were the original inhabitants and the majority of permanent residents in the western part of the NWT, and therefore were entitled to a formal public government. Other Canadians who met the requirements of a reasonable (ten-year) residency rule would be entitled to the same political rights. The proposal contained a charter of founding principles, which would provide irrevocable protection for the Aboriginal rights of the Dene, and for the collective and individual rights of the Dene and other Canadians in Denendeh. Such government would be set up in the western part of the NWT traditionally used and occupied by the Dene but did not include the Inuvialuit in the Mackenzie Delta region, who also have Aboriginal rights. In brief, the proposal was for a "province-like" political jurisdiction with powers similar to those of other provinces, but not identical, as Denendeh would have some powers which other provinces did not. The thirty-one-page proposal set out in detail how this political system could be set up, in nine stages.

To develop the Denendeh proposal, the Western Constitutional Forum (WCF) had been set up in 1980 with representatives of the Dene, Métis, and Northwest Territories. The mandate was to initiate research and discussion and to reach a tentative Agreement in Principle. Public consultations would be important. Included were Inuit representatives from the Committee for the Original Peoples Entitlement (COPE) and the Inuit Tapirisat of Canada (ITC). The division of the Northwest Territories (the eastern part would ultimately become Nunavut) was also on the agenda. In an April 1982 plebiscite, the people of the NWT approved the division. Accordingly, the WCF created two subcommittees, the WCF and the Nunavut Constitutional Forum (NCF). Each was tasked with proposing a boundary between east and west, negotiating with the federal government, and producing proposals for the political and constitutional development of their respective territories.

In 1984, the WCF published "Dene Government – Past and Future." This came out of a discussion between Dene Elders and younger leaders about their model of consensus government for Denendeh. They detailed how the Dene might flourish in a multicultural environment by emphasizing traditional Dene values of sharing, respect, caring, equality, self-respect, and pride. It contained eleven principles:

- The land was created by "the one who provides for all."
- Respect for the natural laws which regulate the cycle of seasons, the rhythms of the earth, and the ways of the animals.
- No individual has the right to own the land. As the ones who come from the land, we have a collective right to use the land

and its resources to ensure our survival as a people. We also have a collective responsibility to protect the land and its resources for our children and grandchildren.
- We take only what we need from the land; we honour and give thanks to the spirit of the land and that which we take from the land.
- The survival of the whole group is more important than the accumulation of individual wealth or status.
- The laws of the Dene which have been passed down to us by our Elders teach us how to respect the land, ourselves, and each other. They teach us how to live in balance and good health and how to protect ourselves and our children. We must continue to live by these laws and pass them on to our children.
- We respect and care for each other. In particular, we honour and provide for our Elders who cared for us and passed on the gifts of generations past. We also honour and provide for our children, who will pass on the ways of the Dene for generations yet to come.
- We come from male and female, and we respect and honour the contribution which both men and women make in working together for the survival of the people.
- We respect and honour our leaders and medicine men and women who share their special skills, knowledge, wisdom, and powers for the benefit of the people.
- Everyone has the right to be heard and to take part in discussion of matters that will affect us.
- We respect the right of the Dene, in family groups, in communities, or in regions, to make decisions, without interference from outside, with respect to matters which affect them in their territory.[30]

"Clearly," the report noted, "the values and principles summarized above have a certain universal human quality. Many of them have been reflected in the cultures of other peoples throughout the world, at different times in history. For the traditional Dene, however, these values and principles were as fundamental as life itself. It not only gave expression to the purpose and fulfilment of human life, but also served the very practical function of ensuring the survival of the people."[31]

While they were willing to define new social, economic, and political relationships based on equality and interdependence, the Dene remained firm in their goal of securing the recognition of their special rights as the people in their own homeland. Nevertheless, despite the amount of time and respectful thought poured into all of these political discussions, Canada kept shrugging and walking away. In 1988, the Nunavut Forum dissolved, and federal funding dropped dramatically. The WCF grew inactive, and 1990 marked the end of any cooperation between the Dene and the government of the Northwest Territories. The decline of the WCF was, in no small part, due to the refusal of Canada and the provinces to embrace the implementation of s.35 of the Constitution, as I'll discuss in my chapter about the Aboriginal Constitutional Conferences. This took the steam out of any willingness to consider any inherent Aboriginal rights to self-government.

Also doomed by Canada was the work the Dene undertook on land claims negotiations. An AIP had been reached in 1990 and was presented to a Dene-Métis Assembly in July of that year. I attended and remember the air was alive with the energy of debate in which delegates wrestled with what they would risk if they rejected the AIP – or whether something was better than nothing. Imagine if they could get a better agreement, more in keeping with the Dene Declaration and the Denendeh proposal! What they'd found on the table instead was so disappointing. They would, as usual, be agreeing to scraps. Canada had proposed joint (Canada-Dene) management boards that would control land and resources. Oh, and the Dene would have to extinguish their title to most of the Northwest Territories in return for getting fee simple title to smaller selected portions. Delegates felt that the provisions for their regions were both inadequate and even less than that accorded to other regions. The AIP was untenable. This sense of deflation, once a First Nation realizes their time and energy has been put into a reconciliative proposal that won't actually be taken remotely seriously, is an experience I encountered again and again.

Canada's insistence on extinguishing rights and title had become a clear pattern since it laid out a comprehensive claims policy in 1973 after the Supreme Court decision in *Calder et al. v. the Attorney General of British Columbia*. In the *Calder* case, the strong dissenting opinion led Canada to set up a claims process to try to get those title rights formally surrendered in return for benefits set out in modern Treaties. Extinguishment was included, for example, in the 1984 modern Treaty that the Inuvialuit of the Mackenzie Delta signed with Canada, as well as in the Tungavik Federation of Nunavut (TFN) Final Agreement of 1993. It was also included in an umbrella agreement signed by the Council of Yukon Indians in 1993. After the Dene's "no" vote on the AIP, different communities decided to negotiate their own regional claims. The Gwich'in Tribal Council signed a modern Treaty in 1992. The Shatu Dene region signed one in 1994, and the Tlicho region signed in 2003. The Dehcho region has never agreed, and Treaty negotiations have only recently started again after being suspended for several years.

Decolonizing Regulatory Decision-Making

On the question of the far-too-cozy relationship between project proponents and decision-makers, not much has changed. While the Supreme Court did conclude that there was a reasonable apprehension that Marshall Crowe would be biased if he remained chair at the NEB hearings, the decision made little difference to the "rotating chairs" culture between industry and government. The SCC decision remains as the authoritative precedent about "apprehension of bias," but it is considered to be an *extreme* example of rotating chairs. The practice of appointing people from industries to decision-making bodies that assess affiliated projects remains rife in Canada.

Today, Indigenous and environmental considerations are still viewed as afterthoughts, to be addressed in terms of impact mitigation. Within the existing framework, project approvals will never be denied based on Indigenous rights or environmental preservation. The courts are complicit, as they have decided that Indigenous peoples must be consulted about project impacts and, in some situations, accommodated – *but only in the very rarest of cases* will their consent be required. In those instances where Indigenous peoples or nations have gone to court claiming that consultation was inadequate and the court has agreed, the very poor remedy has been that government or industry go back and get the "box-checking" exercise right. There is still no committed sense that Indigenous rights and ecological concerns should be integrated into the approval process from the start. If we want to engage in authentic reconciliation, we must consciously engage in decolonization, which means giving equal consideration to a more holistic set of non-Western values.

The churches and other non-profits face new challenges, but they are again called to be more courageous than cautious in responding to the ever-louder call of Indigenous peoples for justice. More and more voices are telling us that. First we took their land, then we took their children, and now we are saying, "we are sorry." But when will we actively support their desire to reclaim what they lost?

On a personal note, this period around the pipeline hearings – being in Yellowknife, travelling to every community in the Northwest Territories, and getting to know so many interesting and inspiring Dene people was, for me, extremely edifying. Protest and prophecy are both powerful, and today, we need to urgently continue our efforts to change the decision-making frameworks. Justice-driven people, including all faith communities, must speak up and, as often as possible, do so in league with like-minded people, or public policy will continue to be shaped by world views that put power before people and greed before caring. Without advocacy, policy pertaining to Indigenous peoples and so-called reconciliation efforts will continue to embrace reconciliation to the sovereignty of the Crown (that is, ongoing colonialism) rather than reconciliation with Indigenous people and their own, distinctive world views.

CHAPTER TWO

Mercury Pollution and the Grassy Narrows Fight for Justice

No amount of money can even come close to compensating the people of Grassy Narrows for the 14 years of horror we have lived with since mercury polluted our river system and way of life.

Grassy Narrows Chief Arnold Pelly, June 1984[1]

The poisoning made international headlines. It was the late 1960s and the refreshingly clear river flowing past Asubpeeschoseewagong Netum Anishinabek First Nation (Grassy Narrows) in northern Ontario had suddenly and unexpectedly grown menacing. Dumped by the ton into the English-Wabigoon River system by a paper mill upstream, mercury settled into the river and lake beds and was absorbed by the numerous species of fish eaten, as they always have been, by the Ojibway people along its shores. These people were now falling ill and dying. To this day, more than fifty years later, the water remains polluted with mercury. It is a national tragedy. A polluted waterway that affected the livelihood and health of non-Indigenous people in any part of Canada would have been addressed decisively and with great urgency. Just consider the Exxon oil spill that affected the coast of British Columbia, or the *E. coli* contamination in Walkerton, Ontario. Public outcries led to swift government action.

Not in this case. Ontario was more concerned about protecting Reed Paper, the multinational company responsible for the mercury poisoning, from financial liability than it was about helping the people of Grassy Narrows and their neighbouring community of Wabaseemoong Independent Nations (Whitedog). Indeed, the province let the paper company off the hook by capping any compensation they might have to pay at $15 million, so that Reed could sell the plant to Great Lakes Paper, a subsidiary of the massively affluent Canadian Pacific Ltd., and dodge responsibility for cleaning up the river entirely.

I was privileged to work with Grassy Narrows as an advocate, a negotiator, and a lawyer in their struggle for compensation, decontamination, and control of their traditional land for more than twenty years, starting in the late 1970s. On my many trips there, I was continuously awestruck by the breathtaking beauty of the area. Grassy is about ninety kilometres northwest of Kenora, on a road that winds through pine and poplar forests alongside sparkling lakes embedded in glacial clay, and ringed by the soft pink granite of the Canadian Shield. Before mercury poisoning, the Ball Lake Lodge on the river system just north of Grassy was a renowned fishing resort visited by American actors, politicians, and executives. Owned by a colourful character named Barney Lamm, since 1945 it had employed many Grassy people as fishing guides and resort workers. The lodge, which occupied eighty square miles of their traditional land, had a chapel with stunning stained-glass windows depicting the fourteen Stations of the Cross. There were gourmet preparations of fresh pickerel, and luxury accommodations. For many generations before the Ball

Artwork 2.1: Mary Ann Penashue, *Nekatentum Uass* (Broken Child)

Lake Lodge, the Ojibway people lived self-sufficiently in their surroundings without having to earn wages. As an Elder said: "The ways of nature were our ways. The rhythms of nature were our rhythms. We did not live off the land, we were absorbed into it, nourished by it, we were a part of it."

But that way of life ended in a truly brutal fashion. Ominous changes first began in the 1920s, when Mounties started scooping up kids in the middle of the night, three or four at a time, to parcel them off to a residential school in the town of McIntosh, thirty-five kilometres south. Ongoing government programs of assimilation culminated in the forced relocation of the Grassy Narrows community from an area of relatively inaccessible islands five miles southeast, to the mainland near the Jones Logging Road. Written records of the relocation have either disappeared or been destroyed, but it was not difficult to reconstruct the motive for moving them. In the early 1960s, indeed through that whole decade, there were repeated attempts by Canada to "modernize" Indigenous life in order to encourage economic development. The policymakers thought of Indigenous people as impoverished by Canadian standards because they were too isolated from Canadian infrastructure. If the infrastructure could not be brought to them, they would be brought to it. In 1961, the Grassy Narrows relocation reflected this policy. The Ojibway had to be connected to electrical lines, a permanent day school, medical treatment, and the Hudson's Bay Company when the logging road came through from Kenora.

Anastasia Shkilnyk, who wrote *A Poison Stronger than Love*, suggests that the relocation was for the benefit of the company, which made some money from tourists and loggers but needed the trade with Indigenous people in order to survive financially.[2] What is clear is that the people at Grassy resisted the move. They regarded the new site as spiritually dead. Some reported seeing evil spirits there. All signs were that it was an unhealthy place to live. The soil was heavy with clay, which made gardening virtually impossible. The animal population was small. The traplines, commercial fishing, and wildlife sites were now a greater distance away, and thus economic pursuits were actually more difficult. Moreover, the government built cheap houses in close proximity to one another, set up in a way that did not respect the traditional clan structure. Grassy folks came to refer to the new reserve as their cage, or corral.

Having kids attend the reserve school often led to adults losing their trapping licences because they needed to stay with their children. Since the 1940s, Ojibway trappers had been required to report their harvest to the Department of Lands and Forests in Toronto. If they did not file paperwork, or meet their seasonal quota, their licence was revoked. This went on even though Treaty 3, signed in 1873, guaranteed the Ojibway the right to pursue their way of life, including hunting, fishing, and trapping, a Treaty right that is protected by the Canadian Constitution. It was also now forbidden to build cabins, however temporary, along the traplines without government permission, making it virtually impossible to maintain the lines.

At least they had their relationship with the Ball Lake Lodge. For a time, according to resident Philip Fobister, "We were in full bloom. Fishing, guiding, everything. We thought everything was going to be okay. Then we started seeing our fish acting weird and dying off. That's when we saw something was wrong."

In the 1960s, a UK-owned multinational corporation, Reed Paper, unceremoniously dumped 9,000 kilograms of mercury, used for bleaching the Dryden-based mill's paper, into the headwaters of the English-Wabigoon River. This invisible neurotoxin poisoned the waters for more than 200 kilometres. Mercury had already, by this time, been identified as a neurotoxin in the food chain. Reed should have known from the Minamata catastrophe in Japan how horrifying mercury poisoning would be in terms of human life and health. The first clear case was reported in Japan in 1953. It was called "the strange disease" because nobody had encountered this type of industrial poisoning before. In 1956, a doctor at the Chisso Corporation hospital reported that an unknown disease of the central nervous system had broken out, and by 1959, it was clear that mercury dumped into the sea by Chisso – a chemical company – was causing what officially came to be known as Minamata disease. Over time, more than 3,000 Japanese people were identified as afflicted, and some estimates put the number at around 10,000.[3]

"The nervous system begins to degenerate, to atrophy," according to one of the early accounts of the symptoms. "First, a tingling and growing numbness of limbs and lips. Motor functions may become severely disturbed, the speech slurred, the field of vision constricted. In early extreme cases, victims lapsed into unconsciousness [or] often uncontrolled shouting. Autopsies show the brain becomes spongelike as cells are eaten away. It is proven that mercury can penetrate the placenta to reach the fetus, even in apparently healthy mothers."[4]

The Lancet medical journal published a study in 1958 about Minamata disease.[5] It announced that mercury-poisoned fish in Minamata's bay caused those who ate it to develop a neurological syndrome similar to ALS. Many of the most acutely exposed victims died; hundreds were severely disabled. Japan's government officially acknowledged this environmental poison in 1969, passed a Water Pollution Act in 1970, and began taking measures to clean the bay and protect the citizenry.

I saw first hand how devastating Minamata disease was on a trip to Japan in 1983, with Raphael and Yolanda Fobister of the Grassy Narrows band. We heard that between 200 and 600 tonnes of mercury had been dumped into the water, poisoning fish later ingested by people with disabling and even lethal results. We attended symposia on mercury poisoning, explained the calamity at Grassy, met with lawyers who had worked with victims, visited special hospitals for children, and held press conferences that were covered by the Japanese print and TV media. Some of the little ones had been so crippled that they were living in a vegetative state. We spent time with Aileen Smith, who along with her husband W. Eugene Smith, both American photojournalists, had written the book *Minamata*, a deeply moving account of the tragedy. In his effort to uncover what was going on, Eugene had been severely beaten by employees of the Chisso Corporation. (In 2020, a movie, *Minamata*, featuring Johnny Depp as Eugene Smith was released.)

At that time, groups of Japanese victims decided to proceed along different routes to compensation. Some let the government make decisions, others negotiated directly with the polluting company, and still others took legal action. There were various settlements, depending on the outcome of the negotiations and court actions, which included some compensation generally related to the severity of the health impacts. We invited Dr. Masazumi Harada, one of the key physicians who knew how to identify the disease, to come to Grassy Narrows and conduct tests of people who had Minamata-like symptoms. He did so, but Health Canada was dismissive of his findings, saying that both his testing methods and results could not be relied upon. In all, Japanese doctors made five trips to Grassy over the years to examine patients. In each case, their findings were met with skepticism by Health Canada, even though the Japanese physicians were the groundbreaking experts on this modern industrial affliction. This equivocation, when Health Canada could have evoked the precautionary principle (taking precautionary measures), was indefensible, as the lives of the people of Grassy Narrows were at stake.

Reed's reckless mill pollution could not have come as a surprise to anyone paying attention. In fact, in 1965, NDP MP Douglas Mason Fisher informed Parliament that Reed's mill "is notorious throughout that whole region because of the fact that by its method of disposing of its waste, it has in a sense ruined a couple of good fishing rivers and lakes and has been a blot, if you like, upon the whole region."[6] How could Reed not have known about the hazards of mercury? Or did they know? It's unconscionable either way. They were a huge UK-owned multinational company with extensive resources. Why, indeed, did Ontario not have in place any regulations and monitoring about what was being dumped into the river? You can't build a lean-to on a trapline, no, but you can destroy an ecosystem if there's profit to be made.

Canada and Ontario responded with a combination of political buck passing, delay, denial of the health impacts (*this is nothing like Minamata*), and refusal to take legal responsibility (*this did not happen on reserve land*), with only token relief, such as offering the communities frozen fish sticks. Just eat these! At any rate, that offer was a complete misread of what life on the river meant to the people of Grassy Narrows. "Fish is not just food," resident Judy Da Silva said, "it's a part of our culture and tradition, it's a part of our spirituality."

In May of 1970, Ontario declared that the fish in the river had *some* mercury, but that it would "go away" in several months. This was a wild guess, wholly unanchored in science. In fact, mercury, which settles into the bottom of a river and gets transformed by bacteria into the more toxic methylmercury, doesn't vanish on its own. Ontario banned commercial fishing but allowed sport fishing to continue. Signs were posted on trees: "Fish for Fun but don't eat the catch." It wasn't very enticing, and the fishing lodges closed. Grassy's main sources of employment and nourishment disappeared. Many of its people showed Minamata disease symptoms, and those who did not lived in daily fear that they or their children or their unborn would fall ill. Some made the agonizing decision not to have children for fear that they would be damaged. Enforced idleness from poor health and the collapse of work – the nearest town, Kenora, is about an hour's drive away – began generating despair. The leaders of the community advocated for regained jurisdiction of over 2,000 square miles of their pre-colonial territory, so that they could revive their traditional economy and rebuild their shattered lives.

Remarkably, Reed Paper Company *continued* to dump mercury until 1975. In 1976, after several years in which Ontario and Canada did virtually nothing in response to the disaster, Grassy Narrows and Whitedog formed the Anti-Mercury Ojibway Group. On 30 June 1977, they filed a legal action in the Supreme Court of Ontario for damages against Reed Limited, Dryden Chemical Limited, and Dryden Paper Company. Two years later, as mentioned, the provincial government let Reed Paper off the legal hook by facilitating their sale of the Dryden plant to Great Lakes Forest Products, without requiring the company to clean up the river or take responsibility for the devastating harm.[7] This added insult to the injury of Grassy Narrows. Ontario could have chosen to support them, but instead they advocated for Reed, pledging that Ontario taxpayers would pay any damages over and above $15,000,000. Their public rationale was that they were protecting mill jobs in the town of Dryden. Those citizens and their paycheques mattered; the Ojibway did not. Canada stood by at the federal level and let it happen. When Great Lakes purchased the mill in 1979, the sale agreement covered them for any ensuing liability. Without Ontario's intervention, the plant would not have been sold, and Grassy and Whitedog would have been in a much stronger legal position for the suit they filed in 1977, as the Japanese victims had been.

In 1979, Simon Fobister, the Chief at Grassy Narrows, asked me if I would come up to discuss the mercury situation with him and his council. Chief Fobister had heard of my work with the Dene and the Mackenzie Valley Pipeline. He was twenty-three when I met him, the youngest Chief in the history of Grassy Narrows, a dedicated, thoughtful, creative, and inspired leader with deep spiritual beliefs. We became good friends. Our work together commenced with a review of the legal action they had filed and how that fit together with a mediation agreement that Grassy and Whitedog signed in 1978 with both the provincial and federal governments. Reed and Great Lakes were not included in the mediation, and Ontario and Canada were not named as defendants in the legal action. The Chief and council had entered the mediation agreement in good faith, so they wanted to participate fully and with vigour. The mediation process was meant to address four issues, the raising and lowering of water levels, the flooding of the reserve lands by Ontario Hydro, the relocation of the reserve, and the pollution of the environment.

The stated goal was to resolve these issues with money or by remedial and mitigatory measures that would contribute to the long-term viability of the communities.

In our discussions, Grassy came to understand that they were in a difficult position. The courts, I explained, were unlikely to consider awarding Grassy ownership of its 2,000-square-mile traditional land use area in a legal action against the paper companies. And they realized that the four mediation goals did not include an expanded land base. The Chief and council doubled down on trying to refocus mediation on the land issue and on care for the victims of the poisoning, as those steps, they felt, were the keys to recovery.

I should note that the mediation process came about in response to an interim recommendation of Ontario's Royal Commission on the Northern Environment. The Commission had been set up by Ontario Premier Bill Davis in 1976 after Andrew Rickard,

Grand Chief of what is now the Nishnawbe Aski Nation, voiced concern that Reed Paper had proposed to log a huge swath of forest near Red Lake in northwestern Ontario. The Commission was to examine the allocation and management of resources in that area. Justice Patrick Hartt served as the first commissioner. He recommended that a ministerial-level committee composed of Ontario, federal, and Aboriginal representatives be formed to resolve, through negotiation, issues raised by its members. One priority would be to address the challenges faced by Grassy Narrows and Whitedog. This resulted in the Indian Commission of Ontario, led by Hartt himself. Meanwhile, J.E. Fahlgren took over as chair of the Royal Commission, which released its final report in 1985.

The Royal Commission recommended that Ontario grant land, including mineral rights, to Indigenous communities north of the 50th parallel to help them meet their needs for food gathering, housing, community facilities, water supply, energy, fuel, and building material. It also recommended that community use areas be designated where Indigenous people had priority access for hunting, fishing, and trapping. Furthermore, until the claims of Grassy Narrows and Whitedog were settled, the Commission advised Ontario not to grant any logging rights to Great Lakes Paper. None of these recommendations were followed by Ontario. Not one of them. How many dollars were spent, how much brain power deployed, how much ink spilled? For nothing. For political window dressing.

Right from the beginning, the mediation process was poisoned by ill will. Ontario was adamantly opposed to the river clean up, insisting that it was impossible, even though Japan had demonstrated otherwise. They were equally opposed to acknowledging Grassy's entitlement to its broader traditional territory. "Nonnegotiable." Canada, meanwhile, basically washed its hands of the whole mess. It was soon clear that Grassy's earnest, almost desperate objectives would not be met.

Remarkably, Ontario maintained that its guarantee to cap corporate liability at $15 million was sufficient public contribution to the matter, even though that was a gift to the paper companies rather than to the staggering First Nations communities. The position of the Elders, Chief, and council that the return of the 2,000 square miles of their traditional land use area – which was supported by the Erikson and Vecsey report, discussed below – held no weight. That Grassy backed up its proposal for jurisdiction over its 2,000-square-mile Grassy Narrows Traditional Land Use Area (GNTLUA) by detailing the importance of the land for trapping, hunting, fishing, berry picking, wild rice harvesting, and selective logging held no weight. Grassy also proposed that commercial logging, fishing, tourist camps, and sport hunting lodges compatible with traditional activities could be licensed and regulated by Grassy Narrows. Again: no weight.

Ontario dismissed the prospect of Grassy stewardship as "totally unacceptable." They said that Ontario would retain control of the GNTLUA for the benefit of "all of the people in the province including 'the Indian people.'"[8] Ontario was prepared, within certain limits, to negotiate access to timber, wild rice, fish, fur, game, blueberries, and commercial tourist resources. That was it. The fundamental clash between the objectives of Grassy Narrows to control and use their traditional land in order to heal, and Ontario's colonial determination to retain ownership continues to this very day. Until recently, when they imposed a partial ban on logging, Ontario continued to grant permits for logging and other uses without the consent of Grassy. Still, they fight on. It's like they're coming to the negotiating table with arrows through their bodies, like Sitting Bull, wounded and still fighting, while the government orders tea.

Because Ontario and Canada refused to seriously discuss the Grassy proposals, the mediation process ground to a halt and was formally ended on 30 May 1981. In those first few years, I made numerous trips to the reserve. Along with attending many long and hard meetings with the Chief and council – Chief Simon Fobister, followed by Chief Arnold Pelly – I formed warm friendships with Bill Fobister, Andy Keewatin, John Beaver, Isaac Pahpassay, and Joe Fobister. Judy Da Silva was and continues to be a gifted and inspirational freedom fighter for Grassy Narrows. All the people at Grassy were and still are wonderful people, deeply committed to justice for their people and their land. I often went out on the English-Wabigoon River system with folks from Grassy to experience its now-deceptive beauty. Greed had turned this paradise into poison. The people were very angry that Ontario retained sole control of environmental stewardship yet had imposed no regulations on Reed Paper. And they were furious that Ontario had bailed out the company. They were also devastated by the pollution and terrified that the health impacts might be as severe as the Minamata tragedy. The company, meanwhile, tried to spin it away as a trifle. "In any sample, you could find perhaps 5 per cent of the population of Toronto that would show symptoms of Minamata disease," Reed Paper CEO Robert Billingsley said airily in a 1976 CBC interview. "Headaches, for example, is a symptom."[9] And that continued to be the company spin, one that Ontario and Canada echoed when refusing to concede anything in response to the Grassy proposals.

Grassy ended the mediation and resolved to build on the support of the many people in Ontario, across Canada, and increasingly around the world who felt outraged at the immoral stance of the companies and politicians. They invited Japanese activists to come to Grassy. They also invited Kai Erikson, a retired Yale University sociologist who specialized in the effects of disasters on human communities, and Christopher Vecsey, then assistant professor of history at Hobart and William Smith colleges, and currently professor of philosophy and religion at Colgate University who specializes in North American Indian history. The two men would evaluate the impact of mercury pollution and relocation on the Grassy community. In their report, Erikson and Vecsey said a cash settlement by itself was likely to aggravate despair in the community rather than alleviate it, because the people of Grassy needed land to regain their sense of independence, and their traditional communion with the environment. They noted that the assimilation of Indigenous peoples, so widely presumed in the 1960s and 1970s by North American governments to be the path forward, was not a meaningful option for most. For every story about an Indigenous person who succeeds in mainstream society, there are hundreds who fail because mainstream society is not neutral about the fundamental beliefs and values that give meaning and purpose to life; rather it is the expression of one specific set of values, European in origin. The report confirmed what Grassy was already telling Canada and Ontario in mediation negotiations: namely, that European values often stand in sharp contradiction with the traditional beliefs of Ojibway people. For example, Europeans typically see the Earth as a storehouse of materials to be exploited by science and technology, whereas Ojibway see the Earth as the mother – the source of all life to be respected and revered. Europeans view plants and animals as physical beings to be cultivated by humans for gain, managed for enjoyment or else exterminated, whereas Ojibway beliefs hold that plants and animals are spiritual beings who provide growth and healing for all creatures.

With respect to happiness, the report noted that Europeans believe happiness is achieved by pursuing material gain and power in human relationships, whereas the Ojibway feel it is achieved by pursuing a vision and fostering a society that actualizes that vision. A person who tries to enter mainstream society carrying a different set of values finds his or her sense of what is real or important attacked by the very way that life is organized. Few people from minority cultures can stand up to this since it comes from all sides and in ways that can't even be seen. The price paid for assimilation is sacrifice of oneself.

Because of the racism inherent in dominant societies, most Indigenous people who make this sacrifice are denied the reward anyway. With all of this in mind, Erikson and Vecsey advised that the most appropriate form of compensation would be a substantial grant of land, ideally close to the current reserve. Grassy should have a home territory in which they could restore the security of their traditional ways and escape the pollution of the river. The lands in question ought to contain sufficient resources to provide an economic base for people in all the ways of nature, so that they can employ their native skills in such meaningful activity as timbering, fishing, trapping, harvesting wild rice, and serving as guides to tourists and sportspeople.

The economic benefits of this arrangement are obvious. Psychological and social benefits would follow. This tract of land could provide a sheltered territory in which the people of Grassy Narrows recover some of the strengths of their Ojibway past, and at the same time serve as a base camp, a place to regroup for those preparing to take their place in the economic structure of modern Canada. Sociologists have long suggested that upward mobility for those who want to participate in mainstream society is easiest for people who know their roots and can draw nourishment from them.

In a world that has begun to recognize the fragility of nature and the scarcity of natural resources, anything the government can do to help the Ojibway people preserve their understanding of and respect for ecology would, in the long run, be a service to all Canadians. The question may not be what the country can contribute to the welfare of the Indigenous inhabitants, but what those inhabitants can contribute to the rest of the world, a viewpoint reflected by the Grassy Narrows Elders. A clear example of this has been Grassy's vehement defence of the old-growth forest in their territory, blockading logging roads until they finally compelled the Ontario government, in 2023, to suspend clear-cutting for ten years. Non-Indigenous people are only beginning to understand the importance of the old forests in mitigating the impact of extreme weather events, as I'll discuss more in my chapter on the Teme-Augama.

These discussions led the band to adopt the Grassy Narrows Traditional Land Use Approach. The Elders spoke of it to me this way: "The Anishnawbe are known to be experienced hunters and food gatherers. It's obvious why they survived all those years before the coming of the early settlers from overseas. The Ojibway provided themselves with everything they needed to survive. They made their homes, clothes, food, weapons, transportation, and medicine. The Ojibway had their own way of worship."

With the 1982 recognition and affirmation of the rights of Aboriginal peoples in Canada's patriated Constitution, hope arose in Grassy that this might cause Ontario and Canada to abandon their approach and take a fresh look at Grassy's proposals for river clean up, care, and compensation for the victims of Minamata and a new land base.

At this time, the situation in Grassy was getting worse, not better. Ten years after the first mercury dump there was still no compensation, no focused care for the poisoned people, and Canadian medical skepticism prevailed over the reality of what visiting Japanese doctors were observing on reserve. There was no river clean up, no economic relief, and no movement towards the new land base. The people of Grassy were suffering, and with that suffering came addictions and family and community breakdown. Public support through rallies and protests was growing, but governments remained what can only be described as cold-hearted. Marc Miller, former minister of Crown-Indigenous Relations and Northern Affairs Canada (CIRNAC), recently acknowledged that "the lack of action on this [Canada's response to Grassy] is an aberration on our history."[10] Yes, it is.

It became apparent that Grassy had to take a more strategic approach, one that would bring some immediate health and economic relief to the community while preserving the option of river clean up and control of the GNTLUA. So, in June of 1984, Grassy signed a $4.4 million compensation package with Canada. Whitedog had agreed to a similar settlement a year earlier. Most of the funds were earmarked for economic development by expanding band-controlled selective logging and wild rice harvesting, as well as setting up a sewing factory to make traditional clothing, arts, and crafts. A social development fund was also established to assist the Elders, which included counselling and crisis services. Grassy and Whitedog also continued to press for a settlement with Ontario and Great Lakes Paper.

The 1984 settlement negotiations got the attention of federal Indian affairs minister David Crombie, who came to understand the importance of Grassy getting agreements with Great Lakes/ Reed and Ontario. Crombie appointed former Supreme Court of Canada Judge Emmett Hall as his envoy in an effort to catalyse negotiations. The Grassy representatives were excited by Crombie's decision to appoint Hall as he, along with Justice Laskin and Justice Spence, had dissented in favour of the Indigenous position in two important Supreme Court decisions: *Calder et al. v. the Attorney General of British Columbia* and *the Attorney General of Canada v. Lavell*, which dealt with the loss of status by an Indigenous woman who married a non-Indigenous man.

Hall joined a new round of negotiations with Ontario, Canada, Great Lakes/Reed, Whitedog, and Grassy Narrows. The two First Nations had negotiation teams led by the Chief and council members, a political negotiator, with me as technical negotiator. Robert Blair, who later became a justice of the Ontario Court of Appeal, served as Grassy's lawyer, and Glenn Sigurdson acted for Whitedog. Some sessions were held in Toronto, some in other locations, and on a few occasions, Emmett Hall came to Grassy. I would pick him up at the Winnipeg Airport when he flew in from Saskatoon. On those long trips up to Grassy Narrows, it was wonderful to hear him reminisce about his career in Saskatchewan and his close personal relationship with John Diefenbaker. He talked about travelling from Saskatoon to Ottawa when he was a young lawyer, and the long train trips that made appearing before the Supreme Court a three-to-four-week journey.

Hall chaired the Royal Commission, which recommended the establishment of federal-provincial health services, leading to the passage of the Canada Health Act. He also authored the Hall-Dennis Report, *Living and Learning*, a review of the public education system in Ontario, and made wide-ranging recommendations for change. Justice Hall was a great Canadian, and it was an honour to spend many hours with him on those memorable drives.

We discussed the importance of a land base if Grassy was to recover from the mercury pollution. Despite Grassy's ongoing insistence that any agreement include river clean up and recognition of the GNTLUA, Ontario continued to declare both goals impossible. The negotiations dragged on. The possibility of moving ahead with the litigation against Reed Limited and their affiliated companies was narrowing: a Pre-Litigation Study by University of Toronto law professor Robert J. Sharpe – later appointed to the Ontario Court of Appeal, from which he has since retired – warned that success at trial would be a long shot. From a cost point alone, he thought it would be virtually prohibitive for Grassy. A particular obstacle was the resolution of health claims of individual adults and minors, and potential health claims of the unborn. This, of course, was a major concern for Grassy. But establishing the liability of the defendants was fraught with troublesome issues, such as establishing quantum of damages. Sharpe also said the law was unsettled on whether Indigenous people could successfully demonstrate a proprietary interest in pollution of a river system outside the boundaries of their Indian Act reserve. Because of that issue he advised that a court might not award Grassy and Whitedog any damages.[11]

Accordingly, Justice Hall advised Grassy and Whitedog that it would be in their best interest to negotiate a settlement instead. At that point, Grassy did two things. It appealed to the public for help to get the best possible settlement, and it developed an internal strategy for the negotiations, seeking care and compensation for the victims of Minamata poisoning and financial compensation as a base for economic recovery while preserving their right to continue the fight for river clean up and ownership and control of the GNTLUA.

In response to the public appeal for help, the *Globe and Mail* ran an editorial headlined "Indecent Delay," arguing that the position of Great Lakes and Reed – that pollution had not been established and the damages to the Indigenous inhabitants had not been proven – was "an attitude that is neither credible nor worthy of a Canadian company with a modicum of social conscience." Great Lakes' failure to produce a fair offer of compensation in the face of an obvious corporate responsibility is "a sad chapter in the history of Canadian business more suited to earlier decades in this century when private enterprise too often made the case for its enemies."[12]

Grassy asked the public to write to Justice Hall, Minister Crombie, and Ontario's premier, David Peterson. It reminded everyone that Great Lakes was a part of Canada's largest company, Canadian Pacific Ltd., whose annual revenue was equivalent to the GNP of New Zealand. In 1984, Great Lakes invested $33 million to build a paper mill in Washington State, and between 1980 and 1984, Great Lakes received $48 million in grants from the government. It could afford to clean up its mess. Grassy called for a boycott of Canadian Pacific Air, CP Telecommunications, Canadian Pacific Hotels like the Royal York in Toronto, Banff Springs Hotel, Chateau Frontenac in Quebec, and so on, as well as Marathon Realty, which had developed thirty-two shopping centres and forty-three office buildings in Canada.

Many First Nations, including Grand Council Treaty 3, the Association of Iroquois and Allied Indians, and the Nishnawbe Aski Nation, responded by writing letters to Hall and the politicians. There was also a groundswell of protest and petition from individuals and non-profits, like the Task Force on Churches and Corporate Responsibility, the Voice of Women, the National Anti-Poverty Organization, the Canadian Wildlands League, and thousands of individuals. There is no question these letters and petitions put pressure on the paper companies and governments to enter into a settlement.[13]

Despite this support, and the commitment and dogged persistence of the Grassy negotiating team, Ontario adamantly refused to even *discuss* including the 2,000-square-mile land base or the river clean up in any settlement. Since Ontario had let Reed and Great Lakes off the hook, those companies sat back with corporate smugness during the negotiations. As for Canada, any "honour of the Crown" had gone AWOL. These realities – combined with the stark certainty that the courts would most likely not rule in favour of a land base and the river decontamination – led Grassy to focus on a settlement that would provide compensation for the victims of mercury poisoning and some socio-economic recovery funding. The fight for their territory would, unfortunately, have to wait.

Finally, in the fall of 1985, after years of work, an agreement was reached providing benefits to victims, as well as funding for job creation and economic development programs. Grassy and Whitedog each received a cash settlement of about $8 million, of which $1 million went towards a health fund and most importantly the establishment of a Mercury Disability Board. As with the earlier settlements with Canada, this pact was no cause for celebration given what people of Grassy and Whitedog had endured – and continue to suffer. You can't put a dollar figure on that.

The settlement was approved by the Supreme Court of Ontario in 1986 and included the provision that Grassy did not waive or release Ontario from any rights or claims arising from the 1978 mediation memorandum of understanding. When submitted to the people of Grassy for ratification, it received overwhelming support, mostly because of the Mercury Disability Board provisions and the fact that it said that the fight with Ontario over the river and the 2,000-square-mile GNTLUA could continue.

As noted above, a critical part of the settlement was the establishment of the Mercury Disability Board via Ontario legislation. As envisioned by the people of Grassy Narrows, this board has turned out to be the most significant part of the agreement. Since its inception on 31 December 1986, 616 people have been approved for benefits, a little over $45 million has been paid out, and most victims continue to get monthly payments. Ontario is required to replenish the fund as necessary, as stipulated in the agreements. Grassy has creatively campaigned for a community mercury treatment facility as well, as Minamata victims were having to travel to Winnipeg for medical appointments, which left many victims without access to proper care and exacerbated their conditions.

On 31 March 1995, Grassy Narrows and Ontario Hydro reached an agreement on the fluctuation of water levels and flooding caused by the construction of hydro dams. Ontario Hydro agreed to pay the First Nation $10 million and also agreed that it would notify Grassy if it intended to build any new hydroelectric generation stations on the English River system or undertake modifications. In such a case, Ontario is required to discuss the reasonable likelihood of incremental adverse impacts in the area with Grassy and is required to enter into negotiations to consider service contracts for the benefit of the First Nation, employment and training for members, natural and social environmental impact prevention, mitigation and compensation for residual impacts, and ongoing monitoring. Hydro also agreed to pay $15,000 per year for fifteen years as scholarships for Grassy student members planning on post-secondary education.

Grassy has kept the pressure on Ontario to negotiate the outstanding issues of control of the GNTLUA and river decontamination, despite the unconscionable refusal of successive Ontario governments to respond to the band's proposals. With remarkable tenacity, they continue to advocate, because the health of future generations is at stake, and Grassy will not give up. The "Free Grassy" movement and the "Grassy River Run" campaign and rallies continue. Remarkable community members like Judy Da Silva are relentless in advocating for Grassy, along with supporters and environmental groups. I continued to work with Grassy on these negotiations until 2017. That year, over *half a century* after the mercury pollution was detected, the Ontario government at last pledged $85 million to clean up the river, but to date has focused on simply "studying the matter."

In 2021, Canada announced $12.5 million for two mercury treatment facilities, one in Grassy Narrows and one in Whitedog. Indigenous Services Minister Miller said that part of the agreement entails putting money in a trust fund to be used by Grassy to treat their people so that they can live (and ail) in dignity, close to their families.

The shameful reality is that, despite some hard-fought achievements, the Ojibway people of Grassy Narrows continue to live in peril. They still suffer from the destruction of their way of life and the health of so many of their people. It could have been different, and it still can be. The hope and the solution both lie in Ontario recognizing Grassy jurisdiction over the 2,000-square-mile GNTLUA. The problem is that Ontario refuses to acknowledge that Grassy *must* have sufficient control over its GNTLUA if it is to rebuild its traditional economy and become self-sufficient and heal itself. Having been at the table over the years with Grassy leaders and negotiators about this, it is clear to me that Ontario is unwilling to share power due to a race-based fear that the men and women of Grassy Narrows cannot be trusted to oversee the area, despite the stark fact that Ontario's own stewardship has often been disastrous.

Ontario's approach continues to be colonial. I do not say that lightly. But the reality is that Grassy came to the negotiating table in good faith, with reconciliation in mind and heart, built into many carefully thought-through proposals tabled between 1983 and 1995 for how they would manage the GNTLUA. Those plans were based on deeply researched and detailed studies for how the land, the flora and fauna, and the renewable and non-renewable resources of the area could be overseen and nurtured. Ontario refused to budge from its position that the province retains control "for the benefit of all of the people of the province including the Indian people." The fact is, the benefit of all of the people means the benefit, primarily, of forestry and mining companies. Forestry companies are granted control by Ontario's Ministry of Natural Resources under Forest Management Agreements (FMAs) – under which "forest management" just means clear-cutting the trees. Traditional land uses, tourism, and related recreational uses are not included in the FMAs. Needless to say, clear-cutting only ruins other possible current or traditional activities in the forest. The cumulative impacts also destroy the possibility for *future* diverse uses.

Grassy commissioned a host of studies about co-managing the land, water, renewable and non-renewable resources, wildlife, forestry, and fishery potentials of the GNTLUA. Grassy also engaged a social reconstruction expert, a child psychiatrist, and medical doctors, all of whom provided advice on community healing. An education group looked at changes to the school curriculum. A social and economic analysis was prepared. All of this work contributed to an overall plan for the recovery and rebuilding of Grassy by drawing on traditional knowledge to build a self-sufficient community. At its core, the Grassy approach was mindful of the importance of restoring a positive personal self-image that fostered an individual and community sense of self-worth in being Ojibway, with a positive ability to choose a direction for the community, and vocation choices that are productive and personally fulfilling; whether the choice be a traditional way of life, a life in mainstream society, or an amalgam of the two.

In its proposals for control of the GNTLUA, Grassy pointed to the recommendations *already made* in the report of the Royal Commission on the Northern Environment. These included that Ontario not grant any additional cutting rights to Great Lakes or any subsequent owner of the Dryden mill until the claims of Whitedog and Grassy were settled, and that a northern land commissioner be appointed to identify and recommend portions of Crown land to be granted to Indian communities north of the 50th parallel after considering the needs of the community.

Adopting those recommendations would certainly be in keeping with the 1985 Declaration of Political Intent signed by Ontario, Canada, and the Ontario First Nations. Grassy urged that negotiations be conducted in a co-operative way rather than the old adversarial manner, to cultivate a respectful and reconciling relationship and embody the sharing of land and resources set out in Treaty 3. This approach would foster an actual negotiation of issues rather than the old "take it or leave it" offers of colonial bureaucrats. Ontario refused to engage in this authentic act of reconciliation. It simply would not bend.

Over the years, Grassy modified its position out of deflated necessity and made several proposals to successive governments that, in lieu of outright ownership and control of the GNTLUA, they would accept co-management with sufficient Grassy control and access to rebuild their traditional economy. The compromises were crafted over many meetings in which the people and leaders wrestled in good faith, trusting that Ontario would meet them halfway and agree to co-management. It was a real privilege to work on those proposals with an amazing array of Chiefs, councillors, negotiators, traditional and non-traditional land, environment and resources experts, all of whom were deeply committed to the people and the land, and all of whom were committed to work for reconciliation with Ontario.

The proposals all noted that the people of Grassy Narrows – by religion, culture, tradition, language, and economics – live in a special relationship with the natural environment. There is suffering when they witness traditional resources being exploited and destroyed by the encroachment of another culture. They wanted to regain some agency *on behalf* of the land. Co-management proposals tabled by Grassy from 1985 to 2000 all featured variants of these central components.

- The GNTLUA would be managed by an area management board that would have an equal number of appointees from Grassy and Ontario, and the board would develop an integrated management plan that prioritized traditional land use and habitat restoration and regeneration.
- Grassy would select certain areas of land and water within the GNTLUA where Grassy would own the land and surface and sub-surface rights.
- Ontario would retain technical ownership of the portions of the GNTLUA that Grassy did not select, but it would be subject to the exclusive harvesting rights of the people of Grassy Narrows.
- Grassy would, by virtue of its traditional land use and occupancy, have the right to share in a percentage – to be established in negotiation – of all royalties and other fees occurring to Ontario by virtue of agreements with other parties for extraction of any renewable and non-renewable resources.
- In aggregate, the revenue from the implementation of the above rights in the GNTLUA would provide ongoing self-sufficiency for Grassy.

The interim and final recommendations of the RCAP were disappointingly, but not unexpectedly, ignored by Ontario. The fact that the province had bailed out Reed Paper and Great Lakes to the severe detriment of Grassy Narrows had been a red flag in the first place.

Grassy renewed its hope for a new partnership with the 1990 election of the NDP government. When the August 1991 Statement of Political Relationship was signed by Ontario and the

Ontario First Nations, Grassy assumed that negotiations would proceed based on that statement. In it, Ontario acknowledged that its relationship with First Nations would unfold based on the recognition and affirmation of Treaty and Aboriginal rights, and on the inherent right to self-government of First Nations that flows from the reality that the Creator gave them their lands, as recognized by s.35 of Canada's patriated Constitution.

In negotiations, the NDP government agreed to set up a conservation authority to manage and set policies for the use of lands and resources in the GNTLUA. Grassy Narrows conservation officers would monitor and enforce the policies. Ontario also agreed that a portion of the royalties and revenues from resources extracted from the GNTLUA would go towards funding the conservation authority. In those discussions, Grassy also asked for a freeze on permits, approvals, and dispositions within the area that did not have Grassy's consent. Some headway was made, but the issue of co-management was a sticking point. Ontario wanted to continue to make all the decisions, with Grassy serving in an advisory capacity.

Unfortunately, good will attempts on the part of Ontario and Grassy to come to some understanding of the extent to which the co-management plan would meet the Grassy Narrows principles for co-management did not lead to any agreement, and in June of 1995 the Rae government fell to the Harris government. In the twenty-seven years since, Grassy has continued, as yet unsuccessfully, to advocate for ownership and control of the GNTLUA.

Overall, the responses of the paper companies, Ontario, and Canada to the mercury poisoning tragedy can only be described as disgraceful. Modest achievements such as the Mercury Disability Board and the Hydro settlement only came from the hard work and unwavering persistence of the leaders and people of Grassy. Former Chief Steve Fobister died in October 2018 at age sixty-six, after suffering from a neurological disorder linked to the river poisoning. He exemplified the spirit of the people of Grassy. For four decades, he fought tenaciously for a better life for his people, despite major health problems. He spoke to me about how a Bible study group on the reserve to which he belonged had struggled to understand what the Ten Commandments mean for their lives. Here's an example Steve relayed about their search for the truth:

> *You shall not commit murder.* You can murder a person in a lot of ways other than physically killing them. You can kill a person's spirit, kill them mentally or take away their pride. We have been killed in these ways by outsiders to the point that we are now striking out against ourselves and others. We don't want to "kill" outsiders, but we need to set things right so we can start loving ourselves and our neighbour again.

I was blessed to have a personal relationship with many Grassy people, including Steve Fobister, Simon Fobister, and Arnold Pelly. Sadly, Simon died in August of 2019 at the age of sixty-three of health issues that were evidently also complicated by mercury poisoning. These outstanding leaders and other remarkable Grassy Narrows women and men taught me a lot about living with integrity and respect for all of our neighbours on Mother Earth. They also showed me what authentic reconciliation can look like. That we cannot see it or don't care – and that we'd rather subject them to fifty years of hell than give their land back – speaks volumes about our failure to love our Indigenous neighbours. Think about it. Fifty years later and the river has still not been cleaned up. Unbelievable and utterly unacceptable. Today, reconciliation with Grassy is not only possible, it is essential. It would mean a new round of negotiations to sort out the details of their control of the GNTLUA, a river clean-up plan, and more urgency in getting the mercury care facility, now finally under construction, properly staffed. There is no reason to fear Indigenous control of their traditional lands and resources. As Grassy has proposed over the years, their management would lead to self-sufficiency based on a more integrated plan that would remove the reckless "management" of forest companies and focus on traditional land uses and forest regeneration. Reconciliation with Grassy Narrows demands that Ontario and Canada come to the table to make this happen.

CHAPTER THREE

The Aboriginal Peoples Constitutional Conferences

The story of how Canada went, in just thirteen years, from an attempt to officially assimilate Aboriginal peoples in 1969 to its 1982 agreement to affirm their rights in our Constitution is a remarkable one, indeed. It speaks to the fortitude and political passion of Indigenous people from coast to coast. It's also a dark tale about our Euro-Canadian leadership.

In 1969, the Red Paper issued by the Alberta Chiefs had called for a constitutional entrenchment of rights, and that campaign intensified in the ensuing decade, as Canada and the provinces began talking about reforming our 1867 Constitution. Federal–provincial discussions started in 1966 with the so-called Victoria Round and continued until the Patriation Round of 1980 and 1981. No Aboriginal delegates were invited. Finally, to call attention to the political cold-shouldering, visionary president of the Union of BC Indian Chiefs, George Manuel, chartered a train in 1980 to ride from Vancouver to Ottawa, which he dubbed the Constitution Express. Money to rent the train from Via Rail was raised at the grass-roots level – a dollar here, ten dollars

Artwork 3.1: Mary Ann Penashue, *Ashtunu* (Innu canoe builder)

there – from across the First Nation communities of BC. Leaders, Elders, and spontaneous volunteers hopped aboard and stopped at every station in the land, attracting media and spreading the message that Aboriginal peoples' rights *must* be recognized in a new constitution.

After 1,000 or so riders arrived in Ottawa, they found a warm welcome from Mayor Marion Dewar, who helped them procure billets and food. They also won support from opposition leader Joe Clark and Governor General Ed Schreyer, who invited them to a reception at Rideau Hall. About fifty of the riders then moved on to New York, to address diplomats at the UN and press their grave concerns. At the same time, the Russell Tribunal, a European human rights organization co-founded by famed authors Jean Paul Sartre and Bertrand Russell, accused North American governments of committing genocide against Aboriginal peoples, partly due to a submission they had received from George Manuel. Public pressure mounted on Prime Minister Pierre Trudeau and the premiers to take these constitutional intentions seriously.

I became involved in the autumn of 1980, at the request of Georges Erasmus, who was now regional Chief of the National Indian Brotherhood (NIB) for the Northwest Territories. In 1982, the NIB changed its name to the Assembly of First Nations (AFN) to make the point that they were Canada's First Peoples, in response to the dismissive assumption that Canada had been founded by the English and the French. Georges asked me to join the NIB legal-technical team to work on how to word a proposed section of a patriated Constitution that would entrench their Aboriginal and Treaty rights. It was a great privilege to collaborate with so many remarkable Indigenous leaders, lawyers, and political advisors from across Canada both internally and in meetings with Canada and the provinces. As we conferred about what "recognition of rights" words to put in the Constitution, the leaders continued pressing the prime minister and premiers to do the right thing, while urging Canadians to support them.

Aboriginal leaders also flew to Great Britain in 1981, asking Westminster to reject any constitutional repatriation proposal that did *not* entrench their Aboriginal and Treaty rights. The nation of Canada could not speak on behalf of Indigenous nations, they warned, because their Treaties had been signed with British monarchs. As they had articulated to the Russell Tribunal in

1980, if Britain did not insist that Aboriginal and Treaty rights be entrenched, "Britain will have completed the process of constitutional development of Canada at the expense of her obligations to the Indian Nations. The result will be to assist the Canadian government in its persistent policy of assimilation of Indian people and expropriation of Indian land, without Indian consent."

The first set of Indigenous constitutional provisions that we drafted were quite detailed and stipulated the inherent right of First Nations to pass their own laws. In all the internal discussions, it was decided that moving away from the Indian Act required a clear constitutional statement that Treaty and Aboriginal rights were *inherent* – meaning that they pre-existed the founding of Canada by thousands of years. They must be recognized in Canada's Constitution as having been granted to First Nations by the Creator, not by Great Britain, Canada, or the provinces. The NIB, Inuit, and Métis articulated that point everywhere they could, including at the United Nations. They asserted their position to a Joint Canadian Parliamentary Committee with such conviction and passion that the committee agreed to recommend, at least, this watered-down provision: "The aboriginal and treaty rights of the aboriginal peoples of Canada are hereby recognized and affirmed." By watered down, I mean that it did not specify those rights as inherent. Still, it was significant; finally, a government body was offering to recognize these rights in the Constitution. With this endorsement in hand, Indigenous advocacy gained new energy across Canada and in Great Britain.

The NIB, Inuit, and Métis reaction to Canada's proposed provision spurred lively debate; some of the leaders and legal-technical team members were jubilant, while others felt disappointed that the provision, as worded, had not been more explicit. (Recall that the initial wording offered by the NIB had specified that Aboriginal and Treaty rights were not contingent upon any other government's definition.) This latter, skeptical group were right to be wary as it turned out. But support for the provision grew with the realization that the provinces would have to be *convinced* to accept any constitutional entrenchment of Aboriginal rights, and convincing them would be a significant challenge, requiring all hands on deck. Eight provinces had campaigned to have the British Parliament reject any patriation package proposed by Canada that the premiers didn't approve of. And in September 1981, the Supreme Court declared that a patriation package required at least some measure of provincial support, which meant that Canada could not include the Aboriginal provision on its own. The court's decision led to another intense round of inter-governmental negotiations in early November 1981. Again, Aboriginal peoples were excluded from these talks, which focused on matters like the Charter of Rights and Freedoms. Indeed, scant notice was taken of Aboriginal and Treaty rights until the last minute. Then it immediately erupted into a contentious issue of power-sharing. Some provinces voiced concern about how the entrenchment of such rights would fetter provincial exercise of constitutional power. Others balked at the lack of specificity. *What* rights, exactly? They demanded to know.

When Prime Minister Trudeau tabled a revised resolution on constitutional patriation in Parliament late in November 1981, the text reflected his impatience with this eleventh-hour wrangling. It omitted the Aboriginal provision altogether and simply decreed that a First Ministers conference on Aboriginal matters would be convened within a year of the Constitution's return. The shock of reading – and re-reading – that resolution, *and not finding the Aboriginal and Treaty rights clause*, was heart-stopping for many of us. The First Nations responded with the same fierce outrage with which they'd opposed the 1969 White Paper. Inuit and Métis people, as well as many non-Indigenous Canadians, also engaged in vehement protests and lobbying. The federal NDP, led by Ed Broadbent, demanded that the Aboriginal rights provision be reinstated. So did many newspaper editorialists. To dodge the outrage, the premiers hastily conferred and decided to put back the provision with an additional word. It then read, "The *existing* aboriginal and treaty rights of the aboriginal peoples of Canada are hereby recognized and affirmed." That, then, would become the text of s.35.1 of Canada's Constitution. S.35.2 declared that Aboriginal peoples included the Indian, Inuit, and Métis peoples.

In my discussions with federal and provincial lawyers at the time, it seemed clear that the word "existing" gave those governments comfort, because they believed that most Aboriginal rights had been extinguished by pre-1981 Treaties. And Canada's new policy for modern Treaty negotiations with those First Nations who had not signed historic Treaties required them to "cede and surrender their aboriginal rights" in return for certain benefits. Hence, modern Treaties would pose no threat either. In other words, allowing the provision back in was an entirely insincere gesture, because the premiers expected it to mean as little as the performative land acknowledgments that so many organizations engage in today. They also permitted a provision that no province could use the Notwithstanding Clause – allowing a provincial government to override Canadians' Charter Rights – to override Aboriginal rights. (What harm in that, since there weren't really any Aboriginal rights?) The Constitution Act further decreed – kicking the can down the road – that a First Ministers–Aboriginal leaders conference must be scheduled within one year of the effective date of the new Constitution. Aboriginal "rights," such as they were, could be worried about then.

Although my strong preference had been to exclude the word "existing," I remember thinking that it was better than having no provision at all. (The usual wall that First Nations get backed up against.) My hope was that, at some point, our governments and courts would shed their settler colonial skin and come to understand that "existing" rights were rooted in the spirit of the historic Treaties – which entailed the sharing of land and not its surrender.

First Ministers Conferences on Aboriginal Constitutional Matters

In the fall of 1982 and early 1983, I spent a good deal of time working with the AFN legal-technical team to prepare for the First Ministers and Aboriginal Leaders Conference scheduled for March. Our preparation was vested in the understanding that s.35 marked a turning away from assimilation towards a nation-to-nation partnership with Canada and the provinces. We believed that the new partnership would be based on an affirmation of Aboriginal and Treaty rights – a *recognition* of rights and yes, that those rights pre-existed conversations at the Euro-Canadian negotiating table. This was an all-important distinction. The Constitutional Conferences would be about unpacking a full box of constitutionally recognized rights, including the inherent right to self-governance, the equal treatment of men and women, unceded land title, and stewardship of resources.

From the outset of the first conference, held in the conference centre renovated from the old Ottawa railway station across the street from the Chateau Laurier, the divide about how s.35 was going to be understood was crushingly obvious. Prime Minister Trudeau, all dashingly attired with a rose in his lapel, said, "We are dealing with a constitution that has yet to define the place of our aboriginal peoples in Canadian Society." The AFN begged to differ. Their sense of place was clear. They were an unconquered people who had agreed to share their lands, not surrender them and lose all right to self-determination. "You, Mr. Chairman, and your people," Kwakiutl Nation leader Bill Wilson, representing the Native Council of Canada, told Trudeau, "Your governments have been involved in nation-building for some 150 years. My people on the coast of British Columbia have been involved for 30,000 years on the same piece of land." He added, "I know there are people here at this table who are more concerned with protecting the power they have, the jurisdiction they have, than ensuring that the lives of Native Indian, Métis, and Inuit people are improved. A change in attitude among all Canadians must solve this problem. And perhaps it can start with this conference." Wilson placed the cards right out on the table.

Premier René Lévesque of Quebec was game to be candid in turn. "This is a political process that is fundamentally a question of power," he said with his characteristic scowl. "Power has traditionally been exercised in several classic ways. Probably the most classic is by the force of arms. And by the strength of numbers ... What alternative is left so that a group can reach a civilized solution? It means accumulating enough power. Ways of exerting pressure, so they can negotiate as equals. That's fundamental."[1] It was self-evident to Lévesque that that power threshold had not been met by his Aboriginal counterparts. They may not have been explicitly, militarily conquered, but they had been overrun. The premiers needn't recognize any rights at all. While he may have been the only politician to voice this view so blatantly, it certainly set the tenor for that and following Aboriginal conferences.

Aboriginal leaders' remarks about needing assurance that s.35 included the right of self-government were interpreted by some pundits at the time as evidence that they understood that s.35 *contained* no spelled-out or inherent rights. In fact, what was being expressed was that Aboriginal leaders understood s.35 to mark the heralding of a new political arrangement, truer to their historic intention in signing Treaties or – in the case of those that had not signed anything – in exercising their Aboriginal rights and title. Section 35 was, in their view, to be a decisive turning of the page from several centuries of power, genocide, and assimilation to a new, "living tree" relationship that grows and matures over time – as opposed to a fixed contract. The Aboriginal leaders saw the harmonization of their constitutionally recognized Aboriginal rights with the longer-standing constitutional rights of Canada and the provinces as the way to achieve the "living tree" relationship. The promise of this new relationship had been heralded by First Nations, Inuit, and Métis in the lead up to the first conference. But it wasn't shared. Instead, they encountered scorn, mockery, and racist derision. When an AFN Elder in full regalia opened the meeting with a ceremonial prayer, Trudeau asked, "Are we going to pray every morning?" The Elder said, "Yes, sir." Trudeau stood up, announced that "everyone should pray to their own God," and intoned aloud, over top of the Elder, encouraging the premiers to join him in the Lord's Prayer. Bill Bennett of British Columbia sat smirking. Bill Davis of Ontario chuckled and blew smoke from his pipe. You could scarcely have invented a more striking illustration of white supremacist arrogance in the context of a nation-to-nation meeting.

"So," Trudeau said to James Gosnell, Chief of the Nisga'a Tribal Council, in a lightly sneering tone, as if teasing a child, "your Creator gave you title [to land]. Did he draw on a map where your mountains stopped, and someone else's began?" At another point, Bill Wilson told Trudeau that he had two daughters who wanted to be lawyers. "Tell them I'll stick around 'til they're ready," Trudeau quipped. All the premiers laughed uproariously. As it happened, it would be his son Justin holding the reins of power when Bill Wilson's daughter, Indigenous lawyer Jody Wilson-Raybould, was appointed justice minister and blew the whistle on his insider dealings with SNC Lavalin. The arc of history is long.

I vividly recall sitting in that conference room and in the AFN caucus, resolving not to be daunted by the frustration, disbelief, sadness, and anger we all felt about "the empty box" positions taken by the prime minister and the premiers. Those positions clearly signalled that the governments were on the old assimilationist road, that Aboriginal peoples and nations were subservient, and that their hard-fought "existing rights" did not, in fact, exist unless Canada and the provinces said so. Which they had no intention of doing. Indeed, at the 1984 conference, now chaired by Prime Minister Brian Mulroney, New Brunswick premier Richard Hatfield, who seems to have had intuitive sympathy for the marginalized, remarked that the First Nations "have been very clear about what they want, and they have acted admirably. I am not very proud of how the First Ministers have responded. I can't discuss self-government with any conviction or any heart when I know we're not going anywhere. We're just not going anywhere." He wasn't wrong, for the following year, Alberta Premier Peter Lougheed said flat out, "We don't accept that there should be more than two sovereign governments, the provincial and the federal." BC's Bill Bennett quickly agreed.

As Gary Potts, Chief of the Teme-Augama First Nation, said to Trudeau, "Mr. Prime Minister, we are tired of fighting a rear-guard action ... to protect the rights of our peoples. It was clearly laid out in the Constitutional Accord that this process was aimed at elaborating on how to recognize our rights in s.35. But it would appear that the federal government and some provincial governments are banding together to erode whatever rights we have, and to ensure our rights will *never* be enforceable in the courts."

In 1982, the Indigenous leaders who negotiated s.35 understood that the full box of rights included the non-contingent, inherent right of First Nation governments to pass their own laws and set up their own institutions based on their own cultural, economic, and political values. Canada's position was that the right to pass laws was a *contingent* right – meaning that it could not be exercised without the consent of Canada or the involved province. Harmonization of laws means that if the federal or provincial government asserts that an action or a law of an Indigenous government lies beyond their jurisdiction (ultra vires), the onus is on the asserting government to prove it. All three jurisdictions must harmonize their powers in a way that respects the other two. But, at the Constitutional Conferences, the prime minister and the premiers simply declared that s.35 itself could only be made meaningful through specific legislation passed by their own parliaments, or by decisions of their own courts.

The historical record of self-governance by Aboriginal peoples got dismissed out of hand. At the 1987 conference, Premier Bill Vander Zalm, a Dutch immigrant to British Columbia, warned of "the disaster to the Native people if the wrong decision was made today"; that is, he would not agree to their self-government because they weren't capable of managing their own affairs even though they had done so for thousands of years before the settler colonialists arrived. How shameful. How stunning. The prime minister and premiers should have listened as Aboriginal leaders unpacked their boxes and spread out for all to see the wonderful array of rights that had been constitutionally "recognized and affirmed." The ethical and moral – the human rights response should have been to set about dismantling the oppressive colonial laws, policies, and institutions that Canada had progressively put in place. From the opening words of Prime Minister Trudeau in 1982 through to the last words of Prime Minister Mulroney at the final conference, there wasn't even any statesmanship talk about a new relationship, let alone any willingness to harmonize rights. The assimilationist spirit and intent that led to the 1969 White Paper was alive and politically active throughout.

"This guy," Bill Wilson later said in total exasperation, referring to BC's Premier Vander Zalm,

> wants to put us back on reserves, and he doesn't want to make any move to liberate Native people in the province of BC. Meanwhile Premier Getty [of Alberta] says, "We want to *define* before we sign." And Devine [of Saskatchewan] says, "We want to make sure how much this costs and who pays for it." Peckford [of Newfoundland] says, "You people aren't as smart as you think you are," and Vander Zalm says, "Look, I'm a heck of a lot smarter than you are, and I can prove it because I made one lousy trip to an isolated Indian village" – and then tells us that he knows what's best for us. Can you imagine the nation-building with Peckford and Vander Zalm? It's impossible. It's like discussing nuclear theory with a newborn.[2]

The four conferences failed to reach agreement on the key issue of whether s.35 was a full-box recognition of Treaty and Aboriginal rights that just needed to be unpacked, or an empty box that could only be filled by what Canada and the provinces agreed to put inside. Between 1983 and 1987, several provinces elected new premiers. AFN National Chief David Ahenakew led the AFN delegation in 1983, 1984, and 1985, and Georges Erasmus led the delegation in 1987. The agendas at all four conferences covered a range of issues, including land, resources, and Treaty rights, but the main focus was on Aboriginal self-government.

And on that fundamental issue, the gap proved a chasm. This was even more egregious when you consider that they all had the 1983 Penner Report to *guide* them in the harmonization of constitutional rights. (The recommendations of the Penner Report are discussed in chapter 9.) A huge amount of time, thought, and energy had already been invested in finding the path forward. These leaders just weren't interested.

My hope at the time of my involvement, and one I continue to hold, was that Canada and the provinces will come to see s.35 as a means towards decolonization. It should be understood as the creation of a new constitutional framework for the harmonization of three levels of government – federal, provincial, and Indigenous. Decolonization must lie at the root of reconciliation. The federal powers in s.91 (except for 91.24) and the provincial powers in sections 92 and 93 need to be interwoven and aligned with the s.35 Indigenous powers. This harmonization would involve Canada's s.91.24 power over "Indians and land reserved for Indians" – the constitutional basis for the series of odious Indian Acts – slowly giving way to the s.35 political power of the Indigenous nations to govern their own lands and affairs.

I understood that harmonization would require discussion and resolution, so that Canada or a province and an Aboriginal government would not be passing laws about the same matter. This harmonization has been underway between Canada and the provinces since 1867.

Yet, premier after premier claimed that they did not understand what s.35 meant. Therefore, they could not implement it. But somehow, they magically knew that it did *not* mean they had to share power. What a contrast to how they read s.91.24. Governments and the courts have never had any problem with interpreting the few words in s.91.24 ("Indians, and Lands reserved for the Indians"). To wit: it was simply assumed that the British

Parliament could give its former colony power over existing Aboriginal nations with the stroke of a pen. Based on those few words, Canada unilaterally passed a series of Indian Acts and policies, and the courts never blinked an eye. Yet, remarkably, when it came to s.35 and Aboriginal rights, the wording was simply too vague to handle.

Over the years, I have often thought about those conferences and reflected on why they failed. I believe the heart of it was that Indigenous peoples saw s.35 as the dawning of a new relationship, and they wanted to talk about and explore that, and feel out its texture. Canada and the provinces were merely intent on defending their turf, by ensuring that whatever s.35 meant, it did *not* mean that they had to share anything. In discussions with lawyers and other officials before and during those conferences, and in listening to the prime ministers and premiers, I was struck by how little they knew about Indigenous peoples; how unaware they seemed to be of Canada's long history of genocide and assimilation. Overall, they did not seem interested in the reality that First Nation, Inuit, and Métis peoples had well-developed societies and political institutions before Westerners arrived. They were not open to listening to the Aboriginal leaders talking about how, finally, after centuries of oppression, s.35 recognized who they were. Canada and the provinces said, "No – we will decide who you are and how, if at all, we will recognize you." When you don't want to look, you cannot see, and when you don't see, it's impossible to recognize. And when you don't recognize the Other, there is no possibility for mutuality and respect. At those conferences, non-Indigenous officials, lawyers, and elected leaders were not thinking of a new beginning, a new partnership. Through their settler colonial lenses, they were only thinking of maintaining their exclusive right to govern.

In their 2016 article "Beyond White Privilege: Geographies of White Supremacy and Settler Colonialism," scholars Anne Bonds and Joshua Inwood write, "If privilege and racism are the symptoms, white supremacy is the disease." Theorized this way, white supremacy is the *defining logic* of both racism and privilege as they are culturally and materially produced. This resonates with me as a credible explanation for Canada's perplexing actions that have made it so very difficult for Indigenous people and nations to regain self-determination. My experience corroborates the conclusion of Bonds and Inwood "that neither white supremacy nor settler colonialism can be relegated to historical context, rather, as they both inform past, present and future formulations of race."[3]

To fully understand colonialism in Canada, I think it important to take in Bonds and Inwood's contention that *settler colonialism* is distinct from *colonialism*. Canada and Australia are settler colonial countries. Rather than emphasizing imperial expansion driven primarily by materialistic or economic purposes, which eventually entail the departure of the colonizer, *settler colonialism* focuses on the permanent occupation of a territory and the removal of Indigenous people in order to build a distinct national community that privileges the colonists' values. Because of the permanence of settler societies, this form of colonization calls for constant maintenance in an effort to disappear Indigenous peoples in Canada. Creating room for settler groups (personally, I prefer the term "invaders" to "settlers") has necessitated the expulsion of Indigenous nations from their long-held traditional lands, sometimes through questionable Treaties, and in other cases via threats, forced starvation, or the spread of disease. For readers who want to learn more about this history, James Daschuk's book *Clearing the Plains: Disease, Politics of Starvation, and the Loss of Indigenous Life* is an important source. The highlights from the report of the RCAP, as I outline in chapter 8, are also a must-read for everyone wanting more information. On the history, RCAP notes that

> [i]ronically, the transformation from respectful coexistence to dominance by non-aboriginal laws and institutions began with the main instruments of the partnership: the Treaties and the *Royal Proclamation of 1763*. These documents offered Aboriginal people not only peace and friendship, respect and rough equality, but also "protection." Protection was the leading edge of domination. At first, it meant preservation of Aboriginal lands and cultural integrity from encroachment by settlers. Later it meant "assistance," a code word implying encouragement to stop *being* Aboriginal and merge into the Settler Society.

Of the doctrine of assimilation, the RCAP noted that it

> was based on four dehumanizing (and incorrect) ideas about Aboriginal peoples and their cultures:
>
> - that they were inferior peoples ... unable to govern themselves and that colonial and Canadian authorities knew best how to protect their interests and well-being;
> - that the special relationship of respect and sharing enshrined in the Treaties was an historical anomaly with no more force or meaning;
> - that European ideas about progress and development were self-evidently correct and could be imposed on Aboriginal people without reference to any other values and opinions – let alone rights – they might possess.

Indigenous peoples continue to live with the settler colonial pressure to complete the dispossession of their remaining land and resources because, according to decisions of Canada's Supreme Court, the sovereignty of the "white" Crown is *normative* – despite the pre-existence of hundreds of "Aboriginal Crowns."

Devin Shaw, a professor at Douglas College in Vancouver, pointed out in 2019 that

> [t]he status quo is settler colonialism: a product of white supremacy, capital accumulation, resource extraction, and Indigenous dispossession. We settlers have made excuses for too long ... When Indigenous peoples demand the recognition of Indigenous title, we deliver land acknowledgements ... When the RCMP invades unceded Wet'suwet'en territory now, we say that all peoples must recognize the rule of law. But Wet'suwet'en claims to title were legally recognized in Delgamuukw v. British Columbia in 1997 ... Every time Indigenous peoples are [encouraged] to wait, for justice will come, only the RCMP shows up.[4]

Musing about the Constitutional Conferences some months later, Georges Erasmus told an NFB documentarian, "When you sit down with those premiers, and you sit down with their prime minister, and it doesn't matter who it is, you actually *see* that they don't have much of an idea of what the world really should look like. They really don't have much of an idea about how people should relate with their environment, and they certainly don't know how human beings should respect each other. They can't build the kind of society that Native people can build. What we're holding out for is how people can live in dignity, how we can take care of the poor, how we can live in balance with the universe."[5]

In other words, the four Constitutional Conferences failed because the First Nations would not accept the crumbs dropped from the Queen's table as if they were lesser, dependent beings.

"When will the Canadian public wake up," asked one of the First Nation delegates afterward, "[a]nd get rid of these jerks who represent them? Because what's going to happen if they reach agreement with Aboriginal people is that we put something in the earth that has never been there before: a relationship between a nation of Indian people, and European people. That's the whole idea of creation, a planting of the seed that was not there before."[6]

Harmonization of constitutional powers means a sharing of power. And sharing power requires a conscious shift away from colonialism. That shift cannot happen without an acknowledgment by each one of us and our political representatives of how the tendrils of white supremacy have shaped our own attitudes, such that we are often unaware of our own racism and how it is embedded in Canada's institutions and policies. Those policies have denied First Nations the social and political space they once had to be self-determining, to be fully witnessed and recognized along with the English and the French as a Founding People of Canada.

After the 1987 conference Prime Minister Mulroney turned his attention to the Meech Lake Accord and to the constitutional revisions for Quebec, preparing to declare the francophone province a distinct society. The accord, of course, required the consent of the provinces. And it was never finalized. Oji-Cree MLA Elijah Harper of Manitoba deliberately initiated procedural delays that prevented the document from being approved before its 23 June 1990 deadline. Harper explained bluntly why he had chosen to do this. He said if the distinct right of Indigenous people to be self-governing would not be recognized, neither could Quebec's desire to be distinct get entrenched in the Constitution.

The next political attempt to tackle s.35 was the Charlottetown Accord in 1992, which entailed amending the Constitution in several areas – a fine-tuning effort after ten years of court rulings on s.35. I was the lead legal negotiator for the AFN at the self-government table that was composed of representatives from Canada, each province and territory, the Inuit, the Métis, and the AFN. We met almost weekly over several months in Ottawa or in a provincial capital to hammer out the text for the Aboriginal rights provisions of the accord. Remarkably, this time, there was promising progress, thanks to new provincial premiers like Bob Rae in Ontario and brilliant First Nations leaders like Assembly of First Nations (AFN) Grand Chief Ovide Mercredi and Ontario regional AFN Chief Gordon Peters. The Accord provisions included the crucial statement that the self-government rights of the Aboriginal peoples were *inherent rights* that were *recognized* in Canada's Constitution – rather than being rights granted to the Aboriginal peoples *by* the Constitution. The Aboriginal rights provisions were part of the package of constitutional amendment provisions approved by the prime minister and premiers and presented to Canadians for consideration in the referendum vote. I continue to be distressed that Canadians narrowly voted against the Accord in no small measure because a voter who disagreed with *one* of the other proposals – entirely unrelated to Aboriginal concerns – had to reject the whole package. This was deeply upsetting because Canada and every province had finally agreed that Aboriginal self-government rights were inherent rights. And all for naught. The baby got thrown out with the bathwater, and our Constitution has never been revisited.

Nowadays, Canada bases its policy approach to s.35 on the low bar set by the courts, to whom it fell to define the rights recognized and affirmed by that section. Faced with the abysmal failure of the Constitutional Conferences, some First Nations went to the courts with the hope that jurists would give a more enlightened interpretation. The first case in which the Supreme Court of Canada considered s.35 involved the Aboriginal fishing rights of Ronald Sparrow, a member of the Musqueam First Nation in BC. In 1984, Sparrow was arrested for fishing in the Fraser River with a net deemed oversized by provincial regulators. Hemmed in by Canadian rules governing their traditional activity, which included the practice of sustainability, Sparrow and the Musqueam peoples went to court. Sparrow was found guilty of violating the terms of his fishing licence by the provincial court, which he appealed all the way up to the Supreme Court of Canada. That court ruled that s.35 lacked sufficiently explicit language to enable the justices to question the right of Canada to regulate Musqueam fishing under its s.91.24 federal constitutional power to exclusively exercise authority over "Indians, and Lands reserved for the Indians." Basically, the court upheld the conclusion of Canada and the provinces that s.35 was an empty box. What the court put in that box was the ruling that even though those fishing rights existed prior to 1982, Canada could infringe upon them, if criteria that the court now set out in this ruling were met. Canada could ban Musqueam fishing, for example, if conservation measures were required. All other fishers would be prohibited *before* the Musqueam, and they would be the first to have fishing rights restored if measures were lifted. But the point is that the Musqueam had managed and regulated the fishery for thousands of years, so why should Canada – rather than the Musqueam themselves – have the final say about fishing policy?

Rather than harmonize s.35 Aboriginal and Treaty rights with federal and provincial constitutional rights, the court said that if certain conditions were met Canada could *infringe* s.35 rights. There was no legal reasoning behind this decision, as many critics have pointed out. It seems clear, however, that the decision was firmly rooted in the court's settler colonial assumption – as per its own ruling – that "there was from the outset never any doubt that sovereignty and legislative power, and indeed the underlying title, to such lands was vested in the Crown."[7] No jurist or law clerk undertook any analysis as to how that vesting came to be despite the fact that the land in question had been used and occupied and governed by Indigenous people and nations for thousands of years. Settler colonialism par excellence! It brings to mind a casual confession by former United States Supreme Court Justice Antonin Scalia some years ago, when he spoke to a Native American woman at a book signing and confided that, when it came to rulings around Native rights, the court was just making things up on the fly.[8]

What struck me about the *Sparrow* decision was the contradictory findings of the Canadian Supreme Court about how to interpret the scant language in s.35 as opposed to similar sparsity in s.91.24, "Indians, and Lands reserved for the Indians." Legally speaking, the court *read down* – interpreted the language in a narrow way – the language of s.35 while, to this day, the court reads powers *into* – interprets the section very broadly – 91.24. This speaks, I think, to the unconscious biases I have been describing. Indeed, since the *Sparrow* decision, the courts and governments have focused on the continued exercise of s.91.24 rights by Canada, rather than recognizing that s.35 is a full box of rights to be exercised by the Aboriginal peoples of Canada. Looked at through a reconciliation lens, this is legally, morally, and ethically unacceptable. It is not reconciliation *with*. It is reconciliation *to*, that is, submission *to* the sovereignty of the colonial Crown. While it may be a position that is more nuanced than that taken by the prime minister and premiers in the Constitutional Conferences, it is nevertheless a glaring continuation of what successive governments have done to eradicate, control, and/or assimilate Aboriginal people and nations.

A few years after *Sparrow*, the Supreme Court heard another case about Aboriginal fishing rights, this time involving a woman named Dorothy Van der Peet, who had been convicted of selling her fresh-caught salmon, which was apparently not a pre-existing Aboriginal right, even though members of the Stó:lō nation, to which she belonged, had engaged in trade and commerce of this sort for centuries. This time, the court established a set of guiding criteria for judges – now called the *Van der Peet* test – which codifies how an Aboriginal right is to be defined. The court interpreted s.35 to require "the reconciliation of the pre-existence of distinctive aboriginal societies occupying the land to Crown sovereignty." That approach was affirmed by Chief Justice Antonio Lamer in the *Delgamuukw* case a year later. In that case, two BC First Nations, the Wet'suwet'en and the Gitxsan, filed a land title claim, which led the court to define Aboriginal title as an exclusive right to certain land, based on the evidence of oral history, but within some limitations. As with s.91.24, what it meant in practice was that Indigenous rights and how they, themselves, perceived them were to be subordinated to those of the sovereign federal and provincial Crowns. In other words, the settler-established Supreme Court gets to decide what Aboriginal rights are. Unfortunately, settler colonialism is alive and well in the highest level of Canada's courts as it is in the federal and provincial halls of government.

To embrace authentic reconciliation, the Honour of the Crown requires that Canada rise above this low bar set by courts and adopt the higher bar of harmonization with Indigenous people and nations. This requires the dismantling of settler colonial policies and institutions, so that Aboriginal people can be self-determining in a pluralistic, progressive country. After the 1987 Constitutional Conference, a First Nations delegate reflected, "People like Mulroney are only entering grade one at this point compared to people like Joe Mathias [Hereditary Chief of the Squamish First Nation in BC]. I don't think they realize how quickly this world is closing in on them, and they are going to seek some solutions in the Aboriginal world. Because that's where they lie."[9]

It is certainly not uncommon for Canadians to argue that the prime minister and premiers today are much more sensitive to Aboriginal rights than those of past years and that reconciliation is underway. My answer is that the dismissive colonial tone of the post-1982 Constitutional Conferences may have ebbed away – the spin doctors have changed that – but the substance of the approach is the same. What governments call reconciliation consists mainly of paying for the horrific consequences of past colonialism. Many residential school survivors have told me that they do not consider compensation for harm done to them to be reconciliation. Nor should they. In most cases, no apologies, no amount of money, can ever come close to easing the life-long and intergenerational trauma they endured and continue to suffer.

CHAPTER FOUR

Paradise Threatened: The Innu of Labrador Fight for Their Homeland – Nitassinan

> We always did our homework, but the federal government never did their homework. Meaning we know who we are. We know what we want. We know what's good for us. But the federal, provincial governments – have to let it go. Let us be.
>
> Innu leader Gregory Penashue to RCAP, June 1992

In June of 2022, I attended the University of Victoria graduation of a young Innu woman named Jolene Ashini. She already had a BSc in geology and was now receiving a law degree plus a doctorate in Indigenous law (JD/JID), being a proud member of the first cohort of students in this groundbreaking program. Sitting with Jolene's family and friends, my mind wandered back to my early days of working with the Innu of Labrador in the late 1980s. I often stayed with her parents Tanien Ashini and Sheila Blake in their trailer in Sheshatshiu. Jolene and her sister Jodie were young girls at the time, and one or the other would kindly give up their small single bed for me. I marvelled at the generosity of the whole family, who had, along with so many other Innu families and their ancestors, endured generations of hardship under the administrative yoke of Canada and Newfoundland and Labrador (NL). Now, here I sat with Sheila and Jodie – who is leading the Innu Nation's archaeological work and setting up a cultural centre – celebrating Jolene's graduation as the first of her nation to become a lawyer. Jolene now practises at Olthuis Kleer Townshend and has moved back to Labrador to continue the work of Innu self-determination that her late father, Tanien, was so instrumental in shaping. I felt very blessed to be part of this multigenerational effort to cast off oppression.

I knew very little about Labrador before my work took me there. A vast, and beautiful peninsula bounded by the Arctic Ocean, the Gulf of St. Lawrence and the Labrador Sea, it is jurisdictionally divided between NL and Quebec – what the Innu consider colonialist lines on a map, because it is overall their homeland, which they call Nitassinan. Archaeologists believe that humans first occupied the area when the ice receded about 8,000 years ago, leaving a spectacular landscape of mesa-like mountains and shimmering ocean inlets. The direct ancestors of the current generation of Innu certainly lived here for several millennia. They mainly inhabited the inland terrain, while their neighbours, the Inuit, lived northeastward along the stunning coastline, with its rugged cliffs and amber and russet scrub grasses.

I remember one summer day when Peter Penashue – later a federal cabinet minister and currently a member of the Innu Nation modern Treaty negotiating team – took me out on Grand Lake, near the town of Sheshatshiu. After a delightful afternoon of fishing and friendship, we boated into Lake Melville, a wide and deep estuary leading into the Labrador Sea. (The Atlantic divides Labrador from Greenland with this sea.) As the afternoon wore on, the waves rose alarmingly, and Peter decided we needed to go ashore for safety. So, we spent a small part of the night in the tattered remains of a long-abandoned tent, but most of it lying on the rocky beach. I will never forget the exhilaration of gazing into that enormous star-filled sky. I got a small hit of the freedom the Innu felt about being in – and on – their land! Unlike the sense given in many mainstream books and movies about the peril of being stranded in the wilderness, for the Innu, it is simply home. That night, the beach was a grand place to be.

Likewise, one winter day when I was in Davis Inlet – the former home of the Mushuau Innu in northern Labrador – I was invited to go with a few of them to check ice fishing nets they had set up some distance from the community. After finding me suitable footwear, our group of six set out on skidoos. I was a passenger, hanging on to my driver tightly; this was no leisurely afternoon ride. It was bitterly cold, and we began to drive into a blizzard. The group decided it was too dangerous to press on. Amazingly, despite the blinding snow, they knew exactly where to find the derelict remains of a tent. We huddled together through the night – at times literally sleeping on top of one another for warmth. At some point, one of the Innu found an old *Playboy* magazine in the tent's frozen folds, placed it close to my face when I was sleeping, and took a picture. (The photo still circulates among the Innu today with different captions.) Rather than feeling stressed during that harsh storm, my friends were playful. On my own, I would quite literally have perished. With them I felt safe. The next morning, the blowing snow had abated somewhat and despite the bone-deep cold – I have actually never *been* so cold – we made it back to Davis Inlet, hungry but cheerful. Overjoyed to be safe, I called my wife, Lois, in Toronto with the news that all was well. "Oh," she said, bemused, "I didn't even know you were lost!" Reflecting on this from time to time, I continue to be awed that the Innu have lived through and survived countless winter storms over many generations, generously helping settlers who would otherwise have died.

Given this tradition of living capably and harmoniously in their environment while welcoming newcomers, imagine the slow-dawning shock of the Innu as European governments began driving them (and their Inuit neighbours) off their lands into static, unsuitable ghettos. If you look at the map of Labrador today, you will see the Innu communities of Sheshatshiu and Natuashish, which (inadequately) house about 3,200 people – with another 23,000 parcelled into Quebec and the communities of Nain, Hopedale, Rigolet, Postville, and Makkovik, where over 2,000 Inuit live. Neither the Innu nor Inuit ever ceded their traditional territory. The Inuit signed a modern Treaty with Canada, NL in 2005, which acknowledged a part of their traditional territory as Nunatsiavut and recognized the Nunatsiavut government. The Innu signed an Agreement in Principle (AIP) in 2011 with Canada and NL. An AIP sets out what has been agreed to date and notes the issues that remain to be addressed in a Final Agreement, which, pending ratification by the Innu people and Canada and NL, will be a modern Treaty. Yes, the Innu have been at the negotiating table to complete the Treaty for over fourteen years since the AIP was signed, more than thirty years after signing the Framework Agreement – the first stage of modern Treaty negotiations. More about that later.

The story of the Innu is one of intertwined themes: the incredible strength, creativity, and heart they have shown in their commitment to reconciliation with Canada and NL, and the dishonourable actions of our governments over many decades that have thwarted their self-determination, as-ever attempting to force the Innu to reconcile *to* the sovereignty of the colonial

Crowns. "I don't know what to say about these people in government," one Innu resident remarked at a "Gathering Voices" session in 1995, where the community came together to discuss their plight. "They think they are our Gods. They think they rule the land, the sea, the stars, and the moon." Said an Elder, "The government was not born in the country on this land. He knows nothing about life in the bush. We know who we are. We know how to survive in the country. I heard the government say he loaned the land to the Innu. How could he say that? We all know God made the world."

As the Innu understand their origin story, they received Nitassinan from the Great Spirit, or Tshishe-manitu. "They are bound in an uninterrupted relationship of reciprocity with the land: the land enables them to live, and they in turn watch over it," wrote the late anthropologist José Mailhot, who spent decades learning Innu ways.

> The land provides eternally for human beings who are eternally its guardians. Land and people are thus connected by strict ties of inter-dependence that imply respect and harmony. This viewpoint is related to the Innu idea of humanity's position in the universe, according to which the human race is not a superior entity somehow placed at the summit of Creation ... They see colonization and conquest as a breach of the natural order, one that violates the principle that each group has its own territory and must remain on it, even if deciding to share it with others.[1]

"When I was a child, I was always in *nutshimit* (the country)," Elder Mary Georgette Mistenapeo recalled to a researcher in 1992. "I never dressed the way I dress now, living in Utshimassits (Davis Inlet). I dress like a White person now. A long time ago, I dressed only in caribou skin. When the White man came, I changed my ways and forgot the ways of *nutshimit*."[2] Although the Innu (which means "human being") are sometimes referred to by non-Indigenous groups as the Montagnais-Naskapi, they see themselves as one people with extensive kinship networks who speak the same language, Innu-aimun. Maintaining that network grew challenging after a 1927 decision of the Privy Council in Britain deemed Labrador to be part of Newfoundland – at the time a British colony. As Innu leader Apetet (Ben) Andrew later put it, "three blokes in wigs signed away our land." This made it difficult for Labrador Innu to hunt with their Quebec families and friends, because the two jurisdictions set different wildlife regulations, none of which were based on consulting the Innu themselves about their deep knowledge of the caribou, porcupine, and partridge. "I wonder if the white government knows where he belongs," Mary Georgette Mistenapeo asked her community during the Gathering Voices community process, "I wonder if he ever hunted on his own land."

The very idea of hunting is fundamentally, cosmologically different for Aboriginal peoples than it is for settler Canadians. In the late 1980s, when my wife, Lois, and I were in Davis Inlet, a remarkable thing happened: legendary Elder Kaniuekutat took us out fishing. I remember my sense that the gods had given us a very special gift. We had a wonderful afternoon on the water, but the joy was in simply being with this revered man, who carried so much wisdom for his people, as he sat so stately and comfortably in his boat with the wind blowing back his jet-black hair against a backdrop of mountains. Kaniuekutat was his Innu name from birth, but he had been baptized as "John Poker" by the Moravian mission in the village of Nain before Catholic priests entered the lives of the Innu. In 1993, at the age of seventy-three, Kaniuekutat told his life story to Norwegian anthropologist Georg Henriksen, as translated by his grandson Thomas Poker, whom I have come to know well as a member of the Innu modern Treaty negotiating team. Kaniuekutat wanted younger Innu to know that they must take care of their language, culture, and traditions.

"In order to comprehend Kaniuekutat and his Innu world," Henriksen wrote in his book, *I Dreamed the Animals: Kaniuekutat: The Life of an Innu Hunter*, "we must think of him operating simultaneously in the realm of the natural environment, where he acts practically and strategically in order to survive as a hunter, and in the spiritual realm of cosmology and ritual which is, the way Kaniuekutat sees it, of no less significance for his physical survival." Henriksen observed that the Innu possessed an animistic cosmology, in which animals and elements, flora and fauna are infused with sentience. "The sun, trees, winds, thunder and lightning, and many other objects in the environment are spirited and can talk ... the animals and the Innu spoke the same language in the distant past. As the Innu see it, their survival in the pre-settlement period was dependent upon them showing respect to the animals and their master spirits."[3]

Over time, the cumulative actions of the governments of NL, Quebec, and Canada – along with the Catholic Church, the Grenfell Mission (which established residential schools), and non-Indigenous settlers – pushed the Innu out of their most fruitful and spiritually important hunting and trapping areas. By the late 1940s, they were in a desperate state due to falling fur prices and a major decline in the caribou herds, obliged to seek relief from the provincial government for even basic foodstuffs. Tsheutshimau – the Big Boss – is how they came to refer to their colonial overlords. Increasingly, their children were educated by missionaries in English, separating them linguistically from their Quebec kin, and truncating their wilderness skills. "I think you would be very devastated if we took some of your children and taught them in our own schools, our own history and our own culture," Innu leader Gregory Andrew later told RCAP. "And I think you would find out that your society was breaking down if we did that. You would have problems of alcohol abuse and problems of child neglect and suicide. The Innu people here, we have a common language and culture and history and territory."[4] *But we have been torn asunder from ourselves and from our land.*

Settler colonialism remained an unshakeable paradigm in 1949 when NL joined Canada and assumed control over the Innu. The island province had long been a British fishing colony whose native inhabitants, the Beothuk, had been driven to extinction in 1829. Now, in merging with Canada, NL was granted provincial jurisdiction over the Labrador Peninsula, and in this political arrangement, the Innu lost all agency. In 1948, there had been some discussion in NL's Department of Mines and Resources over whether it was best to bring the "Indians and Eskimos" under federal jurisdiction. The question was left in abeyance, as if no one cared to figure it out. In the end, the terms of the union made no reference to the "Indians and Eskimos" at all. Essentially, the entire territory was viewed as a province where the Aboriginal peoples were simply assumed to be Labradorians.

In 1950, the federal Department of Justice produced a legal opinion about what obligations Canada might have to the Innu now that Labrador was part of Canada. The deputy minister of justice asserted unequivocally that it was a federal responsibility to carry out all policies directed at "Indians or Indian problems." Yet, despite this clear determination, the federal minister of citizenship and immigration wrote to NL's minister of public welfare in 1953, declaring that Ottawa had *no legal requirement* to assume any responsibility, either financial or administrative, for the residents of northern Labrador. A year later, they changed their minds, up to a point. Canada would assume the cost – below a stated limit – of capital expenditures in the fields of welfare, health, and education, and some administrative responsibility with respect to hospitalization. That was it. It was a spectacular act of nickel-and-diming. For fifty more years, the Innu were denied even the meagre level and quality of Indian Act services accorded to Indigenous people who lived elsewhere on reserves. Canada breached its fiduciary obligations while at the same time erasing all possible means of Innu self-sufficiency.

Industrial incursions into their territory gradually led the Innu to strengthen their collective voice, just as we saw happen with the Dene and the people of Grassy Narrows. "This land is still our home. The White man does things to this land behind our back, without notifying us," Innu Elder Charlotte Rich told José Mailhot. "I think these people are outrageous for damaging our land. The Innu do not go to the White man's land and destroy it."[5] The first alarm bell to sound, arguably, occurred after Canada established the Canadian Forces Base in Goose Bay (CFB Goose Bay) in 1941 without notifying the community. The Innu understood that the war effort was an emergency that justified temporary seizure of their land. Goose Bay was chosen because its proximity to Europe facilitated North America's air-based contribution to the war. But the Innu expected the land back when peace came. After all, from time immemorial, this had been an important area for berry picking, partridge hunting, harvesting medicines, and spiritual and cultural connection. Incredibly, Canada neither returned the land nor offered reparations. To this day, the entire municipality of Happy Valley-Goose Bay – which includes CFB Goose Bay and the civilian airport – is situated on unceded Innu land. Indeed, despite the Innu insisting on it in their ongoing Treaty negotiations, the Department of National Defence (DND) refuses to compensate them for its ongoing illegal occupation of the area.

What DND did with and over that land grew far more egregious as time went on and led some powerfully articulate young Innu leaders and tenacious Elders to challenge the governments of the North Atlantic Treaty Organization (NATO) in the name of their people, which is a tale I will return to shortly.

The second industrial shock arrived in 1969, when NL entered into a contract with Hydro Quebec (HQ) to build a massive 5,000-megawatt hydro project. This involved damming the Churchill River, Labrador's largest waterway, which featured a spectacular, rainbow-forming waterfall second only in grandeur to Niagara Falls. The ensuing flood, which created the Smallwood Reservoir, drowned animals and flushed out ancestral graves. The Innu were horrified. This was not just an environmental but a *spiritual* assault. "We have been gentle and loving to our land," Elizabeth Penashue later observed, "and we use it wisely. With the Churchill Falls Development, all the animals were wasted away in the flooding. They dammed Mista-paustuk (the Great Rapids). Before this, we could see the mist of Mista-paustuk from very far away when we walked through *nutshimit* (the countryside). The government didn't look at the Innu way of life. They never even consulted us. All that mattered to them were dollar signs, the profits, the jobs and the power that would be generated."[6]

CFB Goose Bay began to grow apace. To a large extent, it became a business venture, with DND contracting with foreign governments for flight training, for example, with the UK Royal Airforce in the 1950s. As time went on, the United States, Germany, the Netherlands, and other European countries all began conducting low-level flying exercises with supersonic jets, practising avoiding detection by enemy radar, over Innu territory. Canada had advertised Nitassinan as expansive, uninhabited land ideally suited for training, which European countries couldn't undertake at home due to public outrage at the terrifying fighter jets screaming just 100 feet overhead. During low-level flying, sonic booms occur. Their force is measured in pounds per square inch (psi). Human pain begins at two pounds per square inch, animal pain at a much lower threshold. Sonic booms average four to five psi and can even reach twenty psi. The startle effect, an involuntary reaction to a sudden, intense, random noise, increases cortisol production in the body, weakening the immune system. There are many accounts of the suffering of Innu people from this effect, such as children running off in fright and getting lost, people in canoes overturning as the jets boomed. The caribou and other wildlife began to lose weight and to miscarry their young. Geese fell stunned from the sky. It was like an airshow on steroids, and over the years, the number of flights increased dramatically. In 1980, the base recorded 860 take-offs and landings. By 1988, there were more than 8,400. To add insult to injury, Canada offered CFB Goose Bay to NATO as a site for a full-fledged, tactical-level weapons training facility.

A new generation of Innu leaders, in collaboration with their Elders, began to get organized. One was Tanien (Daniel) Ashini, the father of Jolene and Jodie, who had been elected Chief of the Sheshatshiu First Nation in 1978 at the age of nineteen. Another was Penote (Ben) Michel, born in 1953 and fluently bilingual, who felt passionately about preserving his culture and way of life. With his long, wavy dark hair, neat mustache, and aviator-style sunglasses, Michel cut a striking figure. A third was Peter Penashue, my companion on Lake Melville, who held many Innu leadership positions and was also a cabinet minister in Stephen Harper's government. Another was Apetet (Ben) Andrew, who understood deeply how settler colonialism and its inherent racism would destroy the Aboriginal way of life. These were powerful and prophetic leaders who would not be ignored. Soon after my "counting his fingers" experience with Innu Nation president Greg Penashue, I was taken out on a small boat on Grand Lake by Penote Michel and Tony Jenkinson, a Brit who came to live with the Innu and brought their attention to books like *The Wretched of the Earth* by Frantz Fanon and *Pedagogy of the Oppressed* by Paulo Freire. The purpose of our boat ride was to ensure that I understood "Innu 101," or what their struggle for liberation and self-determination was all about. It was both inspiring and direct enough that I told them – and we laughed – that I knew enough to say "amen" to everything they said, lest I end up on the bottom of the lake. Innu women, whose tales are told in Tshaukuesh (Elizabeth) Penashue's book *Nitinikiau Innusi: I Keep the Land Alive*, were also emerging as tenacious leaders in efforts to resist the Big Boss.

Innu opposition to the flying exercises began conventionally enough, with letters sent to the ministers of the environment, DND, and the Department of Indian and Northern Affairs. But as is so often the case, polite mailings garnered no meaningful responses. So, in 1981, several Innu travelled to the United Nations Human Rights Commission in Geneva and described their predicament, which generated international interest. In 1983, Innu families met at Northwest point near Sheshatshiu for their first National Assembly, to discuss the flights and the threats posed by industrial development. Then, activists from Sheshatshiu and Davis Inlet visited major Canadian cities to inform the public. The same citizens who had listened to the rallying cries of the Dene and other Indigenous groups began to take notice. In 1986, the Paris-based International Federation of Human Rights mandated a five-person mission to investigate;

one of their primary conclusions was that internationally recognized natural and legal rights of the Innu were being violated by the military.

In the spring of 1986, determined to press their case, an Innu delegation toured England, Germany, and Italy to directly accuse these countries of being complicit in Canada's illegal seizure and use of their land. In July of that year, the Canadian Public Health Association released a report on the impacts of low-level flying and recommended a moratorium on any increase. But stopping the *expansion* of flights was hardly good enough. So, Innu families set up a camp at the end of the runways on CFB Goose Bay to protest the arrival of German, Dutch, and British aircraft. They also occupied the practice bombing range near Mininipi, sixty miles south of Goose Bay, and managed to halt all action for two weeks.

The range was again occupied by Innu the following autumn, during a visit of Defence Minister Perrin Beatty accompanied by NATO's survey team. Innu leaders called upon Beatty to visit them for talks but got no response. A long-held stance of "ignoring the Natives" was beginning to crumble, however. That same autumn, rallies and protests in support of the Innu were held throughout Canada and Europe. In the Netherlands supporters entered the airfields at two Dutch airbases to protest their nation's aerial harassment of Nitassinan. In the fall of 1988, the Innu established a significant protest camp at the base. I went there several times. That December, as I moved from tent to tent, I was deeply moved by the emotional displays of anguish, fear, defiance, courage, love, and rage. They were so committed to preserving their homeland for the generations to come, praying for strength from their ancestors.

It was also a time of planning for future actions and determining the role that they wanted me to play as a lawyer. As I mentioned, Innu women emerged as co-leaders in this emancipation struggle. I was deeply honoured to be invited by Tshaukuesh to a women's meeting in her fire-lit tent, with a few Akaneshua (English speakers or European settlers). I was asked many questions, and the discussions were heartfelt, sometimes tearful, always open. In her book, Tshaukuesh later quoted from her diary:

> We've been here for about a month and a lot of Akaneshau have come out to support us. One evening when Betty Peterson [a Quaker peace activist from Nova Scotia] was staying with us, I invited the women to get together for a meeting in my tent. We lit candles and made everything nice. Some other Akaneshau came too, and John Olthuis the lawyer was there. I asked why they never invite Innu women to their meetings ... They didn't answer but I think they thought about it and maybe they realized I was right ... I was invited to speak at Uapush. The military were holding a meeting there and the women were invited. That was my answer.

In March of 1989, the Innu tried five times to re-establish a camp at the end of the runway of CFB Goose Bay. Many were arrested, and eighteen refused to sign the condition for their release, which was that they cease their protest. They were detained in prison for two weeks. That month, the new Conservative defence minister, Bill McKnight, visited Sheshatshiu, aware that Canada could no longer get away with blowing off Aboriginal concerns. On 27 March, the *Evening Telegram*, NL's daily paper, reported that McKnight's visit had done little to improve relations – a remarkable understatement from what I observed at that meeting. Philomena Nuna opened with prayer for the people in jail and read out a statement from nine women detained earlier that week. "There is absolutely no reason why we should be arrested for attempting to camp on our own land," they wrote. "This land does not belong to government or DND." Nine-year-old Carolyn Penashue told the minister that jailing her parents was disrupting her family. Family was very important to her culture, she explained. Ten-year-old Clem Andrews asked, "What is wrong? What did my mother do to be in jail?" Another mother, Manien Michel, told the minister that three of her four daughters were locked up. McKnight was either so unsettled by this confrontation or so indifferent to the issues that he walked out before the Innu had finished speaking and took off in his helicopter.

That Easter weekend, I spent several hours visiting imprisoned Innu who had been moved to the federal penitentiary in St. John's, to discuss strategy for their upcoming trials. Twenty-one of them, some of whom were jailed in St. John's and some in Stephenville, released a two-page Easter letter that asserted, "we're not criminals. We're here because we are exercising our basic human rights." They asked supporters to call on federal politicians to demand that the military activity over Labrador stop and that NATO forces decamp. "People often tell us that we should talk to government instead of protesting, but when we heard that Minister McKnight had walked out, we got stronger because we know that we must keep fighting."[7] By this point, they had gained the backing of many groups, including Project North, Survival International, the Canadian Campaign for Nuclear Disarmament, Project Plowshares Canada, the Green Party of Germany, the International Fellowship of Reconciliation in the Netherlands, Greenpeace International, and the Anti-Slavery Society for the Protection of Human Rights, which is the oldest rights organization in the Western world. To give you an idea of the extent of international awareness, the protests against the flights included demonstrations at the Canadian Consulate in the Netherlands and West Germany, rallies in twenty cities across the United States, occupation of NATO country consulates in Montreal, religious services and vigils in Toronto, and a rally on Parliament Hill. The CODCO comedy troupe staged a street theatre performance called "Goose Bay, Canada's New Ground Zero" in St. John's. David Suzuki visited an Innu protest camp. Bruce Cockburn participated in a press conference alongside me and anthropologist Peter Armitage to spell out Canada's violations of human rights. Gordon Lightfoot added his voice of support.

On 7 April 1989, members of the Alliance for Nonviolent Action blocked traffic in front of the Department of National Defence in Ottawa. Police moved in quickly with a warning, then dragged or carried them to waiting buses. Tshaukuesh Penashue, Penote Michel, and Tanien Ashini were arrested. I spent the better part of a day at the police cells arranging bail for them. By this time, the RCMP had laid over 200 charges against Innu arising from several protests. The Crown decided to go ahead with a "show trial" of four prominent protesters: Tanien Ashini, Peter Penashue, his mother Tshaukuesh Penashue, and Penote (Ben) Michel. Judge James Igloliorte unconditionally released eighteen other Innu who had been jailed for refusing to sign documents agreeing to stop protesting. The other Innu scheduled to stand trial would, he ruled, be bound by the outcome of the trials of the four.

As the trial approached, I asked that all the Innu who had been charged, not just the four facing the show trial, instruct me, as the protests had been a collective effort. So, we had several community meetings in Sheshatshiu. The energy was electric, and ideas flowed fast and freely. At this point, Innu contempt for settler colonialism was at the boiling point. At length, I was instructed to convey to the judge that his court held no jurisdiction over them, since the Innu had never consented to be governed by Canadian law. I could feel the sense of self-worth and agency stirring as consensus emerged about these instructions. So, I filed a pretrial motion urging Judge Igloliorte to declare that his court lacked jurisdiction. True justice, I said, would mean that Canada, the United States, the Netherlands, and Great Britain would appear *in Innu courts facing Innu judges* on charges of illegally conducting military flights over Nitassinan. Accordingly, the motion said, the four Innu accused would not validate the foreign court by entering pleas as "the Innu do not believe that the trial is valid in international law."

Not unexpectedly, Judge Igloliorte ruled that he *did* have jurisdiction. That likelihood had been discussed in our planning sessions, so the next motion I'd been instructed to make was that the venue of the trial be moved closer to the Innu community of Sheshatshiu, in a hall large enough to accommodate all the people who wanted to attend. This the judge agreed to. The proceedings were transferred from Goose Bay-Happy Valley to the Lion's Club building in North West River, just across the water from Sheshatshiu. Such was the hostility of Labrador's settler population that Warren Pike, president of the Labrador North Chamber of Commerce, called for a denial of town services to anyone assisting the Innu in their protests. They should not be put up in hotels, he defiantly declared, nor served food or other necessities. Mr. Pike's words "smell of racism," I remember Tanien Ashini remarking to me. I personally experienced this stubborn, racist stance when trying to rent a car at the Goose Bay Airport. It was only after considerable difficulty and frank discussions with the agency that I was able to lease a vehicle. I got the car but was barred from hotel rooms and wound up staying at the hospitable home of Mennonite Bob Bartel and his family. (Bob supported the Innu and was questioned by Canadian Security Intelligence Service (CSIS) during this time about his "subversive" work.) Sometimes I stayed with Jim Roche, a priest in Sheshatshiu who had spent twenty-one days in jail for accompanying Innu on what NL deemed an illegal hunting expedition of caribou in the Mealy Mountains. I was also hosted by the Innu themselves, often, as I've said, by Tanien Ashini and his wife Sheila Blake, and enjoyed the warmth and resilient good humour of many families who nourished me in their homes with traditional food, family stories, and the richness of their culture.

During trial preparations in the spring of 1989, the community decided a few Elders should appear as witnesses. They wanted the judge to understand that Nitassinan was *their land* and that the runways at Goose Bay, where they had been charged with mischief, had been built on unceded territory. I searched Canadian law for any precedent that would support this argument. And lo and behold, I discovered the "colour of right" concept, a provision in the Criminal Code of Canada that holds that, if you establish that you have an honest belief that what you're doing is lawful (in the case of the Innu, that they were on their land and protesting the trespassing activity of Canada), then that can serve as a valid defence. Once, over lunch with a group of Innu at the Hong Kong restaurant in Goose Bay, we opened our fortune cookies together and mine said: "Canada our home and Native land." We had a good laugh and decided that the theme of the trial should be to bring attention to what our anthem *should* say: "Canada our illegal home on Native Land." This was the determined – and playful – way the Innu approached the trials, determined to honour the teachings of their ancestors, and provide a good future for coming generations.

One morning, I met several Innu women who had been jailed in a small room at the RCMP detachment in Happy Valley-Goose Bay. We had arranged for them to be interviewed by Peter Gzowski on CBC's *Morningside* without informing the police. I sat on the floor with my back firmly blocking the door. As the interview got underway, the officer in charge came bounding down the hall. He banged on the door, yelling, "John! You will be disbarred for this!" He and other RCMP staff had the radio on in their office. I continued to hold the door until Gzowski and the women had finished. When I left the detachment, I was verbally accosted and simply said, "I was doing my job and that includes protecting free speech." (A few years later, while working with the Lubicon Cree in northern Alberta, I ran into the same RCMP officer. We shook hands, talked about the incident, and laughed.)

One witness we called at the trial was Jim Roche, a member of the Oblate Order who had worked respectfully with the Innu for years. He spent considerable time in jail himself, not only for caribou hunting but also because he refused to sign an undertaking that he wouldn't rejoin the runway protests. A NATO training base, Roche testified, "will be the push over the cliff for the Innu people ... the State must recognize that there is much more at stake here than mischief charges. Your Honour must make a ruling on those charges, but everyone in this building knows that that is not the issue at all."[8] When the judge had agreed to move the trial closer to the Innu community, he may not have been prepared for the rounds of applause that rang out at the end of each testimony. The room was filled with both anger and exaltation. Penote Michel testified that Canada was oppressing people and stealing land, resources, and air space. He would continue demonstrating until Ottawa recognized the land as *Innu* land and ordered a halt to the flying. "You can expect to see me back there on the runway and before the court again," he advised. In emotional testimony, Tanien Ashini said, "I firmly believe that this land will become a wasteland and that the Innu people will be destroyed because of low-level flying and the proposal for a NATO base."[9] Peter Penashue testified that protesting at the base wasn't for publicity or money or for claims. He did it because he believed the land *belonged to his people*. "You have not taken us seriously, you have robbed us of everything we had," he said, and broke into tears.[10] The Elders we called to testify, through interpreters, all explained that they had learned from their parents and grandparents that the Creator had gifted the Innu with Labrador.

Remarkably, given the earlier decades of arrogance and indifference, this proud and tenacious group of people were now being listened to. The trial drew daily press coverage from the *Globe and Mail*, the *Toronto Star*, and the *Canadian Press*. An editorial in the St. John's *Evening Telegram* asked why Canada was promoting military expansion at a time when Cold War tensions were easing. "Above all, we have to ask as Newfoundlanders and Labradorians [about] the moral right to impose upon the Innu people a scheme which they find repugnant," the *Telegram* observed. Premier Brian Peckford had advised a NATO site survey team that Labrador offered an environment where "military aircraft can train unencumbered by the presence of towns, villages or large populations." He was so eager to have a new NATO facility that he offered financial assistance for the construction of housing and hangar facilities, thus eliminating the need for "upfront capital expenditures by NATO or the allied nations." The *Telegram* allowed that economic and military development in Goose Bay was obviously something that many Labradorians wanted, but "this matter goes beyond economics ... it has to be asked why this province should welcome military war games of such a nature that they are considered highly offensive in the countries of origin."

In my closing argument, I noted what the Elders had told the court:

Maniaten (Mary Adele) Andrew, who had testified that as a six-year-old child, she followed her parents as they walked, hunted and trapped throughout the land of Nitassinan. She spoke of being herded into the village of Sheshatshiu: "More than forty years of life in the settlement has been enough of a prison for me." Maniaten Andrew went back to walking on her land. [Elder] Matthew Penashue testified that he once caught a partridge, and it took him two years in court and a $20 fine to settle the matter of his crime. *His crime*. CFB Goose Bay is on his hunting ground, he pointed out. He had never given anyone permission to use it, and no one else had either. At the heart level, I know that the evidence of these two Innu Elders summed up both the deep belief and the bewildered trauma of the Innu Nation.

I continued: "The Crown voiced the hypothetical situation of danger – posed by a plane trying to land – to people sitting on the runway. The Innu have given evidence of the *actual* threat to themselves, their families, their animals, and their way of life posed by screeching jets in their river valleys and bombing practices over their camps." As had been agreed to before with the community, I focused on two things in this final argument. One was the legal context of the colour of right defence. The other was the political context. "Nitassinan is the homeland of the Innu," I pointed out.

> It always has been, and it always will be. That deep knowing lies in the very hearts and souls of the Innu people and has been told to the court. That deep knowing cannot be changed by people in London, England, Ottawa, or St. John's drawing new lines on maps ... The Crown has presented some pieces of paper in their attempt to show that the government of Canada has a right to occupy the land where CFB Goose Bay is located. The living title to Nitassinan today is here.

I looked around at the people. "It is present here today in the great-grandparents, the grandparents, the parents, and children. The living title is present in three and four generations of these representative families who will identify themselves." I read aloud dozens of names and asked each person to stand.

"This is the living title of Nitassinan," I said, gesturing towards them.

> Justice demands that this living title be recognized. It cannot be erased by some government somewhere waving a magic wand and saying "presto, Nitassinan now belongs to Newfoundland and Canada." It is either madness or premeditated genocide for a so-called civilized society to deprive a people of their homeland in defiance of the rule of law. The Innu have never signed any Treaty or any other agreement. They have never signed any piece of paper giving Canada rights to Nitassinan. About fifty years ago, the government of Newfoundland and Labrador purported to give Canada a lease to Nitassinan, where CFB Goose Bay is now located. Newfoundland and Labrador had no more right to do that than Chief Ashini has to lease downtown St. John's to the Cree of James Bay. Slow genocide has become an art form in Western society. "Sacrifice a few people for war games, why not? How unreasonable for the Innu to stand in the way of progress." Wonder of wonders, the Innu finally say enough is enough, wrong is wrong, genocide is genocide, justice is justice.

I closed by saying:

> Maniaten Andrew has been in prison in the settlement for forty years. But she is liberating herself. God knows how strong and capable she is in doing that. Matthew Penashue is liberating himself.

Elizabeth Penashue is liberating herself. Tanien Ashini is liberating himself. Penote Michel is liberating himself. Peter Penashue is liberating himself. It is time that our society turn from oppressing Aboriginal people to providing a framework of justice. Your Honour, the Innu have acquitted themselves in this courtroom. The only remaining question is whether our justice system will acquit itself. By acquitting the Innu in the narrow context of the Criminal Code, you will be honouring their struggle for their own liberation. By acquitting the Innu in the larger context of justice for Aboriginal peoples and Aboriginal nations in Canada, you will be making a strong contribution to the liberation of all Canadians. Our liberation from oppressive policies and actions against the First Peoples in what is now called Canada.

When the trial was over, many Innu came to say goodbye to me at the airport. I was so humbled and filled with respect and love for them and their gifts to my life. Sitting in the plane on the tarmac as it pushed back from the gate, I glanced out the window and saw Maniaten and several others through the wire fence, still sending me off, and I cried.

On 18 April 1989, I was in South Africa representing Oxfam in the fight against apartheid when Judge Igloliorte issued his decision. He had deemed the "colour of right" defence to successfully satisfy the definition of an honest belief and a state of fact which, if it exists, would be a legal justification or excuse. He ruled,

> We are not dealing with any land which has been subjected to divestiture through Treaties under the Indian Act. Each of these four persons based their belief of ownership on an honest belief on reasonable grounds through their knowledge of ancestry and kinship. They have shown that none of their people ever gave away any

rights to the land to Canada, and this is an honest belief that each person holds. The provincial and federal statutes do not include as third parties or signatories any Innu people. I am satisfied that the four believe their ancestors predate any Canadian claims to ancestry on this land. A concept of land as property is a concept foreign to aboriginal people. The court must not assume that a 'reasonable' belief be founded on English and hence Canadian law standards. The Innu must be allowed to express their understanding of a foreign concept on their terms, or simply to express what they believe.

"All of the legal reasonings of Canada," he continued:

are based on the premise that somehow the Crown acquired magically by its own declaration of title to a fee of consequent fiduciary obligation to the original people. It is time this premise, based on 17th Century thinking, be questioned in the light of 21st century reality. Canada is a vital part of the global village and must show its maturity not only to the segment of Canadian society that wields great power and authority to summarily affect the lives of minority groups, that the flourish of a pen to yet another 'agreement' or 'memorandum of understanding' resulting in great social and economic benefit, but to all but its most desperate people.[11]

The Innu responded with a statement by Chief Tanien Ashini. "This is a historical day of great pride and joy for the whole people of Nitassinan," he said.

We see it as a further step in our liberation. While we don't need the Canadian court to tell us who we are or what our rights are, we believe the court has recognized the validity and legitimacy that this land and in particular those lands stolen by Canada for CFB

Goose Bay are Innu land. By its decision, the court has questioned the foundations on which Canada has worked in dealing with aboriginal people in attempting to enculturate and assimilate them. While we have always said that we will never stop struggling to protect our land and our life, this decision reassures and encourages us all the more.[12]

A day after their acquittal, about seventy-five Innu entered the military base to deliver a letter declaring that the governments of Canada, the United States, West Germany, and Great Britain were trespassing and should leave. The RCMP, operating on a DND request, barred Chief Ashini from delivering it. Two reporters who were present were told, "take one more picture and you'll never see the camera again."

During the trial of the protesters, Robert Fowler, an assistant deputy minister in the Department of National Defence, told reporters in Ottawa that he wasn't concerned about Canada's chances for getting the NATO training centre. He downplayed the national campaign condemning the flights. Fowler said that NATO was used to petitions and protests; he dismissed the Innu's allegations. Pilots are willing, he said, to avoid areas where "Natives are hunting." Federal trade minister John Crosbie staunchly advocated for the development of CFB Goose Bay and came down hard on the Innu. He accused them of engaging in propaganda to strengthen their position in land claims negotiations. The protests would not work, he said, because the advantages to Labrador were just too great. On land claims, he scoffed – so Innu leaders told me – that they would have to wait their turn.[13] As if they were children, lining up for some sweets. At that time, Canada had a policy of only negotiating six modern Treaties at any time, which created a waiting list. This restriction was dropped after the Innu protested. They were doubtless assisted by then MP Bill Rompkey, who warned that "the dithering and procrastination by Ottawa and St. John's must stop. It is high time all three parties were at the table attempting to thrash out these issues."[14]

Meanwhile, according to St. John's *Evening Telegram*, Igloliorte's decision to acquit the Innu rocked the legal world. "Legal experts say the ruling challenges much of the established case law on aboriginal land claims."[15] A *Globe and Mail* editorial cited the colour of right defence to question whether the Crown owned the land. Could Ottawa not suspend the flying for six months to give negotiations a chance? "The Innu have struggled for years to be heard above the noise of the jets. It is time for serious talk."[16] The answer, apparently, was no.

On 3 April 1990, with the looming reality that a full-fledged NATO base would be established in Goose Bay, with flights increasing to approximately 40,000 per year, the Innu filed an injunction application with the Federal Court Trial Division in Toronto, asking the court to order the minister of national defence to halt all low-level flights over their traditional land. Many Innu came to Toronto for the case and joined local protestors outside the court. The basis of the application was that the defence minister was contravening the guidelines of an environmental assessment review process by continuing to allow training flights while a study of the impact on wildlife was still being carried out. The Innu submission to the federal environmental assessment panel, organized by Peter Armitage, anthropologist and long-term Innu advisor, was called *Homeland or Wasteland: Contemporary Land Use and Occupancy Among the Innu of Utshimassit and Sheshatshiu and the Impact of Military Expansion*.[17] (It also addressed the sensitive and painful issue of sexual abuse of young Innu women by military men.)

The Federal Court ruled that an injunction would harm the economy in Happy Valley-Goose Bay and that, on the balance of convenience, there would be *no* irreparable harm to the Innu if flights continued. This finding was shocking in many ways. It shows that the court was not open to seriously considering what was actually happening to the Innu and their homeland. It was also clear that the judge was upset by the Innu and other protesters demonstrating outside her court, in the Canada Trust Building on University Avenue in Toronto. Indeed, a niggling question in my mind as I argued the case had been whether the lawful protest of the Innu and their Toronto supporters would somehow, perhaps unconsciously, influence the decision of the court. It also struck me that, while lobbying politicians for decisions favourable to vested corporate interests is acceptable to decision-makers, Indigenous protests aren't viewed in the same light. In the case of this injunction, despite all the evidence we placed before it, the court *without any supportive evidence* (because there was none) accepted the federal government's warning that stopping or reducing the number of flights would likely close the base and result in dire economic consequences for the predominately white populace of Happy Valley-Goose Bay. (This never happened.)

    The Innu were considering an appeal of this ruling when they received the news that NATO had shelved its plans for the base. The Innu were overjoyed with this news but vowed to continue to oppose any ongoing low-level flying. Fowler and Crosbie, who had dismissed the possibility of NATO walking away, were caught off guard. There were a few key factors in the NATO decision, including the fall of the Berlin Wall and the fact that digital training for pilots had been perfected, but the Innu protests and their trips to Europe to directly petition the governments obviously played a role. Later, a former US ambassador to Canada told Peter Penashue that Innu opposition had been a critical factor in the NATO decision to abandon its base proposal.[18]

Finally, in 1995, the Federal Environmental Assessment Review Office (FEARO) recommended that the low-level flying continue. That recommendation and Canada's acceptance of it was not as devastating for the Innu as it would have been had NATO forged ahead. Nevertheless, it was concerning, for it confirmed that the FEARO decision-making framework, like that of the NEB and other government agencies, prioritized economic interests. Rather than considering impacts on the Innu way of life and wildlife habitat to be critical factors, the framework focuses on jobs and economic prosperity. It is all, seemingly, about material wealth. Speaking more generally to this point about the fever dreams of gold, Apetet (Ben) Andrew asked RCAP, "How do people expect to get any justice from the European justice system? Especially when it's so well grounded in property rights, because that is what it is. Most of the legal system is all property rights designed to protect the wealthy."

How right Apetet was about justice for the Innu. When the environmental assessment panel released their report on low-level flying (the review of military flying activities in Labrador and Quebec), they appended a letter (see Figure 4.1) from Tom McMillan, minister of the environment in the Mulroney government, when the panel was appointed. Canada loaded the dice! Canada's minister of the environment and minister of national defence told the panel it could not recommend the termination of the low-level flying.

The Innu Nation had tabled a report entitled *Homeland or Wasteland* with the panel. It included the reports of twenty-five experts about the impacts of low-level flying on Innu people and wildlife. The Innu fully believed the panel would conduct its hearings in an impartial manner after a fair consideration of the facts. Imagine Innu anger and dismay to discover that the

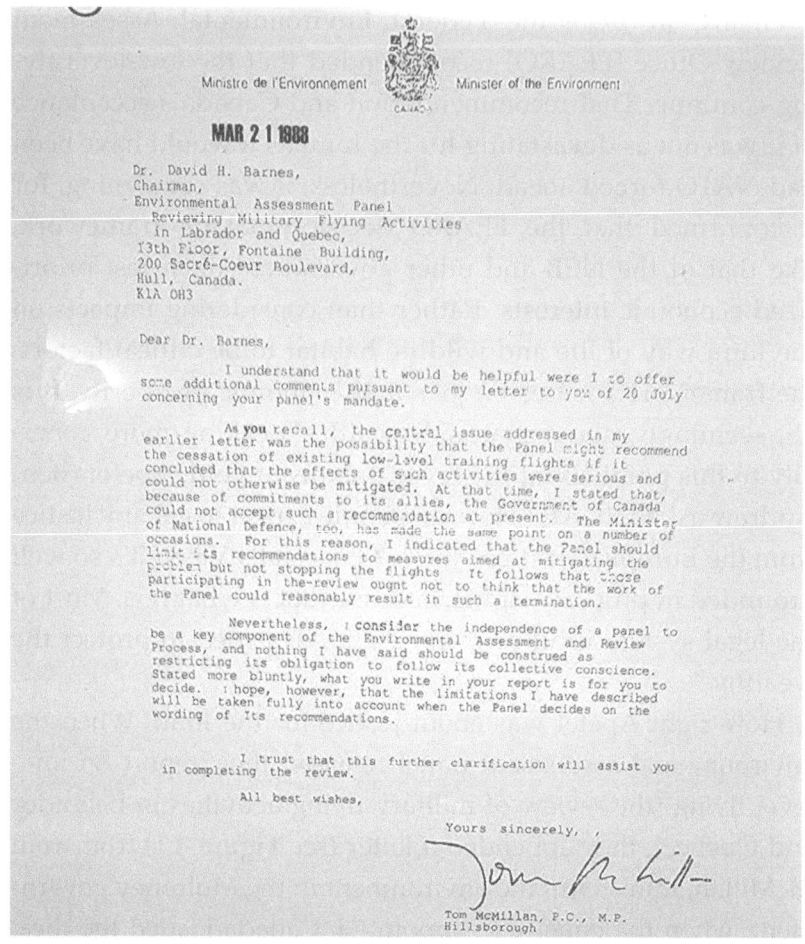

Figure 4.1: Letter from Minister of the Environment Tom McMillan to David H. Barnes, Chairman of the Environmental Assessment Panel Reviewing Military Flying Activities in Labrador and Quebec.

panel hearings were an utter and complete sham, a sham that also undermined the trust of justice-minded Canadians who like to believe that agencies like FEARO, as it was then called, operate independently and objectively without political direction and interference.

Despite what the environmental assessment panel said in its 1990s report and what Canada continues to say, Happy Valley-Goose Bay continued to thrive, even as countries abandoned low-level flying, thus dispelling the myth that the white settlers had faced economic ruin. Over the years, for a variety of reasons, the number of flights has dwindled drastically, and although they still occur, there has been some improvement in notification of Innu communities, and the actual flights are accordingly less disruptive. In the summer of 2024, however, the Department of National Defence (DND) proposed the resumption of low-level flying and began soliciting European countries to once again conduct that flying over Innu traditional land. The aim essentially is to enhance the economy of Happy Valley-Goose Bay and to attempt to convince NATO that such activities count towards bringing our NATO contribution close to the target of 2 per cent of gross domestic product (GDP).[19] The Innu response, once again, was "no military flying or ground-based activity in their territory without Innu consent."

The battle to protect Nitassinan was fought on other fronts as well. In 1994, a nickel deposit was discovered by two prospectors who were looking for diamonds on the North Atlantic shorelines of Anaktalak Bay and Voisey's Bay, near Davis Inlet where the Mushuau Innu lived at the time. Diamond Fields, the company wanting to open the nickel mine, was headed by Robert Friedland, a man renowned [and reviled] as a global prospector with no understanding of Indigenous rights. "With few exceptions," Chief Tanien Ashini said at a miners' conference around this time:

> Aboriginal people across Canada and around the world are witnessing an incredible change on their lands ... Many Innu people remember a time when we had nothing to do with mining or hydroelectric companies, and once they had settled in the communities

of [Sheshatshiu] and Utshimassits, or Davis Inlet, the governments did everything they could to pretend we didn't exist. This was the case only 15 or 20 years ago in my community, and only 6 or 7 years ago in Utshimassits.[20]

Ashini rued the fact that he couldn't use his time to solve problems in his community, or spend it in the country with his family, because he was always fighting to stop or at least be *consulted* on massive industrial developments. In February 1995, Innu men, women, and children travelled together to protest the mine site at Voisey's Bay, handing the camp manager an eviction notice. The company, of course, informed the Innu that they had permits from the province. The Innu then started disrupting their drilling activities and watched impassively while great numbers of RCMP flew in by helicopter from Goose Bay. Once again, they had to face the prospect of arrest just to get invited to a meeting. A discussion was finally arranged between Innu Nation officials and board members of Diamond Fields Resources. I was present at those highly charged sessions with Friedland. They would mark the beginning of negotiations between the Innu and Diamond Fields, which concluded with the signing of a groundbreaking Impact and Benefit Agreement between the Innu and International Nickel Company (Inco), which purchased Diamond Fields' interest in Voisey's Bay in 2002.

The Innu negotiating position for the IBA was based on the following positions:

- Land rights should be resolved before any mining goes ahead. (This position was later abandoned, as it soon became clear that it would take decades to negotiate the modern Treaty.)
- The company is moving too rapidly and should engage in proper consultation and planning; after all, the minerals aren't going anywhere.

- The Innu Nation should negotiate an IBA but proceed with extreme caution given the level of opposition and concern within the communities.
- The company should be prepared to go beyond the requirements of the government's environmental assessment process and accept a broad definition of environmental impacts, one that examines past, present, and future implications for both natural and human environments.
- The company should be committed to an ongoing process of defining its partnership with the Innu Nation. One which allows for meaningful, not just token roles in decision-making.
- The Innu nation should continue to view protests as a viable strategy to address unauthorized mining developments on the land.

Together, the Innu and Inuit went to court to stop the mining company from "project splitting," which is when resource extractors push part of a development without waiting for overall project approval. In this case, Inco was splitting off road construction and an airstrip. The NL Court of Appeal stopped the company. Judges Marshall, Steel, and Green said:

> In this province, as elsewhere, society has been left to grapple with the deleterious, and sometimes tragic effects of development on the health and security of its residents and upon the environment. The recent experience of the devastation of the fisheries through overexploitation bears stark witness to the consequences of the impact which the pace of humankind's activities, especially those driven by economic forces, can have ... As important as are environmental considerations [here the court mentioned *Silent Spring* by Rachel Carson], sight cannot be lost of the economic and social benefits

that flow from the production of these resources ... Nevertheless, they cannot be allowed to control the agenda without regard to competing environmental interests.[21]

After that ruling, the Innu were able to negotiate a memorandum of understanding (MOU) with the Labrador Inuit Association (LIA), Ottawa, and the province, which, among other things, ensured that Innu and Inuit representatives sit on the environmental assessment panel set up to consider the environmental impacts of the nickel mine.

Ashini believed that the MOU was a key first step. "Perhaps more importantly," he said, addressing the mining conference, "it's probably the first MOU in Canada between aboriginal groups and the government where no Treaty rights exist. In signing the MOU, the government has essentially said that they recognize the authority of the Innu government, and we were given the same authority over the process as they had."[22]

Ultimately, the environmental assessment panel recommended that the mine go ahead, but not without land rights negotiations concluded and an IBA settled. Using their usual playbook, both NL and Canada rejected this. They would not give the Innu veto power over the mine, and they could not legally compel the company to conclude an IBA. Remarkably, despite the scaremongering about Innu having a veto, Inco *agreed* that Innu consent was required. And that consent was granted by the Innu in the IBA that addressed the mitigation of the impacts and set out the Innu benefits of the construction and operation of the mine. This supports a central argument of this book – that Indigenous governments must be trusted to make decisions about projects based on relevant considerations, just as the governments of Canada and the provinces do. It is utterly hypocritical: governments feel comfortable with the *concept* of resource governance, but only for them, not in extending a similar power to First Nations. The Innu IBA, which was one of the first major IBAs in the country, spoke to that loudly. The Innu gave consent to the project based on terms and conditions it had negotiated with Voisey's Bay Nickel Company and Inco. A good enough outcome, but like defeating the NATO base, one that could have been achieved with a lot less suffering and sacrifice if Canada and NL had just shown them more respect.

In July of 2002, in anticipation of the signing of the IBA with Voisey's Bay Nickel Co./Inco, the Innu Nation, St. John's, and Ottawa all agreed that the modern Treaty being negotiated would stipulate that the Innu receive 5 per cent of the mine's revenue (or royalties). The Innu could also undertake non-commercial hunting, trapping, fishing, and gathering activities and camp in the Voisey's Bay area, subject to restrictions that may be imposed for public health and safety reasons. The essential importance of the Voisey's Bay IBA and Treaty provisions lies in how they established that Innu approval be a condition *precedent* to any development on their traditional land. Typically, the IBAs signed since by Innu leaders include provisions about workplace conditions, community employment priorities and training, business opportunities, environmental, social and cultural protection, use of infrastructure and facilities, and a percentage of the profits. The upshot of all of this is that what began with one company saying, essentially, "we don't need Innu consent when we have the province's" ended up with industry and politicians conceding that consent was *mandatory*. Recall that all of this happened because the Innu took control of their rights and faced a standoff with over fifty armed RCMP officers.

The Innu have entered several agreements with companies in their traditional land use area since the Voisey's Bay IBA. In doing so, they place an exclamation mark on the reality that, when Indigenous governments have control, they make decisions based on their own determination of the balance between protection of traditional activities and ecosystems and the compatibility of developments.

The exact number of IBAs (or similar agreements going by other names) now signed across Canada isn't clear – most of them are confidential – but I would guess it exceeds 650. In 2015, the Library of Parliament released "Supporting Aboriginal Participation and Resource Development: The Role of Impact and Benefit Agreements." In the coming decades, this paper says, Canada anticipates that its resource development projects will yield investments of around $650 billion. Roughly 1,200 Aboriginal communities sit within a 200-kilometre radius of 180 productive mines and over 2,500 active exploration sites.[23] These projects have the potential to create new social and economic opportunities. IBAs will be a key part of ensuring that. Research from the Northern Development Ministers Forum indicates there has been a big increase in IBAs in the last two decades; notably, the number signed between 2001 and 2010 quadrupled, from 23 to 102, and that momentum has continued. According to the Mining Association of Canada, around 490 agreements were signed between mining and exploration companies and Indigenous communities between 2000 and 2019. These include co-operation agreements, MOUs for exploration agreements, participation agreements, letters of intent, socio-economic agreements, IBAs, and surface lease agreements.

In January of 2023, a First Nation in the Elk Valley region of BC entered an agreement with an Australia-based coal company that gives the Nation – Yaqit ʔa·knuqɬi'it (YQT) – the status of environmental reviewer and regulator for a proposed mining project. "Industry often acts as if Indigenous peoples having a veto is terrifying," Dave Baines of NWP Coal Canada told a CBC journalist, "and what we think is if they are the ancestral title holders, if they are the people with the most rights in the area, we should be treating them like a government. Yes, it's scary, but we're brave enough to say we think we can earn your 'yes,' and we're going to work with you to get that 'yes.'"[24]

On 19 March 2023, the *Toronto Star* wrote about Indigenous involvement in developing clean energy. A 2020 report by Indigenous Clean Energy Social Enterprise identified 197 medium-to-large renewable energy-generating projects with Indigenous involvement, either in operation or in the final stages of planning and construction. The executive director of the Clean Energy Social Enterprise noted that Indigenous communities are so heavily involved in clean energy that they now own, co-own, or have a defined financial benefit in place for almost 20 per cent of Canada's electricity-generating infrastructure and that "Indigenous communities across the country now are, quite literally, the largest change agents for clean energy."[25] This re-enforces the truth that there is nothing to fear and a lot to gain from the decisions that Indigenous communities make about projects that are on their traditional lands or impact those lands or their culture.

Since, as I mentioned, IBAs are often confidential, it's hard to calculate First Nations revenue gains. The only information I'm aware of comes from political scientist Tom Flanagan at the Fraser Institute. Although the institute has strongly assimilationist leanings, the data it collects looks reliable. Flanagan reviewed the records of First Nations as submitted under the First Nations Financial Transparency Act, which requires bands to report own source revenue (OSR). That means money received from sources other than government transfers. Flanagan deduced that, of a combined $11.1 billion in total revenues from 494 nations for the fiscal period of 1 April 2018 to 31 March 2019, about a third – 31.5 per cent – was OSR. Almost all of that revenue likely flows from business agreements. Eventually the IBAs for Voisey's Bay and the Upper and Lower Churchill hydro dams will give the Innu more revenue than they will receive in contribution agreements from Canada.

Statistics Canada uses a Community Well-Being (CWB) index to measure the social health of First Nation communities by income, education, labour force participation, and housing. Flanagan looked at eighteen First Nations showing a significant increase in their CWB score between 2001 and 2006 and, not surprisingly, found that more OSR correlated with higher well-being. By contrast, the CWB of those First Nations where OSR was less than 20 per cent of total revenue had *decreased*. (OSR for First Nations, Flanagan pointed out, is as unequally distributed as income for non-Indigenous Canadians, based on income tax filings.)

Aboriginal groups have expressed concerns about the requirement – in the First Nations Financial Transparency Act – that they report OSR, because Canada has a formula-based policy in place to progressively claw back some of that OSR and use it to reduce the funding it provides to First Nation governments. Although as of November 2024 a moratorium is in place on the application of the OSR claw-back, it is a provision in modern Treaties and the moratorium could be unilaterally removed by Canada at any time. There is a reasonable apprehension that when the moratorium is lifted, the OSR claw-back will be imposed on all First Nations, not just those with modern Treaties. The claw-back is reprehensible for two reasons. First, OSR is compensation generated from IBAs which the First Nation has the *right* to require for projects they consent to, in the case of modern Treaty First Nations on their Treaty lands and in the case of other First Nations on their traditional lands. It is unconscionable for Canada to claw back some of that revenue in order to reduce its financial obligations to First Nations. That is like requiring the victim of a car accident to use a damage award to pay for their ongoing medical treatment in a country with universal healthcare.

The second reason that claw-backs are unjust is that they would forever freeze the CWB gap between First Nations and other Canadians, as a First Nation would not have sufficient OSR to *close* that gap. As Flanagan notes, the StatCan model doesn't factor in security, health, language, culture, environmental integrity, and other measures.[26] It should include the rate of Indigenous infant deaths, suicides, and incarcerations, which are considerably higher than for other Canadians, as discussed in my conclusion. But, even considering the four factors (income, education, labour force participation, and housing), Flanagan says the CWB gap between non-Indigenous and Indigenous communities is 19.5 points, based on a score of 100. That has remained roughly constant for thirty-five years.[27] This is why the claw-back provisions are essentially cruel. They make it impossible for these communities to heal themselves.

In 2014, Canada passed the Extractive Sector Transparency Measures Act, which establishes a framework for foreign and domestic oil, gas and mineral companies to report payments to all levels of government. Specifically, this act requires companies to publicly report payments over $100,000 on a project-by-project basis. These include payments made to Aboriginal governments. Again, the First Nations are concerned that Canada will use this information to calculate claw-back amounts. Economic power enables Indigenous peoples to shed the shackles of settler colonialism. Those communities that do not yet have IBAs or similar agreements are beginning to demand them. They recognize that resource companies are increasingly willing to sign agreements to secure consent for their projects in return for a share of profits and other benefits. It is notable that, while Canadian courts and governments refuse to acknowledge what the United Nations Declaration on the Rights of Indigenous Peoples (UNDRIP) says is the Indigenous right "to free, prior and informed consent" for any proposed interference with their rights, companies routinely agree that such consent is required and seek to obtain it in IBAs. Often, companies take this approach for the very practical reason that it's increasingly difficult to undertake a project without that consent.

NL did not take the Innu land claims and self-government process very seriously until the Voisey's Bay protests. Negotiations happened monthly after the signing of a Framework Agreement in 1996 but lacked urgency until NL decided to further develop the hydro potential of the Churchill River, particularly with new dam sites and reservoirs at Muskrat Falls and Gull Island. It slowly dawned on the folks in St. John's that projects could not go ahead if there was Innu opposition. This was again driven home in 1998, when Quebec premier Lucien Bouchard and NL's Brian Tobin flew to Churchill Falls to stage a photo op and announce their joint plan to build a $10 billion hydroelectric project on the Churchill River. They were met at the tiny airport by 120 Innu protestors who prevented them from coming into town where a press conference had been set up. Instead, a diminutive Innu Elder took Bouchard's chair, her eyes crinkling as she smiled mischievously behind his name placard. When Tobin was succeeded by premier Danny Williams, it was clear that NL's wish to harness Labrador's natural resources would not happen unless he addressed key issues – including reparations for the Upper Churchill hydro project, which had had such devastating impacts on Innu lands. On 26 September 2008, after several months of intense bilateral negotiations in which I took part, including one memorable all-night session, both parties signed the Tshash Petapan, known in English as the New Dawn Agreement.

Tshash Petapen, which is available online, stipulated that the Innu would have outright ownership of 5,000 square miles of land. On 9,000 square miles of additional land, they have substantial specified rights, including the right to pursue IBAs for major developments, based on negotiations that are subject to arbitration in the event of disagreements. An additional 13,000 square miles has harvesting rights. Also included in the overall agreement is the establishment of the 4,131-square-mile Akami-Uapishk-KakKasuak, or Mealy Mountain National Park, with substantial Innu management and access rights. Further, in terms of the existing Upper Churchill hydro project, NL will pay the Innu $2 million a year, indexed at 2.5 per cent, and an annual amount equal to 3 per cent of the dividends received by the province after 2041.

The year 2041 is extremely significant, as that is when NL will begin to receive the full benefit of Upper Churchill – which through all these years has been flowing to HQ by virtue of the terrible deal NL had to make in 1969 to finance its construction. With production capacity of 5,428 megawatts, the Upper Churchill hydro-generating station is one of the largest in the world – annually producing 1 per cent of global hydroelectric power. HQ purchases the bulk of the power at extremely low prices, as per their deal, until 2041. By that date, HQ will have earned an estimated $150 billion from the sale of the energy. (In 2019 alone, HQ's revenue was $28 billion – compared to $2 billion for NL.) So, even 3 per cent of the province's post-2041 Upper Churchill revenue will be very substantial for the Innu and can be used to close the socio-economic gap with other Canadians.

For the Lower Churchill Project, Nalcor paid the Innu $5 million annually from 2010 – the date the project was sanctioned –

until 2020, the date of the first power production. The IBA states that after the first power production, the Innu will receive 5 per cent of the annual after debt net cashflow (or $5 million, whichever is greater). Because of the huge cost overruns of construction on the project, the Innu will only receive the $5 million annually for the foreseeable future. Among other provisions, the Lower Churchill IBA set out an Innu business participation target of $400 million for construction with job priority for qualified Innu workers.

Canada, of course, expressed annoyance that the Tshash Petapen included a bilateral Innu and provincial Treaty AIP but, nevertheless, they were willing to use that AIP as the template for negotiating a tripartite agreement. That AIP, along with the Upper Churchill Redress Agreement and the Lower Churchill IBA, were all formally signed in Natuashish in November 2011. Interestingly, Peter Penashue, one of the Innu negotiators for the Tshash Petapen, had been elected by then as a Conservative Member of Parliament and was appointed to the federal cabinet. So it was, in fact, federal minister Penashue who signed on behalf of Canada at a moving ceremony.

Before this book went to press, HQ finally agreed to compensate the Innu for its role in the construction of the Upper Churchill Hydro dam. The Innu had sued HQ, and the court date was approaching, but more importantly, in 2025, HQ had entered an agreement with the Government of NL to build a new hydro project at a site on the Churchill River called Gull Island; the company understood Innu consent for that development would be required. So, in late June 2025, both parties signed an Agreement in Principle. HQ will contribute $87 million to an Innu Reconciliation fund over a sixteen-year period as well as 3 per cent of the dividends it receives from the Upper Churchill dam for as long as that dam produces power. The AIP also sets out the terms for HQ's collaboration with the Innu Nation in the development of future facilities in the region, such as the Gull Island Power Generation Station. The agreement is "in principle" because it will not proceed unless it is approved by the Innu people in a ratification vote to be held in the fall of 2025.

Many generations of Innu People have suffered from the impacts of the Upper Churchill power dam over the last 50 years, and many are no longer alive to consider ratifying this compensation agreement. Obviously, HQ's awareness that its plans to construct future power dams in Labrador would stall out unless the Innu lawsuit about Upper Churchill was settled played a significant role in their decision to sign. "Better Later than Never" is certainly true, but hopefully the history of the Upper Churchill project will help proponents of other projects understand that free, prior and informed Indigenous consent is required for them to proceed. This is particularly important since Prime Minister Carney's Building Canada Act was passed by Parliament on 20 June 2025. The act authorizes the Carney cabinet to fast-track projects it considers to be in the national interest. This adds urgency to the requirement that these "national interest projects" not proceed without the consent of the Indigenous peoples whose lands and rights will be impacted.

There is much left for the Innu to do as they recover from the onslaught of British imperial and Canadian greed. But I do believe that my old friend and colleague Tanien Ashini would be proud that his daughters, Jolene and Jodie, lawyer and archaeologist, guardians of their culture and their rights, are carrying forward the fight to protect Nitassinan and provide a more hopeful future for the Innu of Labrador.

CHAPTER FIVE

The Struggle of the Teme-Augama Anishnabai for Old-Growth Trees and Their Land

"Years ago, when we went somewhere new," Second Chief once explained, "a different lake or a different portage, [the adults] always tied a tree for us, to tie us to the land. I've tied them for my grandchildren."[1]

Among the rising young Indigenous leaders of the 1970s was Gary Potts, Chief of the Teme-Augama Anishnabai (Deep Water by the Shore People). I first met Potts at the Assembly of First Nations meetings in 1981 and 1982. He had worked as a trapper in his beloved home territory of northern Ontario until he felt compelled to get into politics in order to defend his land. Gary was a force to be reckoned with, a charismatic speaker with an engaging smile and a twinkle in his eye. We became friends – he sang "Forever Young" at my relationship commitment ceremony in 1991. But first, I joined with him and the people of Teme-Augama to attempt to stop the heartless logging of their magnificent old-growth forest. The Teme-Augama territory, known as N'Daki Menan, lies about 400 kilometres north of

Toronto, an hour's drive beyond North Bay. It is an exquisitely beautiful wilderness, with deep-water lakes that flow one into the other over misty waterfalls. I was awestruck when Gary led me into one of the last remaining ancient forests in the world, the first of many walks we took on 3,000-year-old trails which the Teme-Augama call *nastawgan* (traditional paths). White and red pines, some centuries old, towered ten and fifteen stories above the ground, part of an intricate and highly evolved ecosystem that sustained life for innumerable plants and animals. The pine forest was a habitat for endangered golden eagles and had large nesting concentrations of great blue herons, ospreys, and pine warblers.

The Teme-Augama were not opposed to logging as such. They just wanted to preserve the old growth, protect wildlife habitat, and do selective harvesting rather than clear-cutting. As Chief Potts put it, "it all comes back to having a feel for what you are working with. A craftsman knows his tools, a farmer his lands, the Teme-Augama know the bush." Canada, however, had entered the age of corporate forestry. More trees were felled in the fifteen years between 1978 and 1993 than in all the previous fifty, mostly by a handful of multinational companies paying provincial governments for the privilege of quick profit. The governments, in exchange, were earning $23 billion per year as of 1992/3 and directly or indirectly employing 900,000 Canadians.[2] The cathedral-like forests of Teme-Augama, teeming with life, were being rapidly razed to the ground by industrial-scale clear-cut operations. "You gotta have shade for animals, you know," Elder Walter Becker mused sadly in front of his hunting shack in a documentary at the time, about the calamity of clear-cutting. "They can't be sitting out there in the open sun all day. It's not good for them."[3]

On one of our strolls, Gary took me to the conjuring rock, a sacred place on the shore of a lake called Shis-kong-abikong.

This is where the people have come for generations, to listen to what the spirits tell them about their survival and care of the land. They feared that logging would expose Shis-kong-abikong and damage its spirit.

Many non-Indigenous people and organizations also began expressing alarm about the incessant destruction. An article in *Maclean's* in 1989 noted that "Jon Grant, president of the Quaker Oats Co. told the Conference Board of Canada in Toronto last month that on a flight over the Teme-Augama woodlands in early October, 'we crossed tracts of clear-cut woodland that were as appalling to see as shots of deforestation in the Amazon rain forests.'"[4] In the 1970s, when mechanized logging kicked into high gear, the industry was "almost completely unaware of environmental issues," writes the journalist John Vaillant about the decimation of old growth in British Columbia, where "there was only sporadic replanting of logged areas, and conservation, as we know it today, was negligible."[5] The only people who could see the catastrophe unfolding were the experienced Indigenous stewards – who had been sidelined.

When he became Chief in 1972, one of Gary Potts's first acts was to file a legal land caution, warning that roughly 10,000 square kilometres of territory fell under his nation's care, as it had for thousands of years; they had never ceded it. This put the public on notice that they should be cautious about buying or leasing land within N'Daki Menan. The caution effectively halted all development except logging; the government of Ontario was legally responsible for any issues concerning the licences it issued. Despite the caution, another 500 square kilometres of timber got harvested from N'Daki-Menan, and Ontario licensed a further 2,000 square kilometres for clear-cutting. By Ontario, I do not mean the men and women living their lives – as immigrants and working-class people and scientists and artists – who were largely unaware, at this point, of the Teme-Augama and their need to protect their forest. I mean the men who lunched together at steakhouses on Bay Street and schemed up new ways to get rich, confident that they would have politicians and judges on their side. Timber was a commodity. That had always been the settler colonial approach. It was there for the taking until there wasn't a twig left.

In the 1970s, Ontario also began considering approval of a ski resort on Chee-bay-jing (Maple Mountain) – a sacred Teme-Augama site. Potts and his community, who had been confined to a one-square-mile reserve called Bear Island, joined forces with environmentalists to push back. This new assertiveness, taken together with their legal caution, prompted Ontario, in 1983, to establish the Lady Evelyn Smoothwater Provincial Park – a wilderness of 720 square kilometres. But that same year, Ontario's Ministry of Natural Resources assured lumber companies that all was not lost: they could extend the existing Red Squirrel Logging Road farther into the old-growth forest. Construction began in 1984, without the completion of a required environmental assessment. The Teme-Augama, environmental groups, and some local residents set up a protest blockade in June 1988, which evolved into the largest peaceful civil disobedience protest in Canada – until the BC Clayoquot Sound logging protests five years later. Over 300 protesters, including Ontario's soon-to-be-premier Bob Rae, got arrested for participating. Many other prominent Canadians, including Margaret Atwood and Bruce Cockburn, strongly advocated to save the old-growth forest.

In the winter of 1989, the Teme-Augama Wilderness Society (TWS), a non-profit citizen's coalition dedicated to the research and conservation of Ontario's wilderness, published a report about Teme-Augama's forests. As Chief Potts had told me on one of our walks, the forest included the only known complete network of *nastawgan* – traditional Aboriginal trails – on the continent. It also held one of the largest concentrations of archaeological sites on the Canadian Shield. TWS (currently active as Earthroots) called on people to tell Premier David Peterson to "Stop the logging of Temagami NOW" and to "Preserve this world treasure for future generations."

While the Teme-Augama welcomed the support of non-Indigenous activists, they wanted more focus on their rights; the reality was that what TWS called "this world treasure" was their *homeland*. Their struggle to regain stewardship had been ongoing for over a century. Some Ojibway and Cree clans in northern Ontario had signed what was known as the Robinson-Huron Treaty of 1850, but the Teme-Augama did not, as confirmed in an 1883 report by the deputy superintendent of Indian Affairs. They had never surrendered their traditional title. Indeed, as a result, from 1857 to 1882, they never received government funding. Finally, stressed to near starvation by the fur trade, they did request that an Indian Act reserve be established for them, and an area on the south shore of Lake Temagami got surveyed but was never set aside because Ontario refused to transfer the land to Canada. It wasn't until after 1971, when the federal government purchased Bear Island on Lake Temagami from the province, that Teme-Augama First Nation was established, with Gary Potts as leader. And, indeed, this only happened because Ontario threatened to evict the people from their homeland for failure to pay provincial taxes and other levies.

In 1982, Ontario and the Teme-Augama went to court over who, in fact, had title to the N'Daki Menan. The four-month hearing, and a subsequent appeal to the Ontario Court of Appeal, ruled against the Teme-Augama. I was not involved in these court actions, but the Teme-Augama First Nation engaged me to seek a temporary court injunction (legally called an interlocutory injunction) to stop construction of the logging roads and restrain Ontario from licensing the harvesting of old-growth red and white pine. They had appealed the negative title decision of the Ontario Court of Appeal to the Supreme Court of Canada and wanted road construction and more timber harvesting to pause while the Supreme Court considered their appeal.

As part of my preparation for the court proceedings, I spent many delightful days with the Teme-Augama people on Bear Island. It was inspiring to be engulfed and embraced by the gentle spirit of the land. We talked there about what the courts would consider in an interlocutory injunction application. First, was there a serious issue to be considered in the appeal to the Supreme Court of Canada? Second, would the plaintiff, in this case the Teme-Augama, suffer irreparable harm if the temporary injunction wasn't granted? And third, on balance, would the inconvenience to Ontario – if the temporary injunction got approved – outweigh the positive effects for the Teme-Augama? A week before our court date, the Supreme Court of Canada agreed to hear the title appeal case, so I argued that there was, indeed, a serious issue to be tried. Namely, the title to the land in question. With respect to irreparable harm, I said what I thought should be blatantly self-evident, that cutting down centuries-old pine trees and destroying an ecosystem was an irreparable act of harm. It would never grow back. Indeed, the Teme-Augama "could not sustain the blows of the road and this harvest," I argued. Continued logging would "cause irreparable and irrevocable harm that would finally lead to extinction of the old growth forest after years of mismanagement."

Finally, with respect to balance of convenience, I argued that surely the inconvenience to Ontario and the loggers, in waiting for the Supreme Court to decide the title case, was far less egregious than destruction of the old-growth forest.

Justice Philip of the Ontario High Court agreed that the issue of whether it was the Teme-Augama or Ontario who had title was a substantial one. Yet, to my dismay and to the utter distress of the Teme-Augama, the judge went on to find that the serious issue of the ownership of the land had *already been decided* by the courts. Accordingly, he said, "There is not before me at this time, therefore, a serious or substantial issue to be tried." He noted that the trial judge in the title case (Justice Steele) had found that the Teme-Augama people had no right, title, or interest, so Ontario had the right to issue letters of patent to grant, sell, lease or otherwise convey or dispose of the lands without their consent. "It is my view," Justice Philip said, "that I should not grant injunctive relief at this stage as it would have the effect of conferring the right on the Teme-Augama to prevent the harvesting of timber as if they had title to the lands ... I do not have such jurisdiction under those circumstances to grant injunctive relief in my view." But, in fact, as he implicitly said at the beginning of the above quote, the issue was not that he could not grant an injunction because he did not have the legal right to – but, rather, that he decided to exercise that right by refusing to grant the injunctive relief despite his acknowledgment that the title of the land issue was a substantial issue and was yet to be addressed by the Supreme Court.

What was so disappointing was that the judge actually viewed the decision of the Ontario Court of Appeal as the end of the road for the Teme-Augama when, in fact, the judicial process was not complete. The Supreme Court could still reverse the ruling of the Ontario Court of Appeal, yet the judge appeared to rationalize his decision by incorrectly claiming that the Teme-Augama had made no attempt to stop harvesting before this trial. It was such an affront. In the words of Chief Potts, the Teme-Augama "have vigorously protested all encroachments, including timber harvesting in N'Daki Menan since 1877."[6] Further, Justice Philip narrowed the impact of any new logging roads on the Teme-Augama by saying that construction would not *specifically* affect the band's ability to trap and fish, whereas granting the injunction would detrimentally affect the status quo of the lumber companies, their employees, and their communities, thereby causing irreparable harm. He added that "this court is not the forum to determine the forest management problems of the province of Ontario."[7]

In all these findings, Justice Philip ignored what Gary Potts had told him in his affidavit. Potts said, "The cumulative impact of the forest roads and the resulting timber harvesting in N'Daki Menan has decimated the traditional way of life of the Teme-Augama Anishnabai people. Construction of the Goulard Road and the extension of the Red Squirrel Road is the 'straw that will break the camel's back,' as the destruction of the old growth will decimate our traditional pursuits of hunting, trapping, fishing and gathering." That, Potts continued, "will contribute to the on-going decimation of our entire social structure, including our religion, culture and political and economic institutions, which all derive from, and are nourished by our relationship with the land."[8]

This issue of *cumulatively* impacting Indigenous life on the land is a hallmark of settler colonialism. Residential schools are the example we tend to focus on, but, over time, the government issuance of licences for mining, logging, and other activities constitutes "death by a thousand permits." The courts enable this by only considering "impact" one project at a time, based on the three-pronged test for granting injunctions (noted above), which excludes *cumulative impact* as a measure of irreparable harm. In some recent non-injunction cases, the courts have looked at whether a series of encroachments amount to the extinguishment of an Aboriginal right, rather than a justified infringement on those rights. Those findings are encouraging, and hopefully more courts will do likewise. It is imperative that there be a clear remedy for the extinguishment of a way of life. Otherwise, the approach of the courts will continue to fly in the face of reconciliation with Indigenous nations, continuing to entrench the non-Indigenous devotion to economic interests as paramount over all others. In the Teme-Augama case, the economic growth paradigm assigned more importance to preventing temporary layoffs than to preserving an ecosystem flourishing with life. Governments can grant relief to workers and businesses, as they did during COVID lockdowns, but they cannot resurrect centuries-old trees. In this injunction application, the Teme-Augama presented the court with the option of redefining the criteria for irreparable harm. The court refused. That speaks volumes.

Even today, injunctions – as demonstrated again in the 2021 anti-logging protests at Fairy Creek in lower BC[9] – are aimed at restraining protesters rather than logging. But there are encouraging signs that values are shifting for an increasing number of Canadians. Perhaps the courts will reflect on what actually constitutes "irreparable harm" and adopt a more appropriate, holistic test, which in the Teme-Augama case would have meant focusing on the irreparable harm of destroying an old-growth forest and, with it, a good deal of Teme-Augama spirituality and culture. Speaking more broadly, when considering injunction applications, the courts must take this holistic approach in determining whether there is a serious issue to be tried, what constitutes irreparable harm, and where the balance of convenience lies.

The stubborn focus of our courts has entrenched in Canadians an idea that reconciliation is about Indigenous people and nations having to reconcile *to* the sovereignty of the Crown. Moreover, it's simply wrong for the courts to try to wash their hands, as was the case in this injunction, by saying, in effect, "it's a government forest management problem, not a matter for the courts." In fact, court injunction decisions are rarely impartial in that they are based on reinforcing the narrow and increasingly discredited notion that economic loss to Canadians is the only conceivable consideration. If authentic reconciliation is to happen, it is far more important that the courts recast their criteria for defining irreparable harm than it is for Canadians to make land acknowledgments at conferences and galas.

The Logging Road Blockades

On 2 November 1989, a few days after the injunction dismissal, the Teme-Augama called on supporters to join in a seven-week blockade of the Red Squirrel Road. Gates were set up at the west and east ends of the road, and Chief Potts met with Premier Peterson in a last-minute attempt to get Ontario to cancel construction. Peterson refused, although he reiterated Ontario's earlier commitment to discuss outstanding issues in the relationship between Ontario and the Teme-Augama. (In 1988, his cabinet minister, Ian Scott, had offered the Teme-Augama $30 million and 100 square kilometres if they dropped their title claims. The Teme-Augama refused to do so, as their urgent concern was protecting the old-growth pine. Would you offer the Pope, say, a bucket of cash and a bigger house in exchange for blowing up the Sistine Chapel?)

Potts asked people to come, en masse, to blockade on 11 November, Remembrance Day. Many of his ancestors and the ancestors of other First Nations people had fought as allies of the British in the War of 1812, as well as the First and Second World Wars. They had served Canada when Canada needed them, and it was long past the time for their rights to N'Daki Menan to be recognized. Four generations of Temagama stood on the Red Squirrel Road. "Never again, never, ever again, would the Temagama Anishnabai [be] on the verge of extinction," Potts later said, of seeing his people make their stand.

After the failed injunction application, Chief Potts and I had extensive discussions about our anger and sorrow, and about the next steps. There were going to be arrests, and the logging road builders would surely apply for their own injunction to end the Teme-Augama blockade. So Chief Potts announced that the blockades would be peaceful, and he urged people not to resist arrest. He also issued an eviction notice to Ontario and the logging companies. NDP leader Bob Rae defended him, saying that there should be a moratorium on logging until the Supreme Court ruled on Teme-Augama's "historic claim, a claim of ownership, a claim of stewardship."[10]

As expected, Ontario responded swiftly with their own application for a temporary injunction. I argued on behalf of the Teme-Augama that this be denied; the blockades were there to stop the irreparable harm threatening the forest. Unsurprisingly, the Ontario Court granted the interim injunction, and a hearing for permanent injunction was argued on 17 November. In short, it was a re-run of our application to *stop* the road construction and the logging, except, of course, this time I was arguing against the injunction. The issues of "irreparable harm" and "balance of convenience" were the same as in the previous case. Justice O'Leary said that Justice Philip had already concluded – in rejecting the Teme-Augama application for an injunction – that irreparable harm would result if construction on the road did not go ahead. He refused to reconsider that issue. The court decided that "[o]nly at its peril will society allow anyone to flout the law" and that "[t]he Attorney General as protector of public rights and the custodian of the public interest is entitled to seek an injunction against those flouting the law." He added, "In such case, the Attorney General does not have to show that irreparable harm will result if the injunction is not granted."[11]

In dismissing my argument that an injunction wasn't necessary, since Chief Potts had made it clear that the Teme-Augama and their supporters would not resist arrest, the court said, "the whole purpose for the injunction is to bring home to anyone who might be tempted to obstruct the construction that hereafter he will face being held in contempt of court if he obstructs the work and not just the penalty he might have otherwise incurred."[12] He prohibited protestors from being within 300 metres of construction works.

In March of 1990, I made a second application for an injunction, on behalf of the Teme-Augama as licences to harvest 17 square kilometres of old-growth forest had just been granted. This meant that *a third* of the remaining old growth would be gone before the Supreme Court even heard the title case appeal. Justice McRae found that, despite the issuing of those new logging licences, he could find no reason to overturn the 1989 decision. Colonialist capitalism must go full steam ahead. The construction of the Red Squirrel Road extension was completed just before Christmas.

The Arrests and Trials

In all, 225 people were arrested for blockading Red Squirrel Road from Remembrance Day through December of 1989. I was asked to defend ten of them, including Chief Potts. The others were: second Chief Rita O'Sullivan, Elder Mary Vosdingh and Elder Reynold Turner of the Teme-Augama First Nation; John Agouni, a member of the Sheguiandah First Nation on Manitoulin Island; Frank Beardy, a former Chief of Muskrat Dam First Nation; and Chief Patrick Madahbee, Aundeck Omni Kaning First Nation on Manitoulin Island. Also three members of religious orders: Father George Leach, Sister Faith Sherlock, and Reverend Dennis Drainville, at the time an Ontario MPP representing Victoria Haliburton and chair of the NDP government caucus.

All of the accused except Drainville instructed me to inform the court that they would not enter a plea to the charges, as they did not believe the court had jurisdiction over them. They felt that entering a plea would be disrespectful to the Teme-Augama people and ancestors, as the trials were being held in a building located in N'Daki Menan, the Teme-Augama homeland. They also asked me to inform the court that, historically, the Teme-Augama Nation had its own laws and justice system, and no one had ever given Canada or Ontario the right to make laws to govern their collective or individual action as citizens, or as guests of the Teme-Augama. They could not enter pleas to charges that they had committed an illegal activity when, in fact, it was Ontario that was, and had been, committing prohibited activities in N'Daki Menan for many decades.

It was not they who should be on trial, when Ontario had violated its own law in the context of the Canadian justice system by authorizing the construction of Red Squirrel Road and the logging of the old-growth forest before the Supreme Court of Canada had heard the Teme-Augama title claim appeal. Provincial Court Judge Robert Fournier listened carefully and respectfully to these submissions but dismissed them, declaring – as Justice Igloliorte had in the case of the Innu protesters – that the court did have jurisdiction. He entered pleas of "not guilty" on behalf of nine accused. Reverend Drainville entered his own "not guilty" plea. Despite having to proceed to trial, each of the defendants I represented felt empowered that their concerns and their sense of dismay and anger at Ontario's failures had been expressed and quite respectfully heard.

As Judge Fournier later noted in his reasons for judgment in the case of Chief Potts, "In itself, that type of offence is not usually considered overly complex, however, because of the flavour of the circumstances surrounding the commission of this particular mischief, perhaps it becomes one which is indeed complex; this explains why such a great deal of time has been dedicated to the consideration of the relevant issues."[13]

So, the trials began. Each morning, I gathered with the Teme-Augama and their supporters around a sacred fire that was kept burning for the duration. It was a time of meditation, a time to give thanks for the Blessings of the Creator, a time to remember and thank the ancestors for their stewardship of the land and the old growth, a time to pray that the Government of Ontario would receive wisdom to protect the white and red pine and recognize the Teme-Augama title to N'Daki Menan, a time to support and care for those who would take the stand that day to explain why they had blockaded the road, and to be strong when they were cross-examined, a time to pray for the judge, a time to express feelings of fear, hope, and resolve. Elders reminded us daily to act honourably and out of respect for all, including those who would testify against the accused. Around the sacred fire those mornings in the community with so many spirit-filled people, I entered a liminal space, one of deep connection to the sacred.

Some evenings, I drove over the ice road to the Bear Island reserve to participate in powerful sweat lodge ceremonies, but usually my nights were spent in trial preparation. As with the Innu, it seemed appropriate here to employ the "colour of right" defence. That defence is very difficult to argue successfully, especially for non-Indigenous defendants, as the courts make a distinction between a "moral right" and a "legal or lawful right." A plea either of ignorance of the law or moral objection to a law will not succeed as a colour of right defence. But, based on what each of the accused told me about their sincere belief that the Teme-Augama owned the land on which they were protesting, I was prepared to make the colour of right argument at their trials. Although the accused gave moving evidence about their beliefs in each trial, Judge Fournier ruled in all cases except for Chief Potts that the accused knew what the law said; namely, they were aware that two Ontario courts had ruled that the province owned the land, and thus their claim did not meet the criteria for a successful colour of right acquittal. Eight of them were fined. In the case of the ninth, Reverend Drainville, Judge Fournier issued a twenty-six-page written judgment explaining why he was guilty. I will return to that in a moment.

First, I want to discuss the judgment in which Judge Fournier *acquitted* Chief Gary Potts by accepting the colour of right defence. On 28 November 1990, it took the judge fifty minutes to read his extremely thorough and well-reasoned judgment. He began by saying:

> I'd like to thank everyone involved in this trial for their patience. It's been a long night for me. There is an expression in the Northern Territories, Mr. Potts, which goes something like this – it says "Before you judge a man, walk a mile in his moccasins." Before judging you, I must say that I walked at least twelve hours and I'll let you figure out the mileage.

I had asked Chief Potts to provide a history of the Teme-Augama on N'Daki Menan. The Crown objected, but the judge allowed it. Potts was as quietly charismatic as ever. He spoke honestly, clearly, and with deep conviction and emotion. He wore his Chief's medallion, featuring a water bird with outstretched wings. N'Daki Menan, Potts explained to the court, was once divided into fourteen traditional family territories, with names and numbers assigned to each. The territorial boundaries were based on watersheds and heights of lands, or demarcated by creeks, rivers, and points on lakes. These family territories were passed down from one generation to the next, following the paternal line. In the event that a given territory could not be passed on in this fashion, the heads of families would decide how to reassign the lands. This provided an element of certainty and security for all members of the nation. When the Europeans arrived, they imported concepts of jurisdiction and ownership that held no meaning for his people, Potts explained. This wasn't merely an ownership dispute – it was a fundamentally alien matrix.

Chief Potts was not breaking any laws, because although he respected "the rule of law," in his honest opinion, in these circumstances, the state of the law was not settled. Chief Potts was informed by police officers that the construction company wanted access to the land and that he ought to remove himself. He replied, "No, I won't. This is Teme-Augama Anishnabai land. I cannot remove myself from it." When the presiding officer read the notice about him interfering with the lawful use of the property, Potts replied, "For the record, Sgt. McClair, it is my duty to inform you that this is not the property of Carmen Construction. It is not the property of the Ontario government. It is the property of the Teme-Augama Anishnabai and has been for 6,000 years and will be for at least another 6,000 years if the Creator keeps our land strong."

They were torn and offended as a people, Potts told Fournier, and began to view the Red Squirrel Road extension as a symbol of the "rape" which was being perpetrated on the motherland.

They felt they must do something to protect her. But they wanted to continue to protest non-violently, as they had done for the past century. "The people felt that they would continue to deal in a very honorable way, because at the end of the day, we wanted our honour intact; even if our land had been stolen from us by whatever system brought in from Europe dictated."[14]

In his long decision leading to the acquittal of Chief Potts, the judge reviewed the history of protests as these related to what he called "the rule of law." He noted that civil disobedience is a time-honoured method of drawing public attention to claims of fundamental freedoms or human rights. We do not cease to witness shining examples to this day, he said, pointing to such notables as Martin Luther King Jr. and Mahatma Gandhi. Chief Potts may well be on his way to becoming a contemporary example, Fournier mused.[15]

The key to the court's finding was Chief Potts's testimony about the choice he made – and urged all protesters to make – to protest peacefully when they could have vandalized construction equipment or placed boards with nails across the roads. Moreover, a European justice system being applied to the Teme-Augama Anishnabai, a system foreign to their way of life, was, the judge said, a troubling aspect which, in the court's view, deserved to be addressed. He referred to the Innu case, quoting Judge Igloliorte's comments:

> Since the concept of land as property is a concept foreign to the original people, the court must not assume that 'a reasonable' belief be founded on English and hence, Canadian law standards. The Innu people must be allowed to express their understanding of a foreign concept on their terms, or simply express what they believe ... the Crown has presented to me recent cases which only emphasize the concept of land as property from an English law viewpoint.[16]

Like the IQ test administered to schoolchildren years ago, which reflected the understanding of the maker of the test, rather than the person tested, there lies in this an inherent bias. "In this particular case," Fournier said, "if the court is to make a determination which is based on a truly 'subjective test' it must take into account the inherent bias that Judge Igloliorte refers to and which Chief Potts has evidently experienced firsthand."[17]

Justice Fournier concluded that it could not be said that Chief Potts did not have the honest belief – and the right to take the action – that he did and acquitted him. Unlike the other Indigenous accused, who were found guilty, the judge seemed to have taken into account Potts's leadership in insisting, out of respect for his ancestors, that the protests be peaceful.

Reverend Dennis Drainville, on the other hand, was convicted despite his sense of *moral* right. On scrutiny of the evidence, the judge found, it was clear that Drainville knew what the law of the land was that pertained to "legal ownership," but that he just strongly disagreed with it. The court understood Drainville's dilemma. When confronted with the legal reality that Ontario had title to the land, his own moral sense dictated Teme-Augama had the rightful claims, so he chose to be morally correct rather than "law abiding." In his decision, Judge Fournier recalled Drainville's testimony about the biblical passage, "Render unto Caesar the things that are Caesar's, and unto God the things that are God's," namely, Drainville saying:

> that we constantly have to be aware that there is a point at which we owe God our allegiance and our actions, our care and our concerns, and the decision as to where these two realities meet is the responsibility of the citizens of this country. It is wrong for any citizen to willfully disobey the law and to do so is unacceptable, but there are laws that are greater in the supremacy of God, and

it is those laws that speak to the heart, mind and soul. For me, to deprive the native people of this country and in this province was such that I had to heed that call when the invitation came and that is why I stood with my brothers and sisters on the Red Squirrel Road.[18]

Drainville could have resolved the conflict between "the moral rules of God" and the "rule of law" by standing on the side of the road and protesting, Judge Fournier said, rather than obstructing construction. Right after he was convicted, Drainville told the court that he would block the road again if the people asked him to. They have been abused and oppressed by governments and the legal system for centuries, he declared. "The native cause is just and right." Sentencing him on 13 February 1991, Fournier remarked, "Here is a person who, as an elected member of the provincial parliament, has sworn his allegiance to Her Majesty the Queen, and yet displays very little respect or recognition for the rule of law which is the very foundation of the system which elected him in the first place ... Though the adoption of several disobedient methods in the promotion of numerous good and noble causes is quite common, there are instances, such as in this case, where it is unlawful and cannot be tolerated."[19] Reverend Drainville was sentenced to a week in jail and a fine of $750. He went on to become the Anglican Bishop of Quebec from 2009 to 2017 and is now retired. I think about Dennis from time to time as I ponder why it is that so many religious leaders today are so guarded about speaking truth to power.

In 1991, the Supreme Court of Canada dismissed the Teme-Augama's appeal. The Court said, "It was unnecessary, however, to examine the specific nature of the aboriginal right because that right was surrendered, whatever the situation on the signing of the Robinson-Huron Treaty, by arrangements subsequent to the

Treaty by which the Indians adhered to the Treaty in exchange for Treaty annuities and a reserve."[20] The Court did find that Ontario breached its fiduciary obligations to the Teme-Augama by failing to meet some of its Treaty obligations, but said those matters were under negotiation between the parties and did not alter the fact that the Teme-Augama Aboriginal rights had been extinguished.

For the Teme-Augama, the decision proved devastating, but still, some progress had been made. During the mischief trials, negotiations led to a memorandum of agreement between the Teme-Augama and Ontario government about stewardship and management of four townships. It was the intention of the parties to expand on that agreement over the next decade so as to ultimately encompass all of the motherland. Potts said, in his testimony, that it was his dream to blend his peoples' ancient land use systems with modern administrative methods. That, in his view, was true Canadianism.

There have been four rounds of discussions between Ontario and the Teme-Augama since then but, still, no agreement. The latest round – still underway as of this writing – began in 2020. In 1993, the Teme-Augama rejected an offer made by Ontario of 115 square miles, $15 million, and a larger shared stewardship. Six years later, Teme-Augama proposed a settlement based on that offer, but Ontario said no, and removed their offer from the table. In 2000, the Teme-Augama accepted an Agreement in Principle (AIP), but some families of the larger Teme-Augama Anishnabai objected, and so it was never completed. In 2001, Canada joined the discussions, and in 2003, Teme-Augama and Ontario agreed that there would be 127 square miles of reserve land, $4 million in economic development, and $20 million in compensation. The Teme-Augama, who include among them non-status people, objected to the settlement, so it wasn't completed. In August of 2009, Chief Potts suspended negotiations, which only resumed recently. Sadly, Gary Potts died on 3 June 2020, but his legacy lives on. Gary was a good man, a delightful friend, a fearless, charismatic leader, and a compelling advocate for N'Daki Menan and its people and trees.

Teme-Augama and Earthroots continue with their struggle to safeguard the old-growth forest. After the blockade, the Ontario government issued the Teme-Augama a land use plan, with several provincial parks and conservation areas established to protect just half of Teme-Augama's remaining old growth. Since 1996, Earthroots has worked to preserve the remaining unprotected forest along with Indigenous sacred sites. They have also advocated for low-impact recreation in the area, such as hiking and canoeing, which has raised public awareness about the uniqueness of the region. Nevertheless, Earthroots notes, nearly twenty years after the Red Squirrel blockade, Teme-Augama still isn't fully protected.

Earthroots has had extensive involvement in the planning of the Teme-Augama Forest Management Unit. Right now, they are voicing several concerns about the changing climate, and the effects of increased access on the Teme-Augama canoe culture, the importance of intact forest landscapes, and problems with the enhanced forest inventory. The war in the woods continues.

"What we're finding," Potts said at the time of his trial:

> is that the governments realize that they've run into something that they can't control. They've run into a spirit – a spirit that rises from the Canadian soil through human beings that have been here for thousands of years, that they could not kill. They could suppress it, but they could not kill the spirit of the Indigenous peoples of Canada. And the Canadian people have nothing to fear from that.[21]

CHAPTER SIX

The Struggle for Healing Among Mushuau Innu of Labrador

I once had the pleasure of caribou hunting with Penote Michel and Tanien Ashini in northern Labrador. The expedition involved a five-hour Skidoo trip, pulling a Komatik (a sled to carry caribou). I had never personally piloted a Skidoo and it was – to say the least – challenging to keep up with the two Innu leaders. My Skidoo belonged to Larry Innes, who at that time lived in Labrador as the Innu Nation environmental advisor. At one point, racing around a corner, I flew off the Skidoo and landed in a deep drift, while the machine kept plowing through the snow and glanced off a tree. (I think Larry, who now heads up OKT's office in Yellowknife, has forgiven me the slight damage to his Skidoo.) After a good laugh and some good-hearted kidding from Penote and Tanien, we continued on and arrived at their chosen campsite. I admired the skill Penote and Tanien showed in setting up camp, including cutting small trees for tent poles. It was so easy and natural for them. They issued me playful instructions to tramp down the snow for a tent base, gather spruce boughs for the floor, and fetch wood to feed the quickly

Artwork 6.1: Mary Ann Penashue, *Ueishenu* (Lost Innu soul)

assembled wood stove. They also instructed me in Innu outdoor washroom protocol, which included wading to the selected spot in waist-deep snow.

It was thrilling to be part of the pursuit of hundreds of caribou on the frozen lake, watching them scatter and head for cover on the banks while Penote and Tanien teased each other about their shooting prowess or lack thereof. I then watched the butchering of the felled animals, to be stored in the komatiks for transport back to Sheshatshiu where the meat would be distributed to the Elders. But first, I sampled the unbelievably tasty caribou cooked on the traditional Innu stove by master chefs Penote and Tanien. Food that fresh, from wilderness to table in the bright, clean air, tastes amazing. The memory vividly warms my heart and sometimes brings tears to my eyes, as both of those creative and bold leaders, good men and caring friends, would later die far too young.

Innu have been hunting caribou for millennia, of course, and it felt sacred to be able to experience that hunt. I remember Penote and Tanien reflecting on their people's struggle to stay connected to the land, given so many disruptions and forced relocations. They lamented the historic and ongoing attempts of governments to drive them off, and the heartbreaking costs to Innu families and communities. As I write, the History Channel is broadcasting a new season of its reality series *Alone*, in which ten non-Indigenous outdoor adventurers compete to outlast the others in isolated camps in Labrador, having to hunt and trap their own food. As they slowly starve and lose their mental fortitude in an unfamiliar wilderness, you are reminded of two things. One is that being expert in the bush has to do with your *intimate familiarity* with that landscape and its animals. It's a matrix of knowledge based on prior experience and inter-relationship. The second thing is that you cannot survive long in isolation. Everyone works together.

Recently, I asked Innu Elder Tshaukuesh (Elizabeth) Penashue, a strong, determined, and brilliant Innu matriarch who has become a dear friend, how many descendants she had. She said over eighty. She then asked about me, and I told her I had four children and three grandchildren. "Oh, your poor man!" she teased, with her affectionate chuckle. Large families are one important way in which the Innu continue to foster their communal interdependence with each other and the land. This is key to understanding how thoughtless settler colonial policies implemented by career-building government officials destroyed those harmonious relationships and left the Innu so profoundly vulnerable.

A case in point is the Mushuau Innu, who traditionally lived hundreds of kilometres to the north of where I went hunting with Penote and Tanien. This Innu community has been relocated three times since 1947. The herding around of First Nations people to suit government objectives has happened across Canada and, as I mentioned, was a contributing factor to unravelling the fabric of the Grassy Narrows community. But in the case of the Mushuau, the series of relocations has been particularly destabilizing. Their decades-long effort to reclaim a sense of agency and communal health has been nothing short of remarkable.

In the early 1900s, fur-trapping for profit was still promoted by the Hudson's Bay Company, who had a depot on the coast at Davis Inlet. The Mushuau Innu relied on the caribou hunt, tracking their annual migration patterns for their food and for spiritual and cultural practices. But non-Indigenous fur traders wanted to trap marten, whose fur was valuable in Europe, so they attempted to restrict Innu access to prime hunting areas, which interfered with caribou hunting. In the first half of the twentieth century, missionaries and traders essentially made the administrative decisions about the Innu, rather than government officials, who were far away and didn't much care. The restricted access to caribou – as traders set between 300 and 600 traps each year for themselves – led to periods of starvation, which contributed to disease, including growing incidences of TB, which caused the Innu to grow increasingly dependent upon the missionaries and traders. It became a vicious circle.

In those years, the Mushuau summered in Voisey's Bay near the site of the present nickel mine, as well as at Davis Inlet farther north along the coast, socializing, trading, and repairing equipment. Then they would typically move back to the interior. But as they lost food sources, they spent more of their time on the coast; government supplies were offered to them exclusively through the Hudson's Bay depot at Davis Inlet. Since the missionizing Roman Catholic priests also travelled by sea to Davis Inlet, they eventually, in desperation, settled there. In 1942, NL took over the Hudson's Bay depot after the company pulled out due to dwindling profits, but then NL decided to close it altogether in 1947 soon after it deemed it necessary for the Mushuau to become economically productive in a Western sense. They moved the Mushuau Innu people by ship far to the north, to a settlement in Inuit territory called Nutak where, as the government saw it, there was a more convenient depot and harbour. The director of the Division of Northern Labrador Affairs, Walter Rockwood, wrote:

> But one fact seems clear, civilization is on the Northward march, and for the Eskimo and Indian there is no escape. The last bridges of isolation were destroyed with the coming of the airplane and the radio. The only course that now is open, for there can be no turning back, is to fit him as soon as he may be able to take his full place as a citizen in our society.[1]

After the arrival in Nutak, the Mushuau were provided with tents, clothing, and food. Some of them lived initially in storage shacks. But this was a barren landscape. They were completely cut off from the land they knew and their only way of being in the world. They couldn't find saplings suitable for their tent poles, for example. Their sense of orientation and mastery vanished.

They had never hunted seals. They were so unhappy, so puzzled and angry that at the end of the second winter, they walked all the way back south to Davis Inlet. Despite the Mushuau literally voting with their feet, NL continued to discuss relocating them to force their integration into the settler economy. (In part this was related to a larger provincial vision of moving outpost Newfoundlanders of all backgrounds to more centralized, economically productive locations.) Officials pondered herding the Innu to North West River, a non-Indigenous community across a narrow waterway from the home of the Sheshatshiu Innu. (North West River was the first fur-trading post in Labrador, established by French trappers in 1743.)

The Roman Catholic priest in North West River felt the Mushuau should be moved to his parish, to be under his influence, while the priest in Davis Inlet, Father Frank Peters, supported relocation to a new site just twenty miles from Old Davis Inlet, which was *his* sphere of influence. Father Peters had become, by all reports, a very powerful figure in this area. The Mushuau elected not to go to North West River, a decision reached by consensus rather than formal vote but undoubtedly influenced by Peters, who reportedly assured them that he would arrange for warm, snug houses.

What happened next was a classic case of colonialism in action with disastrous results. Father Peters decided, in conference with government officials, that the Innu should move to a place that was later named Davis Inlet on Iluikoyak Island, because it was a good place to build a wharf. Many Innu told me that the priest often made decisions for them, including appointing members to the community council and nominating the first-ever Innu "Chief." It was clear by now – in the mid-1960s – that governments owed a fiduciary obligation to the Innu. Yet, incredibly, that obligation apparently didn't include assessing whether

Peters's chosen island location had an adequate water supply. Wells were dug for the Catholic mission house, the school, the teachers, and the homes of non-Indigenous people. That was it. The poorly insulated houses built for the Innu were of squalid quality. Up to this time, they had always lived comfortably in tents, including caribou hide tents, so they could easily move around following the herds or other game. Now, they were allotted permanent structures that were cold, leaky, and prone to mould. They had bathrooms with toilets and sinks – but no running water. So, what was the point of this "White Man's upgrade?" I went to Davis Inlet many times and trekked over to the community pump, imagining how troublesome it would be to do this day in and day out, in all kinds of weather. In the depths of winter, people couldn't bathe properly, and washing their dishes and tables was a tiresome chore. It was the ultimate empty promise, coaxing a people who were well-used to keeping themselves warm, dry, and clean in their own way to accept such humiliating conditions in their own homeland.

Critically, the move to the island also cut off the Mushuau from their caribou hunting grounds for significant periods of the year. Given that a key hunt was tied to the annual migration of the animals, when sometimes hundreds would be harvested for food, this was calamitous. They couldn't provide for their families and kin as they had always done. They were reminded every day that white people knew better and apparently deserved indoor plumbing when they did not. The government policy to turn them into civilized citizens on a forward march, integrated seamlessly into a Canadian economy, tore away at everything they knew about living on the land. Many Mushuau Innu today still point to this move to Iluikoyak Island as a major contributing factor to widespread addictions amidst personal and community collapse.

It may not have been on the national radar, but a 1992 internal memo in Health and Welfare Canada leaked to the Innu Nation stated that:

> The situation remains critical in Davis Inlet. The lack of health and social services, poor living conditions and jurisdictional confusion has resulted in the existing crisis ... There are other conditions that have been described graphically in various press reports about Davis Inlet. A chronic level of alcoholism, gas sniffing, domestic violence, and other social dysfunctional living conditions that most Canadians would find totally unacceptable. Minimal numbers graduated from secondary school and even fewer from post-secondary institutions, and excessively high rates of attempted and actual suicide.[2]

Then, in 1992, the lack of water flow for a functioning fire department contributed to the deaths of six children trapped in a flaming house. It was this tragedy that prompted the community consultations published as *Gathering Voices*. "That day woke us up," Chief Katie Rich later wrote, "made us think about our children and what needs to be done. Our children don't have to live like this. They have the same hopes and dreams as any other child."[3]

At around this time, Innu leadership called on the Canadian Human Rights Commission (CHRC) to investigate several transgressions against them. These included the abdication by Canada of its responsibilities when NL joined Canada. The Innu were entitled to compensation, they argued, after five decades of severe underfunding at a time when their means of self-sufficiency had been destroyed. University of Ottawa law professor Donald McRae noted in his 1993 report to the CHRC, "This inaction by the government of Canada constitutes a failure by a fiduciary to act in the best interest of the individuals to whom it has an obligation. It is a failure to live up to the standards that most Canadians would expect of their government, and it is a failure to meet the standards required by the international community of states in respect of the protection of basic human rights."

"The full magnitude," McRae noted,

> of what has been lost to the Innu cannot be restored by the payment of compensation. They cannot be 'compensated' for the social and cultural loss they have suffered as a people ... A real remedy in the present circumstances would address the actual problems faced today, one that ensures that they are able to be in the economic, social and spiritual situation they would have been in if governmental responsibilities had been properly exercised and appropriate human rights standards met.

A failure to provide the Innu with adequate living conditions at (the New) Davis Inlet also led, almost inevitably, to the criminalization of the community. There were domestic disputes, alcohol-related infractions, petty thefts. The RCMP – whose officers didn't speak their language – would lay charges, which were then adjudicated by provincial judges alighting on the island from time to time. The Innu were typically encouraged to plead guilty, often to charges they didn't understand. They saw Canadian law as completely out of touch with their traditional way of addressing conflicts. At one point, a *Globe & Mail* journalist got hold of a trial transcript from Davis Inlet and noted that the conditions were "chaotic." The judge complained throughout and kept threatening to move the whole court elsewhere.[4] The quality of legal defence was terrible. The interpreter didn't speak the local dialect, and it appeared that, willy-nilly, Judge

Hyslop sentenced members of this disoriented community to serve time in far-off penal institutions. If it was justice the Innu were getting, it was rough. Even though they sent some of their young people to train as Aboriginal police – known as peacekeepers – at the First Nations Tribal Police Institute in BC, for a time they worked with the RCMP but were treated as inferior flunkies. Finally, in December 1993, after the triggering effect of the fatal house fire, Chief Katie Rich banned the court from Davis Inlet. "We were saying that the whole justice system does not work for the Innu," Chief Rich said, "and does not meet our needs to heal."[5]

The provincial minister of justice, Ed Roberts, and Chief Judge Donald Luther flew into the community to discuss more acceptable forms of justice. After their meeting, the weather turned, so there were no flights for five days and Minister Roberts was not happy. The Innu jokingly told him they would not clear the skies until he agreed to everything they wanted. In the end, they did win some concessions from him. This is but one example of the good humour they maintained despite all the subjugation they continued to encounter. The community began working on an alternative justice diversion project. While the Innu may share several values expressed in Canada's criminal code, they prioritize those values differently. Certainly, they do not share the emphasis on judgment, punishment, and taking "the offender" away from the community, unless there is no other effective way of dealing with the situation. Wherever possible, the Innu believe that a transgressing group member should stay *in* the community so that he or she can acknowledge and change their behaviour. Punishment without healing moves a person further out of balance, they say, and often leads to more unacceptable behaviour. The sentence circle technique, in which members of the community are asked to speak on how to address an issue, is integral to Indigenous justice and more appropriate than a non-Indigenous judge intoning from on high. Innu policing protocols reflect the principles of justice diversion. A Council of Elders would be set up to divert the disputes away from the Western system.

The Mushuau submitted a proposal for community policing to the regional RCMP commander, but discussions broke down when the RCMP insisted on having discretion to decide whether they would enforce bylaws passed by the Mushuau Chief and council. The issue was not whether the Mounties would have the normal discretion of laying or not laying charges for an infraction under the law, but that the RCMP wanted the discretion to decide whether an Innu law *was* a law they would enforce. For example, if the Innu government banned alcohol and drugs from the community, the RCMP wanted the right to decide if they would enforce that law even though they had no discretion and were legislatively obliged to enforce laws passed by NL. Such unvarnished colonialism deeply impacted daily life for the Mushuau.

Within months of Chief Rich banning the court from Davis Inlet, Justice Minister Roberts lost patience and decided to send the court back. He assigned up to 100 RCMP officers to rotate to protect the judge and other court officials that he was sending back into the community. But the Innu blocked the local airstrip with debris. Roberts retaliated by announcing that NL was suspending modern Treaty negotiations, discussions about turning over more responsibility for health and social services to the community, and negotiations about relocation of the Davis Inlet to a more suitable location on the mainland. To resolve this stand-off, Innu representatives and provincial officials met in St. John's. Because Chief Rich had been charged with contempt of court, Roberts objected to her being there.

Innu Nation president Peter Penashue protested, and Roberts and his entourage of bureaucrats left the meeting. This counterproductive posturing from the province went on for years. I worked with the Mushuau Chief and council to draft community policing objectives as part of a community policing agreement in which Chief and council bylaws would be enforced and the RCMP would recognize Innu peacekeepers as equals. But to date the RCMP refuses to do so, and the government of NL refuses to order them to do so even though they had the authority to do so. The issue of an Innu police force is an outstanding one at the modern Treaty negotiating table. However, an independent study of policing issues in the Innu communities is underway and the Innu hope Canada and NL will agree to a Treaty provision that there will be an Innu police force. Canada and NL will agree to a Treaty provision to discuss the matter but not to a provision that says a policing agreement will be negotiated.

Meanwhile, the Innu continued to pressure the federal government. In 1993, Davis Inlet community leader Simeon Tshakapesh used a home video camera to film some Innu children staggering about, dazed and unhinged, after sniffing gasoline, expressing their desire to kill themselves. He sent the tape to international media. It proved such a powerful and haunting depiction of Innu despair that it renewed public outrage at how cruel NL and Canada were being. After intense negotiations, the federal minister of Indian affairs agreed to a statement of political commitments that had been proposed by the Innu to address several key issues. It was a privilege to work with the Innu leaders to negotiate these commitments, which were a very important milestone brought about by both international pressure and the creativity and persistence of the Innu. In this statement, the minister recognized that Canadians were deeply concerned with conditions affecting the Mushuau Innu and affirmed that Canada would continue to take emergency measures to improve conditions. It also said that Canada would resume the modern Treaty negotiations and would fund the relocation of the Mushuau Innu to a place the community had selected, which was on the mainland at Little Sango Pond, which they named Natuashish.

The Innu were heartened by Canada's response, but everyone knew that a relocation from Davis Inlet would only succeed if the social infrastructure was rebuilt as well; they were beyond the point of settling for better and warmer houses with indoor plumbing. This was a community that had been shattered. Indeed, the 2002 follow-up report of the Canadian Human Rights Commission by Don McRae and Constance Backhouse would note that "from the outset it was apparent that social, cultural and economic reconstruction were as critical to the relocation as the physical relocation of the Mushuau Innu."[6] On 15 June 2001, the federal cabinet approved the Labrador Innu Comprehensive Healing Strategy. It sounded promising as a headline but, as usual, intergovernmental progress was glacial. The Innu had been asking for an alcohol detox centre, for instance, but nothing got off the ground; they had requested a safe house for victims of domestic violence, but that never got green-lit. Without key pieces of infrastructure for healing, efforts would be useless. In 2011, the Innu proposed that they lead the strategy themselves. Issues identified in the healing strategy they adopted underscored with hard facts the degree of their suffering. The Sheshatshiu suicide rate was 75.7 per 100,000 people, with the Natuashish rate more than double that. Those are stunning figures. The Canada-wide rate at that time was eleven suicides per 100,000 citizens. As for violent crime, the rate in 2010 was 23.39 charges laid per 100 people in Natuashish compared to the general Canadian population rate of 1.28 charges. Innu drug, alcohol, and solvent use was four to six times greater than in the general Canadian population. Infant mortality rates for First Nations generally were 6.4 per 1,000 live births – while the average rate among the Mushuau Innu was three times higher than that. Life expectancy had fallen to forty-eight years. By contrast, in the year that the community was first moved to Iluikoyak Island, they had the lowest annual mortality rates in Labrador, according to Norwegian scholar Elisabeth Thorring Dalsbo.[7]

In 2014, the Innu finalized their Innu Healing Strategy, which set out fourteen priority areas. Each has a specific vision for change which fits into the overall objective. Implementation is a practical exercise overseen by an Innu Round Table Secretariat (IRT). There are five-year planning goals. The IRT is staffed by a highly qualified group of Innu workers with an intimate understanding of the community. Their plans arise from two sources: *Gathering Voices: Finding the Strength to Help Our Children*, and a second inquiry supported by RCAP and published as *Gathering Voices: Discovering Our Past, Present and Future*. These important community-led initiatives, both ably facilitated by Camille Fouillard, were designed to assist the Innu in deciding what they wanted for their future and the future of generations to come.

The view of the Innu was that the root cause of their social problems was their progressive and near total disempowerment by white strangers and agencies, most notably the Roman Catholic Church and the two levels of government. That disempowerment began in the early nineteenth century but accelerated after the Innu were forced to the Labrador coast by the absence of caribou in the interior in about 1916, and again with the decline of fur prices in the late 1940s. Above all, for the Mushua Innu, it was their relocation to Davis Inlet in 1967. The Innu Healing

Strategy was designed to restore the agency that had been taken from them. The plans included a comprehensive list of measures required for the Innu to take control of health, social services, education, training, policing, and enhancing the traditional economy. The planning itself energized them as they felt they had taken a crucial step in regaining self-determination. Year over year, the Innu feel stronger, more confident, as the future begins to look brighter.

In many respects, the work of the Round Table is devolution work, which means it focuses on devolving administrative power to Innu authorities, power which Canada continues to exercise under s.91.24 of the Constitution, with NL wielding provincial powers as both governments resist recognizing the Innu inherent right to self-government under s.35.

For example, the administration of education has been "devolved" from the province to an Innu school board. This is extremely important in terms of capacity and policy development and hopefully will be the base for a transition to full Innu governance once the modern Treaty is in place. With respect to education, RCAP recommended Indigenous-controlled education systems, with Indigenous language assigned a priority. The Innu now have their own education authority, although for years NL insisted on dictating certification of teachers and approving the curriculum. Their standard for this, of course, was what non-Indigenous students learn. The Innu kept reminding them that this is a very colonial approach; many of the teachers assigned to Innu schools know nothing about Innu history and culture and do not speak Innu-aimun, while children entering school often *only* speak Innu-aimun. The Innu want a curriculum that focuses on their history and their relationship with colonial governments and that incorporates instruction on the land so that Innu children can learn from Elders. In July 2022, Innu leaders and their negotiating team met with Premier Andrew Furey to address the outstanding provincial Treaty issues. It was finally agreed that the laws passed by the Innu regarding both the school curriculum and teacher certification would be "reasonably comparable to that of Newfoundland." Some details still need to be worked out, but agreement on the words "reasonably comparable" – thankfully – removes decades of provincial opposition.[8]

As I mentioned, in 2002, professors Donald McRae and Constance Backhouse prepared a follow-up report for the Canadian Human Rights Commission. This one considered the RCAP recommendations and Canada's international human rights commitments and obligations. While Ottawa began to provide some direct funding to the Innu, it had not provided them with access to all federal programs available to on-reserve people. Negotiations around self-government, undertaken after the 1993 report, had been suspended. Most of the RCAP recommendations on housing, education, culture, language, and health had not been implemented in Labrador. The foot-dragging had continued apace. With Innu increasingly taking control, progress is being made on some immediate issues. At the request of the Innu Round Table, Canada and NL launched an inquiry into the treatment of Innu children in provincial care. That inquiry – announced in 2017 – got underway in the spring of 2022, after some wrangling over terms of reference and financing and was still underway in October 2025. Among other matters, it will focus on understanding the systemic causes of mistreatment of Innu foster care children, and its cultural and community impacts. It will also probe several individual cases of children and youth caught up in the system who lost their lives. Former Innu Nation Grand Chief Anastasia Qupee, retired provincial court judge James Igloliorte, and retired Memorial University social work professor Mike Devine are the three commissioners.[9]

The Innu road towards healing and self-determination is long and winding, with many potholes and washouts along the way. But they continue to walk to their longed-for destination of reconciliation *with* Canada rather than *to* Canada. Completing the negotiation of a just and equitable modern Treaty is critical for a bright future for the Innu and that will be discussed in the next chapter.

CHAPTER SEVEN

The Road Home: The Innu of Labrador and Modern Treaty Negotiations

In 1990, Tanien Ashini, then thirty-one years old, took part in a symposium on Aboriginal self-determination sponsored by the Assembly of First Nations. He explained who his people were and observed that:

> Sometimes politicians in Britain or Ottawa or St. John's, Newfoundland sit down and draw lines on maps and say that we're a part of Canada. Or that past laws say that we're subject to Canadian or Newfoundland jurisdiction. The truth remains that there is no moral or legal basis for these claims. It is only the Innu people, by agreeing with the government of Canada, that can give Canada or Newfoundland any jurisdiction or shared jurisdiction over our lives.[1]

For Ashini, the prospect of extinguished rights, to simply be wiped out by Canadian officials in modern Treaties for their own benefit and purposes, was a non-starter. "At the heart of our struggle is that we are a nation of people," he said. "We've never

Artwork 7.1: Mary Ann Penashue, *Tshiatutet* (On her journey)

given up our right to be a nation by signing any Treaty or agreement and we will insist that our right to be a nation is recognized in any agreement that we enter."²

Why, he asked his listeners, do we all find ourselves on small, assigned patches of land with shoddy buildings and often undrinkable water? "Reservations" he continued, "were designed as temporary places where First Nations people would be 'stored' until they realized that living on the land was no longer possible." What Ottawa is prepared to accept as Indigenous self-government, from the Innu perspective, is nothing less than a final step to assimilation. "Are there any self-respecting people anywhere who would agree to self-government without a land and resource base and adequate jurisdictional powers?" he asked, arching his brow. "I think not."[3] Later that year, Elijah Harper incorporated these comments into his address to the European parliament.

The Innu, like other First Nations across Canada, understand that their inherent right to govern themselves was entrenched in s.35 of Canada's Constitution in 1982. A good part of regaining their sense of dignity and agency involves them making their own decisions about where and how to live rather than being dictated to by priests, traders, and administrators. Referring to the notion of the inherent right to govern, Innu community leader Apetet (Ben) Andrew told RCAP commissioners in the early 1990s that white people

> seem to be afraid of it. Sure, they should be afraid of it because I think it means what it says, inherent. It's not something that can be passed on from the Europeans when it was there already. And I think that *"inherent,"* to me, means we should be able to do what we want on our lands. Why should I define to Joe Clark what I want to do on those lands, when they're mine? Why talk about claims policy when we have to do all that research to prove that we occupied that land for thousands of years? Why doesn't Canada do that? Why doesn't Quebec do that? Why doesn't Ontario do that? It's not negotiations, it's all dictations by the Federal government and the province. It's not negotiating.[4]

In 1976, the Innu formed the Naskapi Montagnais Innu Association (NMIA) to improve their situation and protect their land. The late Bart Jack was formidable at that time in fighting for Innu rights and achieving some increase in funding through agreements in which Canada contributed to services that NL had been providing. But another important objective for the NMIA was to prepare a land use and occupancy study, as required by Canada's comprehensive claims policy established that same year. Anthropologists Adrian Tanner and Peter Armitage worked on that with the Elders. Canada conditionally accepted the study in 1978 and formally accepted the claim in 1990. However, Ottawa had a policy of only negotiating six modern Treaties at any one time, which is why Minister John Crosbie told the press during the low-level flying crisis that the Innu would "have to wait their turn." Innu pressure forced Canada to abandon that position, which opened up the modern Treaty process to them without further delay, as well as to others who wanted on the list. Negotiations for a Framework Agreement, the first stage of setting an agenda, began in 1991.

One of the key reasons the negotiations have gone on for decades is that Innu are *not* willing to simply accept what the government-mandated scripts – read like cue cards by bureaucrat-negotiators – say about an issue. The first meeting with the Innu negotiating team took place in a cramped and smoky room in Sheshatshiu. I have been at that table with the Innu for over thirty years with mostly three or four days of table negotiations a month and numerous side table meetings in between. I still remember how gobsmacked the negotiators from St. John's and Ottawa were at that first gathering. They explained their "land claims" negotiations policies, which included that Innu would give up their Aboriginal rights and title in exchange for the benefits that would be set out, which would in effect be a contract and not a government-to-government living Treaty. The Innu responded by saying, in essence, "we also have a negotiating policy, and that is that we are not claiming any land or resources from you, since the land and resources belong to us. It is *you* who are claiming our land and resources."

Oddly enough, at the beginning of this process, the lead negotiators for Canada and NL were both former priests: Denis Chatien for Ottawa and Ray Hawco for the province. Jim Roche, then the Catholic priest in Sheshatshiu, often joined the Innu at their request. Particularly in winter, with the windows closed and almost everyone sucking on cigarettes, we sometimes had to wave our hands to clear the air and see who was on the other side of the table. I have now been with the Innu at the table for decades, and sometimes it's with a chuckle that I remember these early sessions.

One thing remains pretty consistent in the meetings: the government negotiators come to the table with positions on issues they have no personal mandate to alter. All they can do is declare them. Those positions are rooted in Canada's comprehensive claims policy of 1973, which was designed to get the surrender of any existing Aboriginal rights and title. The dissenting judgments in the Supreme Court of Canada decision in the *Calder* case said there may well be unextinguished Aboriginal rights and title in areas of Canada (like Labrador) that did not have historic Treaties. Canada's policy was therefore *to extinguish* rather than to *recognize and implement* those rights. Unfortunately, that position hasn't budged in nearly fifty years, despite the patriation of the Constitution in 1982, the Penner Report, RCAP, TRC, and MMI-WGI. This focus on surrender of rights turns Treaty negotiations into contract negotiations aiming to nail everything down in excruciating legal detail. Canada's system moves at a snail's pace, with layers of bureaucrats having a say in any script changes proposed by the Innu. NL can move faster – as they demonstrated in the Tshash Petapen negotiations – when they want something (in that case, to build another hydro dam on the Churchill River).

The Innu Treaty negotiating team includes representatives from Sheshatshiu (currently Sylvester Antuan, Gregory Nuna, and Peter Penashue) and three from Natuashish (currently George Rich, Damien Benuen, and Thomas Poker.) Longtime Innu leaders Prote Poker and Mark Nui also attend the Treaty negotiation sessions on behalf of Innu Grand Chief Simon Pokue. George Rich and Peter Penashue, both long-term stalwart Innu leaders, have been at the table for almost all of this time. I have been there now for thirty-four years, my colleague Nancy Kleer for over twenty, and Larry Innes for almost that long. Over that period, the federal and provincial negotiating teams have changed several times, leading to substantial Innu frustration about having "to once again educate new people."

There is, in my experience, a profound disconnect between First Nation communities trying to get things done and remote bureaucracies that don't truly understand and in some cases don't really care about what's at stake.

In October 2000, Canada suspended the modern Treaty negotiations with the Innu of Labrador, citing too many competing priorities, namely health initiatives and the relocation of the community. The Innu, by contrast, felt that a modern Treaty was the *key* to addressing their entire government-to-government relationship. The Innu position was consistent with the RCAP recommendations. Where communal health was concerned, for example, the RCAP pointed out that regaining control over holistic delivery systems and culturally appropriate ways of healing were critical for Indigenous empowerment. RCAP noted that a crucial role for self-government lay in providing:

> the affirmation and conservation of aboriginal cultures and identities as fundamental characteristics of Canadian society ... It should be understood that self-government does not mean bringing

aboriginal nations into line with predetermined Canadian norms of how people should govern themselves. It is the re-instatement of a nation-to-nation relationship. It is the entrenchment of the Aboriginal right of doing things differently within the boundaries of a flexible Canadian Charter of Rights and Freedoms and international human right standards.[5]

Ironically, one of the reasons that Canada wanted to postpone self-governance negotiations was that it was too busy creating Innu *reservations* in Sheshatshiu and Natuashish. There is almost a Kafkaesque logic at work in some of these "dances around the table" as I've observed them. In the mid-1970s, by now thrust frighteningly into poverty, Innu community members had asked the federal government to register them under the Indian Act. If that was the only way they could get basic services, then so be it. NL's premier opposed it at the time, warning that they would then lose provincial education and housing benefits, which would amount, in his view, to a backwards step. Nevertheless, this discussion about registration continued into the 1980s, by which time the Innu were very cognizant of the fact that, across Canada, most Indigenous nations were trying to get *out* from under the suffocating Indian Act. As a step in that direction, Donald McRae argued that

> [t]o require the Innu to be so registered would be to elevate form over substance. It would be nothing more than a symbolic act of subordination – to legislation that the Canadian Human Rights Commission itself has described as 'outdated and paternalistic.' There is no reason why the federal government could not act directly without imposing the process of registration under the Indian Act on the Innu.[6]

The deputy minister of Canada's Department of Indian and Northern Affairs (DIAND) wrote to the Innu Nation in December 1997: "With self-government currently under negotiation, it appears that registration ... is an unnecessary step to take and then undo under a self-government regime."[7] So, Innu leaders sought instead to obtain equivalency of status. They would receive all the benefits to which status Indians on reserve were entitled, while land claims and self-government were negotiated and, accordingly, Canada would have fulfilled its constitutional responsibilities. That position was acknowledged in an Agreement in Principle signed by Peter Penashue, president of the Innu Nation, the Chiefs of Sheshatshiu and Mushuau, the premier of NL, Brian Tobin, and the federal minister of Indian affairs and northern development, Robert Nault. The province was to facilitate the transfer of land for the settlement of Innu land claims. Canada and the province were to work to transfer control over education programs. There was to be an agreement on Aboriginal policing. Legal arrangements for Innu governments were to be put in place, and all committed to the "expeditious conclusion" of the process.

It turned out, however, that Canada was *not* prepared to grant Innu all the benefits to which status Indians on reserve were entitled. One sticking point was tax-exempt status. The Innu argued that since they were entitled to be registered, equivalency meant they could also receive tax exemption. This had implications not only for individuals, but also for the expenditures made by the Innu Nation and the First Nations of Sheshatshiu and Davis Inlet. There were other complicating factors arising out of the fact that the Innu were not living on reserves. Sheshatshiu and Davis Inlet were simply incorporated entities under provincial laws. This means that they were limited in their ability to enact bylaws and to regulate matters within their communities, such as access to alcohol. Some felt that it might be possible to create new mechanisms and legal vehicles outside of the Indian Act to establish equivalencies. Ottawa deemed this too cumbersome. In the end, Innu leaders concluded that registration under the Indian Act was the only way they could achieve actual equivalency, so in March 1999, they held a referendum in Sheshatshiu and Davis Inlet and garnered their people's go-ahead, albeit as a reluctant last resort. Peter Penashue said, "Either we walked away from the table because we didn't get the full loaf as we had sought, or we accepted the quarter loaf that was being offered to us. We're not jumping up and down, but we recognize it's a step. And I think it is a significant step."

Still, officials within DIAND resisted. So, Innu leaders again took things into their own hands – because this wasn't a matter of debating hypothetical what-ifs – their communities were in *crisis*. In September of 2000, they travelled to Ottawa to camp on Parliament Hill. It was a remarkable event. I joined them on the march and afterward, when they pitched their tents on the lawn in front of Parliament, built their fires, and shut down the government. I vividly recall buses loaded with tourists driving up and looking bewildered that they couldn't go into the building. The Innu stood on the steps and announced their mistreatment. Federal bureaucrats, undercover police, and clothed RCMP officers moved in and about the encampment. We had many discussions with these officials and police and security folks about why the Innu were protesting. It was a very peaceful occupation without threats of violence or eviction on either side. It certainly got the attention of the minister of Indian affairs, Robert Nault. After five days of protest, he offered to discuss Innu registration and reserve creation with his cabinet colleagues before the end of the year.

The need for cabinet approval grew urgent after yet more disturbing public revelations of gas sniffing by Innu children in November 2000.[8] International attention intensified, prompting the prime minister and Health Canada to order a comprehensive background report, which finally resulted in cabinet directing registration and reserve creation in June 2001 – about two years after the Innu had reluctantly voted in favour. Many bureaucrats sincerely thought it was a backwards step to have an Indigenous group register under the Indian Act when so many wanted out. Nevertheless, the die had been cast when Ottawa refused to provide genuine status equivalence. Reserve creation is a long and detailed process, because lands need to be surveyed, and both private and provincial interests looked after. "It should have been just so simple," Peter Penashue later told the Canadian Human Rights Commission. "Eight years (since the 1993 CHRC report) they are starting to do what should have been done in 1949."[9]

Some of the outstanding issues at the Treaty negotiating table are encompassed in a third CHRC report issued in 2021, after the Innu began keeping a "report card" on Canada's foot-dragging.[10] The report identified the following failures or non-responses from Ottawa:

- Canada's failure to meet its obligations to the Innu under the United Nations Convention on the Rights of the Child.
- Canada's failure to meet its human rights and "Honour of the Crown" obligations in its Treaty negotiations – including by insisting that the Treaty be a contract that extinguishes Aboriginal rights and title in return for specified benefits, rather than a "living tree" Treaty that implements those rights and harmonizes them with the rights of Canada and NL over time.
- Canada's insistence that the Innu right to pass laws be subject to federal and provincial approval of those laws.

- Canada's insistence that, even after the Treaty is signed, Canada can unilaterally make changes to it without Innu consent.
- Canada's demand to have the power to claw back Innu own source revenue from IBAs so as to reduce the level of federal funding for programs and services, perpetuating the socio-economic gap between Innu and other Canadians.

Recommendations on these matters had been made in the 1993 and 2002 CHRC reports but were ignored by Canada. The third CHRC report – by Celeste McKay Consulting Inc. and Professor Donald McRae (the third report with McRae's participation) – was released in St. John's on 9 August 2021. I was there to hear the reflections of Marie-Claude Landry, chief commissioner of the CHRC, Innu Grand Chief Etienne Rich, Innu Deputy Grand Chief Mary Ann Nui, Sheshatshiu First Nation Chief Eugene Hart, and Mushuau First Nation Chief John Nui.

"I am excited with the recommendations in this new report that Canada should make a commitment to conclude a Modern Treaty with the Innu in three years and should abandon its positions on key issues such as own source revenue, s.87 taxation benefits, extinguishment and contingent self-government rights," said Grand Chief Rich. "The Innu want to sign a good Treaty so that we can govern ourselves and control our own land and resources with adequate funding to deliver the same level of programs and services to Innu that other Canadians take for granted."

"Canada and Newfoundland and Labrador, I hope you are listening," said Sheshatshiu Innu First Nation Chief Eugene Hart. "Other Canadians do not face these lingering symptoms of colonialism. The Innu have waited a long time for justice, and many Elders have died sadly wondering why Innu people have not been treated fairly. To honour their memory and with hope for the well-being of Innu today and Innu of future generations, I hope that Canada will move quickly and sincerely to implement the recommendations of this CHRC Report."

"In looking at the good recommendations, I was thinking about the well over 3,000 people whose future depends [on them]," said Deputy Grand Chief Nui. "The report says, 'what is needed is new gestures by the federal government to be taken at the highest level' ... On behalf of the Innu of Labrador I call on Prime Minister Trudeau to immediately order the closure of these gaps."

"This is the third CHRC Report," Mushuau Chief John Nui reminded those present. "I think it should be the last one."

Will it be? The Innu table negotiators are pressing Canada to accept the CHRC recommendations and to conclude the Treaty expeditiously. Ottawa must abandon its stubborn positions on key issues, one being that, even if it agrees to the terms and conditions for the contingent exercise of Innu law-making powers, the Treaty must stipulate that funding for the implementation of those laws, as well as for running the Innu government, be a responsibility shared between the Innu, Canada, and NL. This is reprehensible because a just Treaty would have Canada provide the required funding in return for all the land and resources that the Innu yield up. Besides, St. John's itself refuses to accept this approach; they consider that their Treaty contributions are fully met in the land and resource provisions of the Treaty.

Another intransigent federal stance is that any fiscal agreement to fund the Innu government be in a separate agreement that is not Treaty protected, subject to periodic renegotiation. This leaves the Innu and other First Nation governments with serious fiscal uncertainty. The only cash they have otherwise is own source revenue from IBAs.

Substantive equality in funding Innu programs and services is fundamental. Substantive equality is a basic tenet of human rights law and policy in that it focuses on equitable outcomes. Canada's current approach to the fiscal provisions in the Treaty is based on a formula approach that does not adequately relate to the actual responsibilities of the Innu set out in the Treaty, nor to the substantial deficit in Innu program and service infrastructure which started in 1949. In short, the CHRC recommendations for the positions that Canada must take if it is to meet its human rights obligations in its negotiations with the Innu are critical if the Treaty is to bring honour to the Crown, and if the Innu people, who understand a great deal about human rights because of their ongoing resistance to colonialism, are willing to ratify the Treaty. The Innu trust that Canada will adopt these CHRC recommendations at the highest level so the Treaty can finally be put in place and become a beacon for reconciliation with Indigenous people.

Since Confederation, Canada and the provinces have managed to harmonize the brief listing of their constitutional jurisdictions without exhaustive legal contracts, and it is certainly possible to extend that harmonization to Indigenous governments. What is absent is the political will. Recently, Canada, BC, and the First Nations of BC who are negotiating modern Treaties have agreed to try a new approach, which focuses a bit more on recognition of rights and the possibility of updating Treaty provisions from time to time.[11] The Innu have long pressed for the same living tree Treaty approach.

As it stands, the Innu Treaty is over 500 pages long, with more than thirty chapters covering everything from migratory birds, fisheries, forest resources and plants, water management and rights, national parks, protected areas, Innu heritage, place names, environmental assessments, land use planning, non-Innu access to Labrador Innu lands, Innu jurisdiction for child, youth and family services, and education. Before COVID, negotiating sessions rotated between Ottawa, Sheshatshiu, St. John's, and Natuashish. Currently there are more online sessions than in-person negotiating sessions because of federal budget constraints. There are also a number of side tables to discuss contracting and job opportunities, fiscal arrangements to enable Innu government, an Innu police force, more access to fisheries, and the legal provisions that will provide ongoing certainty about the post-treaty relationship of the parties. In between negotiating sessions and side table meetings, the Innu team holds community consultations, letting people know what's being discussed, and canvassing opinions.

While more and more Canadians understand what's at stake, thanks to the remarkable resilience, creativity, and eloquence of First Nations leaders, the overall infrastructure of politics and justice remains infused with white supremacist and capitalist fixations. Rose Gregoire, a late Innu leader, told the RCAP commissioners at a session in Sheshatshiu back in the early 1990s that she was hesitant to present to them because she feared it wouldn't make any difference. "No doubt when this Royal Commission has finished its mandate, another Royal Commission will be created to explore or find answers to this Commission's findings. It is a never-ending cycle that goes on and on, and still the first issue will never be answered."[12]

Since 2011, the Innu, Ottawa, and St. John's have been engaged in final Treaty negotiations. That is an incredibly long time to turn an already quite detailed AIP, which contained several footnotes setting out issues that had not been resolved, into a final draft. In October 2024, after more than thirty years since negotiations began and thirteen years since the AIP was signed, senior officials from the Innu, Canada, and NL joined the appointed table negotiators and spent seven days in St. John's in an attempt to resolve the twelve major outstanding issues. Success was limited as for some major issues Canada's and NL negotiators did not have the required cabinet mandates to agree to Innu proposals. Seeking new cabinet mandates is a long process, particularly for Canada. In the case of NL, there are several outstanding matters, including will they agree to the living Treaty concept, will they commit to Innu policing, and will they agree that air or land-based military activities on key lands where the Innu have rights require Innu consent? With respect to Canada, a key outstanding issue is Innu reparations for the fifty-year period (1949–99) in which Innu were denied the funding provided to Indian Act First Nations across Canada. In their 2021 Canadian Human Rights Commission Report on the Human Rights of Innu of Labrador, Celeste McKay and Donald McRae recommended that "[t]he federal government should make a new commitment to the conclusion of the Modern Treaty negotiations with the Innu in accordance with its human rights obligations" and that "[s]uch a commitment must ensure that the negotiations will result in remedying the wrong done to the Innu by the failure of the federal government to exercise its constitutional responsibilities to them for a period of 50 years." The Innu refer to this as "the fifty-year gap issue." Regrettably, at the October 2024 extended Treaty negotiation session, Canada announced it would not address the issue in the Treaty as it was not an "aboriginal rights issue." What, the Innu ask, could possibly by more of an Aboriginal rights issue than the denial of their Indian Act rights for fifty years? The Innu are currently discussing if they will seek redress for the fifty-year gap in the courts or by submitting a "special claim" to Canada as the Innu people have said they will not consider ratifying the Treaty without a settlement for the fifty-year gap. Included in the list of issues that remain outstanding is the Innu proposal that Canada agree that it will not claw back any portion of Innu OSR, as such a claw-back would mean that the Innu would not have the resources they require to close the economic gap between the Innu and other Canadians. Late in June 2025 the Innu received the good news that Canada agreed to a Treaty provision that the Innu government and the Innu First Nation governments will never have to pay any tax on OSR money they receive unless Canada revokes all or a portion of the current OSR protection from taxation provided in s 149(1)(c) of Canada's Income Tax Act unless Canada abrogates or derogates that protection for all indigenous governments that have similar self-governance characteristics. The remaining list of outstanding issues list also includes the Innu proposal that air and land military activities on land where the Innu have rights require Innu consent and that the federal government should abandon its position that Canada can infringe Innu Treaty rights with the approval of the courts but without the negotiated consent of the Innu. Canada will not table details of its Treaty compensation and ongoing Innu self-government funding offers to the Innu until 2026, at which time the Innu will need to assess whether they will have sufficient funds to provide adequate programs and services to the Innu people and close the socio-economic gap. So, it will be some time yet before the Innu negotiators decide whether they can initial a final Treaty draft with the negotiators from Canada and NL. The initialed draft will then be presented to the Innu people in an intensive community consultation process before it is submitted for consideration in a ratification vote. If the Innu people vote in favour, Canada and NL's ratification processes will begin. The Innu hope and pray that the long and intensive process of negotiations will end with a modern Treaty that harmonizes their s.35 constitutional rights with those of Canada and NL.

CHAPTER EIGHT

Groundbreaking Blueprints for Reconciliation with Indigenous Peoples and Nations

Most First Nations and other Indigenous Peoples face the same implacable settler colonialist mindset that so deeply challenges the Dene, Grassy Narrows, Teme-Augama, and Innu of Labrador. If Canada had paid heed to the blueprints for decolonization provided – *at its own request* – in the Penner Report of 1983 and the RCAP Report of 1996, a number of obstacles might well have been surmounted by now. We have since received the TRC calls to action and the action plan of the MMIWGI.

The good news is that, due to the inspiring determination of Indigenous peoples, it is beyond argument now that Canada and the provinces and territories must embark on serious decolonization efforts guided by the analysis and recommendation of these groundbreaking reports. All are available online and make informative reading for everyone interested in advancing reconciliation. Here, I want to summarize some of their findings.

1. Penner Report

In 1983, a year after the repatriation of the Constitution, a special House of Commons committee tabled the Penner Report on Indian Self-Government in Canada. Liberal MP Keith Penner chaired the all-party inquiry, which comprised three other Liberal members (Warren Allmand, Raymond Chénier, and Henri Tousignant), two Progressive Conservatives (Frank Oberle and Stan Schellenberger), and one New Democrat (Jim Manly). Remarkably refreshing bipartisanship. The committee appointed Roberta Jamieson as ex-officio member of the committee for the Assembly of First Nations, Bill Wilson as liaison member from the Native Council of Canada, and Sandra Isaac, liaison for the Native Women's Association of Canada.

The mandate was to consider how the Indian Act might be amended to remove provisions that discriminated against women and to report to Parliament on prospects for Indigenous self-government. Committee members were directed to take account of what transpired at the first Constitutional Conference of March 1983. There, the meaning of s.35 of Canada's patriated Constitution got addressed, as I've discussed. Specifically, that it recognized and affirmed Aboriginal and Treaty rights. Since that was to be the first of several conferences in which Canada, the provinces, and Indigenous peoples' representatives considered s.35, there was some hope on the Indigenous side, at least, that the Penner Report and its recommendations would shape the discussions. It was a logical assumption.

The Penner Committee gathered in oral testimony, written submissions, and research projects. Witnesses were invited to address matters relating to the structures of government, the process of achieving self-government, fiscal relationships, the delivery of services, economic development, and Treaty and Aboriginal rights. They released their findings in October 1983 in plenty of time for discussion at subsequent conferences. Astonishingly, this didn't happen. The Penner findings are as relevant today as they were forty years ago. If Canada and the provinces actually embrace reconciliation with the Indigenous peoples of Canada, the Penner Report offers a clear pathway.

"Old, distorted, paternalistic notions about the 'protection' of Indian people and nations must be discarded," the committee declared in its report. "The elements of the new relationship would be as follows:

- Recognition of Indian First Nation governments, with powers and jurisdictions appropriate to a distinct order of government within the Canadian federation.
- Fiscal arrangements suited to self-governing entities.
- A secure economic base, including land, water, and resource rights, which, together with educational and community services appropriate to modern society, would strengthen the culture and economy of the First Nations.
- Equitable settlement of claims to restore capital trust accounts, resources, and lands to the First Nations.
- Legally enforceable agreements between the federal government and First Nations to implement the new arrangements.

The committee then gave very concrete elaborations about how the new relationship could and should unfold. It also recommended the setting up of a Ministry of State for Indian First Nations Relations, with a duty to promote the interests of First Nations rather than dictate to them. Harold Cardinal had recommended this concept fifteen years earlier in his response to Pierre Trudeau's White Paper.

What needed to be clarified in the Canadian mind, the committee felt, were the "Conflicting Views of History" wherein Europeans like Jacques Cartier were depicted as "discoverers" and "explorers" of a virgin territory that did not, in fact, already have "productive, cultured, spiritual, intelligent civilizations comparable to those in Europe at the time of first contact." Canadians were poorly instructed in this history, contributing to prejudicial assumptions about First Nations peoples. "Indian people see Canadians respecting their own traditions and ancient doctrines such as Magna Carta, while at the same time regarding the Royal Proclamation as antiquated and Indian tradition as inappropriate for modern times."

Furthermore, the committee noted, Canadians had to develop a more acute awareness of their own culpability in the distress, disarray, and poverty of Aboriginal peoples in order to overcome stereotypes about "drunks" and "bums" unworthy of popular respect.

> Particularly relevant to this report on Indian government is the view held by non-Indians, that political structures were unknown to Indian people prior to contact with Europeans. Contrary to this view, most First Nations have complex forms of government that go far back in history and have evolved over time. They often operated in accord with spiritual values because religion was not separated from other aspects of First Nation life ... Witnesses gave evidence to the Committee of how these Indian political concepts had directly affected non-Indian institutions. Specifically, they described how the political philosophy of the Iroquois Confederacy had been incorporated into the Constitution of the United States.

The committee learned about particular forms of First Nation government. The Haudenosaunee (People of the Longhouse), for example, had had a formalized constitution that Elders recited to the community every five years. It entailed a democratic system wherein each extended family chose two leaders, a man and a woman, to speak for them at various governance meetings. "Debates on matters of common concern are held according to strict rules," the Penner Report summarized,

> ... that allow consensus to be reached in efficient manner, thus ensuring that the community remain unified. A code of laws, generally expressed in positive admonitions rather than negative prohibitions, governs both official and civil behaviour. Laws are passed by a bicameral legislature made up of senior and junior houses. A council of elders oversees the general course of affairs. Since officials are chosen from each extended family, the system is called "hereditary." While the commonly held belief is that hereditary chiefs hold dictatorial powers, these leaders are actually subject to close control by their people and can be removed from office by them.

This was a perfectly sophisticated and ancient form of self-government that had been outlawed and suppressed by Canada. So, allow the Haudenosaunee to resume their own structures of governance. Reconciliation would invite them to do so as their inherent right.

A second significant section in Penner deals with the potlatch, a social system used by many First Nations that has all the necessary elements to maintain continuity, good government, and a sense of identity while permitting people to conduct their own affairs and determine their own destiny. As late as 1951, Canada prohibited potlach functions, seizing items of ceremony and symbols of governance and, in some cases, jailing those who attended potlatches.

All of this was, in some ways, surprising news to the parliamentarians of the 1980s. "The Committee values the understanding it gained during the course of its hearings," the report noted. "Indian people are faced with an array of bureaucratic and legislative obstacles that limit their ability to act. Foremost among these is the complexity of governmental structures for dealing with issues of concern to" them. Indeed, during the hearings, Indigenous witnesses expressed sharp concern about the committee acting, essentially, as a front for the legislation proposed by John Munro, then minister of Indian affairs and northern development, who was still tinkering with Indian Act amendments. Munro wanted to devolve municipal-style powers to bands under s.91.24 rather than focus on how to harmonize s.35 powers with the constitutional powers of Canada and the provinces. Indigenous governments, they emphasized, should not be viewed as junior governments.

In a full display of bipartisanship, the committee rejected Minister Munro's proposals, which envisaged "Indian Governments as municipal governments [failing] to take account of the origins and rights of Indian First Nations in Canada. A major objection is that permission to opt in would be a favour granted to bands that the Minister of Indian Affairs, in his discretion, deemed to be sufficiently 'advanced.' The paternalist role of the Department would be maintained."

The Penner Committee heard from over 500 witnesses, and the recommendations it made were seminal. They charted a truly reconciling course for Canada that, if followed, would have brought about the kind of decolonization that all justice-minded Canadians could support. It is an incredibly sad reflection on the prime ministers and premiers of the 1980s that they never even seriously discussed, much less adopted, the Penner recommendations – as if that very subject wasn't what they'd gathered to ponder together in three subsequent conferences. It is actually unforgivable. Think about how unique the bipartisan agreement on this fundamental issue was when you observe how fractious our government committees are today. Yet, none of the Penner findings were addressed in the Aboriginal Constitutional Conferences that ensued.

The committee recommended, quite specifically proposed

> that the right of Indian peoples to self-government be explicitly stated and entrenched in the Constitution of Canada. The surest way to achieve permanent and fundamental change in the relationship between Indian peoples and the federal government is by means of a constitutional amendment. Indian First Nation governments would form a distinct order of government in Canada, with their jurisdiction defined.

While I agree that an amendment would be ideal, the failure to achieve that in the Constitutional Conferences and the Charlottetown Accord is no reason to delay harmonization any further. Section 35 is a sufficient basis for a third order of government without need for explicit constitutional definitions for each head of power.

"Many witnesses," the committee noted,

> emphasized that, in seeking to establish Indian First Nation governments they did not wish to create divisions that would weaken Canada. Their objective is to change the relationship of Indian First Nations to other governments not to fragment the country. In their opinion, the exercise of political self-determination is a necessary step toward national unity. Canada would be strengthened, not weakened as a result.

In discussing the process for establishing Indigenous self-government, the Penner Report quoted the Bella Coola British Columbia District First Nations Council:

> The proper way to define and establish relations between our Indian governments and the rest of Canada is not through legislation or constitutional amendments, but by a basic political agreement, a covenant or social contract. A basic compact will respect the principle of the equality of peoples. It can be an integral part of the Canadian Constitution while it serves as a constitution confederating Indian Nations in Canada. But as a social contract, it cannot be changed without the consent of both sides. As a part of the constitutions of both parties, each side will be required by Canadian law, by traditional aboriginal law and by international law to respect its terms.

The Bella Coola District Council had brought to the committee's attention that the Berger Inquiry Report (described in the Mackenzie River Valley chapter) had also discussed Indigenous self-determination. The Dene had called for a social contract between the Indigenous nations and the political institutions of Canada. This approach of a covenant is profoundly evocative. At its core, it means a government-to-government agreement to reconcile assumed Crown sovereignty with the pre-existing sovereignty of Indigenous nations. It means a meeting of hearts and minds around sharing constitutional power. This is precisely the reconciling route that Canada and the provinces should have embraced in the Constitutional Conferences after 1983.

Included in the Penner Report are detailed proposals about the structures and powers that First Nation governments should have. The committee recognized that Indigenous governments would change over time and that a wide variety of governmental styles would emerge that reflect historical and traditional values, location, size, culture, economy, and a host of other factors. By entering into over 600 Impact Benefit Agreements, First Nations have since demonstrated that they are prepared, for example, to consent to developments on their traditional lands. That reality decisively quells the oft-voiced fear that First Nations governance – and, therefore, control of resources – will stop development in its tracks.

Importantly, the committee noted that: "Agreements between Indian First Nations and the federal governments would be political settlements, not airtight legal contracts." It recommended the formation of a special tribunal to mediate jurisdictional disputes between First Nations and other governments. Regarding fiscal arrangements, countless First Nations reiterate today what the Penner Report cited then, that it "should appear self-evident that without Indian people having ultimate control over finances, the exercise of self-government is impossible. Economic development becomes irrelevant, if not impossible. The current system is demeaning, irrelevant and counter-productive in terms of nurturing mutual respect."

Had Canada adopted these key recommendations of the Penner Report, reconciliation with First Nations would be in full bloom. It is not too late to implement them.

2. Royal Commission on Aboriginal Peoples 1996

In 1991, the Mulroney government established RCAP shortly after the Oka Crisis, a prolonged stand-off between Mohawk protestors and Quebec police. RCAP was asked to explore solutions to the challenges affecting relations between Indigenous peoples, the Canadian government, and society as a whole. It was headed by Georges Erasmus and René Dussault, and it ultimately produced a five-volume report.

Unsurprisingly, RCAP's conclusions were very similar to those in the Penner Report from thirteen years earlier. The commission concluded that the centuries-long Crown-Indigenous relationship had been built on false premises and misleading promises that led to removing Indigenous peoples from their homelands, suppressing their governments, and undermining their identities and cultures. Residential schools and a succession of Indian Acts were among the policies arising from those premises. As with Penner, I urge everyone interested in reconciliation to burrow into this often-disturbing treasure trove of history. It's long – 4,000 pages!!! – so you might want to start with the recommendations and then move to the more detailed sections on colonial prejudices, policies, laws, actions, and history that the commission addressed in crafting its recommendations.

RCAP called upon Canada to renounce the concepts of *terra nullius* and the Doctrine of Discovery and to renew a relationship based instead on mutual recognition and respect. Treaties should be revisited with a more "just and liberal interpretation" referencing oral history. "Once spirit and intent of the specific Treaties have been recognized and incorporated into the agreed understanding of the Treaty, all laws, policies, and practices that have a bearing on the terms of the Treaty should be made to reflect that understanding."

An inherent right to self-government is an existing Aboriginal and Treaty right under s.35 of the Constitution, RCAP argued. Such a right provides a "substantial degree of immunity from federal and provincial legislative acts, except where, in the case of federal legislation, it can be justified under a strict constitutional standard."[1] In key areas of jurisdiction, "Aboriginal peoples have the capacity to implement their inherent right of self-government by self-starting initiatives without the need for agreements with feds or provinces."[2] For jurisdictional clarity, Parliament should enact an Aboriginal Nations Recognition and Government Act "to establish the process whereby the government of Canada can recognize the accession of an Aboriginal group to nation status and its assumption of authority as an Aboriginal government to exercise its inherent self-governing jurisdiction."[3] There were many more explicit recommendations on how all of this could be concretely achieved, which you can read online.[4]

As with the Penner Report, very few of these systemic and structural recommendations have been implemented by successive governments. But, as with Penner, it is entirely conceivable to begin this process now.

3. Truth and Reconciliation Commission 2015

The TRC was set up in 2008 to fulfil one of the terms of the Indian Residential Schools Settlement Agreement. The Honourable Justice Murray Sinclair was appointed as the chairperson, and Chief Wilton Littlechild and Dr. Marie Wilson were appointed as commissioners. After hearing from more than 6,000 witnesses, most of whom were survivors of residential schools, the commission released its report in 2015.

"Getting to the truth was hard," the commissioners noted in the preface, "but getting to reconciliation will be harder. It requires that the paternalistic and racist foundations of the residential school system be rejected as the basis for an on-going relationship ... Reconciliation is not an Aboriginal problem; it is a Canadian one. Virtually all aspects of Canadian society may need to be reconsidered." The commissioners noted that their report, which includes ninety-four calls to action, was intended to be a "reference point in that important discussion."

While all the calls to action should be responded to positively and decisively, the following – in my opinion – are particularly crucial for moving along the path of reconciliation with Indigenous peoples. The call to commit to the recognition and implementation of Aboriginal justice systems. The call to fully adopt the United Nations Declaration on the Rights of Indigenous Peoples as a framework for reconciliation and to develop an action plan to achieve that. The call to co-develop a Royal Proclamation of Reconciliation to be issued by the Crown, building on the Royal Proclamation of 1763 and the Treaty of Niagara of 1764, and reaffirming the nation-to-nation relationship.

Also crucial are the calls to adopt legal principles that accept Aboriginal title claims, "once the Aboriginal claimant has established occupation over a particular territory at a particular point in time," and that the "burden of proving any limitation on any rights arising from the existence of that title shifts to the party asserting such a limitation." In other words, the onus should be on, let's say, Ontario to convince a court why the people of Grassy Narrows or Teme-Augama can't live as they see fit within their acknowledged territory.

TRC called for the establishment of a National Council for Reconciliation. This would be an independent oversight party tasked with evaluating Canada's post-apology progress, "to ensure that government accountability for reconciling the relationship between Aboriginal peoples and the Crown is maintained in the coming years." (As it stands, it falls to non-profit organizations like the Yellowhead Institute to track how many calls to action the Canadian government has responded to in a given year.) TRC additionally proposed the funding of Indigenous law institutes to deepen understanding of Indigenous laws and enhance access to justice in accordance with unique, individual Aboriginal cultures. It called upon Canada to pursue a transparency policy around legal opinions pertaining to Aboriginal and Treaty rights.

In its December 2022 assessment of Canada's response to the TRC, the Yellowhead Institute, an Indigenous-led think-tank based at Toronto Metropolitan University, noted that the calls to action that "address structural change in this country remain largely unfulfilled." While survivors of residential schools are ageing and many of them have died, "some of the ongoing structural issues that are still in place in Canada are continuing to harm yet another generation."[5]

As of 2023, according to the Institute, only thirteen of the ninety-four calls have been completed. The TRC analysis about systemic issues are consistent with the findings of Penner and the RCAP. A great deal of thought and effort also went into *Reclaiming Power and Place* in 2021, the final report issued by the National Inquiry into Missing and Murdered Indigenous Women and Girls. MMIWGI commissioners Marion Buller, Michèle Audette, Qajag Robinson and Brian Eyolfson had been mandated to investigate all forms of violence against Inuit, Metis, and First Nations women and girls, including 2SLGBTQQIA people. In the preface, Chief Commissioner Audette pointed to statistics showing that "between 2001 and 2005, homicide rates for Indigenous women were nearly six times higher than for non-Indigenous women."[6]

As *Reclaiming Power and Place* points out, "Broadly seen, colonial processes were often set up around what genocide scholar Patrick Wolfe has called 'the organizing grammar of race.' In other words, only by categorizing Indigenous Peoples through legislation and other means could colonial forces begin to control them, as well as to dispose of them. As Wolfe maintains, 'Settler colonizers come to stay; invasion is structure, not an event.'"[7]

In introducing their "Calls for Justice," they describe their recommendations as legal imperatives; they are not optional. They follow international and domestic conventions and laws as well as Indigenous rights laws, including the Charter, the Constitution, and the Honour of the Crown. Everyone, not just institutions and governments, has a role to play in responding.

It is not too late for governments to dust off these reports, read the recommendations they themselves paid for, and implement them. We have the blueprints. Now is the time for them to see the light of day, whoever takes power in Ottawa and at the desks of premiers across the country. Reconciliation can't be viewed as a left or right political issue, because it is actually a nation-to-nation concern. In the next chapter, I will describe what I view as essential and significant changes – including land back to Indigenous peoples and the dismantling of Canada's departments of Crown-Indigenous Relations and Northern Affairs Canada (CIRNAC) and Indigenous Services Canada (ISC) – that could and should be addressed without delay.

CHAPTER NINE

Doing Our Part for Reconciliation with HEART

"What can we do? We want to do our part for reconciliation."

I hear this question frequently after speaking engagements with university students, law school classes, churches, and community groups. It arises in chats with friends and neighbours, even in spontaneous conversations at airports and pubs.

I say: "Dismantle, Dismantle, Dismantle!!!"

That surprising answer is always my response. Explaining what I mean is the theme of this concluding chapter. I continue to be deeply driven by the mandate Georges Erasmus and the other Dene offered me when I first began this work. If I wanted to help them, they said, I and other non-Indigenous people had to work to dismantle the colonial institutions, policies, and attitudes that make it so difficult for them to fully reclaim their self-determination, to have the political, economic, social, and cultural space to live as they see fit on their traditional lands, which they will govern with their own laws. *As they see fit* is important, because Indigenous peoples have unique histories, beliefs, and cultures.

Artwork 9.1: Mary Ann Penashue, *Tuentum* (Drummer and Caribou Spirit)

A one-size-fits-all solution will not accommodate their rich diversity.

Awareness of Canada's ongoing colonial approach to its relationship with Indigenous peoples has grown substantially over the past decade, in part due to the TRC Report. That has been accompanied by dismay at Canada's sluggish implementation of its recommendations, with almost no action on the calls for structural change. Many people know about the MMIWGI, which produced its own calls to action. National Indigenous Peoples

Day is 21 June. Orange Shirt (Every Child Matters) Day – Canada's National Day for Truth and Reconciliation on 30 September – is now a federal holiday. Indeed, Orange Shirt Day events have been so exhaustively covered by the media that a neighbour of mine – who is very committed to reconciliation – told me her book club had grown tired of superficial coverage. Where was the actual redress?

European reporters travelling with the pope on his 2022 visit to Canada were said to have been shocked by the number of homeless living on the streets around the Sacred Heart Church in Edmonton, where Pope Francis met with Indigenous people. They came to understand how hollow a papal apology was without a real action plan. When the United and Anglican Churches of Canada apologized in the late 1980s and 1990s for the harm they caused through their residential schools, Indigenous people both within and outside the churches acknowledged the apologies but to this day have not accepted them, as they are still waiting for concrete evidence of commitment to systemic change. Stolen lives cannot be restored, but lands can often be returned and there can be reparations for stolen resources.

Canada has decried the illegal annexation of parts of Ukraine by Russia. And rightly so. But what about the continued occupation of Indigenous land here at home? That, too, must be seen for what it is. Canada's claim that it champions reconciliation lulls people into believing that real change is happening. But, in fact, governments and institutions like the Canada Energy Regulator (formerly the NEB) as well as the courts continue to resist structural shifts in their thinking and action.

Redress entails the sharing of political and economic power. The idea that it is too onerous or impractical is a myth. We can do what is necessary without upending our own roots or investments. Consider, for instance, the fact that only 11 per cent of

Canada's land mass is privately owned. A huge majority of this vast country has been deemed Crown land, which was once – and should be again – shared with its original Indigenous stewards. Systemic change requires the dismantling of colonialist assumptions about who is entitled to what. Surely, this Land Back initiative is not too much to ask of Canadian governments in the mid-2020s, who say they are committed to reconciliation and control the bulk of our forests and mountains and waterways.

Most Canadians view reconciliation with others to be a good and honourable goal when they face personal and communal differences. They resist, however, being told to reconcile themselves *to* the sovereignty of another. Sovereignty is defined as supreme power and authority. It means submission. It implies oppression. It generates powerlessness. It leads to abuse. It erodes dignity. Yet that is exactly what the courts have decided that reconciliation for Indigenous peoples means. All liberation movements are fuelled by the desire to be free of the bondage entailed in being reconciled to the domination of the other. Women and girls continue to liberate themselves from institutionalized discrimination. Black Lives Matter focuses on breaking free from structural racism. Most people understand these quests.

What, then, are those of us who acknowledge that colonialism is still thriving meant to do? How do we decolonize? In their 2012 article "Decolonization Is Not a Metaphor," Eve Tuck and K. Wayne Yang argue that one thing we need to do is avoid "a set of evasions or settler moves to innocence"[1] that divert attention away from the need for systemic change. The moves to innocence they describe include:

- Settler nativism – the location or invention of a Native ancestor in "an attempt to deflect a settler identity." This has occurred among some remarkably prominent people, such as Nancy Reagan, Senator Elizabeth Warren, author Joseph

Boyden, and singer Buffy Sainte-Marie. By claiming that they, too, are Indigenous, they appear to be trying to avoid the complicity of being colonizers.
- Fantasizing adoption – the myth-building idea, long at work in North American literature and culture, that the white settler comes to revere Native ways and gets adopted approvingly by tribes or nations whose world view the settler will carry forward into the future while the tribe or nation dies tragically away. This approach often leads to cultural misappropriation. This "settler fantasy of mutuality based on sympathy and suffering" lies at the heart of James Fennimore Cooper's novel *Last of the Mohicans* and Kevin Costner's film *Dances with Wolves*. It is a fantasy of forgiveness without allowing for any Indigenous future.
- Colonial equivocation – "the notion that we are *all* colonized." I understand this to be a move to innocence to justify the colonization of others by claiming that at some point we have all been the victims of colonization. Tuck and Yang assert that decolonization is a different project altogether, but in fact is all too often subsumed into the directives of other human rights projects.
- Conscientization – focusing on "decolonizing the mind" as if that could stand in "for the more uncomfortable task of relinquishing stolen land." Examples that spring readily to mind are the land acknowledgments now performed from the stage before concerts and conferences, or the rush to hire Indigenous faculty or to recruit Indigenous board members, as if inviting them to join colonial settler society is their just reward; this leads non-Indigenous folks to think they are participating in systemic decolonization. Actor Cliff Cardinal's one-man show in the spring of 2023 scorched land acknowledgments as a prime example of a move to innocence for so many well-meaning people.

I agree with Tuck and Yang that decolonization "is not about converting Indigenous politics to a western doctrine of liberation; it is not a philanthropic process of 'helping' the at-risk, and alleviating suffering; it is not a generic term for struggle against oppressive conditions and outcomes." As they point out, the intentions of many people who recognize injustice and want to do something about it may be loving and sincere, but, "We are asking them/you to consider how the pursuit of critical consciousness, the pursuit of social justice through a critical enlightenment, can also be settler moves to innocence – diversions, distractions, which relieve the settler feelings of guilt or responsibility, and conceal the need to give up land or power or privilege."[2]

I am consciously coming to understand how often I, myself, indulge in these moves to innocence, which tempt me to accept that reconciliation to colonialism and assimilation is the best we can do. But when I focus on the more than 700 recommendations for structural change made by Penner, the RCAP, TRC, and MMIWGI, I regain my conviction that non-Indigenous citizens must not only work for reconciliation with our Indigenous neighbours, but that it is eminently achievable.

This requires a mutually acceptable process in which both sides can discuss past wrongs and build a new relationship featuring equal power, common goals, and mutual good faith. That is reconciliation *with* the other – not to the desires or framework *of* the other. A true, authentic process of reconciliation requires a level table for dialogue, not one tilted to Canada's side. Over the many years that I've been at negotiating sessions, it has been clear to me that most federal representatives, including policy experts, have never even heard of the Penner and RCAP reports, or, if they have, their instructions are to ignore those recommendations in modern Treaty negotiations. These blueprints that contain detailed guidelines for the dismantling of colonial institutions, policies, and attitudes go ignored. Canada isn't committed to dismantling, so it focuses on benign and low-stakes initiatives like changing the words in our citizenship oath.

However creative and hopeful and politically resilient Indigenous people have been, too many roadblocks still sit in their way. Picture the folk of Grassy Narrows, surrounded by their traditional boreal forest, who are not allowed to protect it because it is off reserve. The river is still slowly killing them because they are denied use of their land and resources required for healing and rebuilding their culture and economy. Dismantle! Dismantle! Dismantle! The Dene struggle against the Mackenzie Valley Pipeline is a modern David and Goliath story. The ten-year moratorium on development – to give the Dene time to negotiate their land claims – was a remarkable dismantling victory, but Canada reneged on it in a matter of years by approving the Norman Wells pipeline. Systemic change took one step forward and then fell back.

I have written about the remarkable resurgence of Indigenous peoples politically when they defeated the 1969 White Paper designed to complete their assimilation and wipe out their historic rights – instead achieving entrenchment of Aboriginal and Treaty rights in Canada's patriated Constitution. Yet, we saw the disgraceful positions of Prime Ministers Pierre Trudeau and Brian Mulroney and the premiers trying to shore up their colonial powers. They did so even though they had the Penner Report in hand as a guide for decolonization.

Faced with the political refusal to implement s.35, First Nations went to the courts, but when the first court decisions were rendered, the sovereign Crown at both the federal and provincial levels had already made it clear that they had no intention of sharing power with Indigenous peoples. The courts had the opportunity to adopt a new, non-colonial interpretation of s.35 that would have recognized what the Penner Report called a *new distinct order of government* within the Canadian federation. The justices could have said that s.35 meant that the three constitutional governments – federal, provincial, and Aboriginal – must harmonize their powers. But they refused to do so. In the case of the Teme-Augama, we saw that the governments and the courts both put the interest of the logging companies before the rights of the Teme-Augama people and the survival of the old-growth forest – as if such prioritization were self-evident. These groundless legal assumptions must be dismantled! Recall the independent legal opinion offered to the people of Grassy Narrows stating that the court would likely rule against them with respect to the pollution clean up – because the English-Wabigoon River system lies outside their reserve. But the river system is *in their traditional territory. It is we who took it away from them!*

I applaud all the efforts individuals and groups are making to understand Canada's shameful history of both genocide and assimilation, and to gain deeper insight into our personal racism. But reconciliation cannot just be about addressing the symptoms of colonialism. Unless policies aimed at tackling poverty, high rates of incarceration, suicide, addiction, physical and mental illness, and the denial of basic human rights, including the rights of children, are rooted in a new foundation of harmonization with Indigenous people, they will continue to fail.

I am convinced that we, as Canadians, can do much better than that. In 2021, the federal government passed legislation that promised to implement the United Nations Declaration on the Rights of Indigenous People. This is a start. First Nations have repeatedly demonstrated that they are ready and willing to harmonize. In the Charlottetown Accord, Canada and every province agreed that the Constitution would recognize Aboriginal governments as one of the three orders of government and that Aboriginal peoples have the inherent right of self-government. As noted earlier, I was at the self-government table as negotiator for the AFN when that provision was worked through. That unanimous wording was a *reconciliation with* statement, and there is no reason why it cannot be included in modern Treaties and accorded to all First Nations. So, it's time that – with the support of non-Indigenous Canadians – governments move beyond addressing mere symptoms.

Agenda for Reconciliation with First Nations

Many people tell me that when they write to their MPs, MPPs, or MLAs about Indigenous matters, they get a "thank you for your letter" response and nothing more. If they do receive something further, it's a rote listing with a favourable spin on what the government is doing. I offer this agenda of items for your consideration, some or all of which you might propose to elected officials at all levels of government. In the preceding chapter, I touched on the key recommendations of the Penner Report, RCAP, TRC, and MMIWGI to show how much thought, energy, and resources have already gone into visions of systemic change. It is important to remind both politicians and bureaucrats of the recommendations *already made to them* by commissions and inquiries over decades.

What Would Dismantling Look Like?

Now that the pope has renounced the Doctrine of Discovery,[3] it would be wonderful if his successor would also *repudiate* it as a continuing paradigm, for it remains the basis for Canada's colonialism just as it was used to justify European sovereignty over all of the Americas. On first glance it might seem that renouncing and repudiating are the same. However, in my view, rooted in many discussions with Indigenous people, "renouncing" means abandoning the doctrine – while "repudiation" entails acknowledging that the doctrine, which led to genocide, should never have been asserted in the first place. Repudiation was called for in both the RCAP and the TRC. On 21 June 2021, Canada passed the United Nations Declaration on the Rights of Indigenous Peoples Act (UNDRIP Act),[4] which purports to implement the UNDRIP resolution passed by the UN General Assembly in 2007. Canada was one of the few countries that did not support the declaration at the time of its passage. UNDRIP says that "all doctrines, policies and practices based on or advocating superiority of people or individuals on the basis of national origin or racial, religious, ethnic or cultural differences are racist, scientifically false, legally invalid, morally contemptible and socially unjust." The declaration asserts that "indigenous peoples have suffered from historic injustices as a result of, *inter alia*, their colonization and disposition of their lands, territories and resources, thus preventing them from exercising, in particular, their right to development in accordance with their own needs and interests."[5] These are compelling words.

Canada's 2021 UNDRIP Act includes some strong introductory language:

> Whereas the government of Canada objects to all forms of colonialism and is committed to advancing relationships with indigenous peoples that are based on good faith and on the principles of justice, democracy, quality, non-discrimination, good governance and respect for human rights.

And:

> Whereas the government of Canada recognizes that all relations with indigenous people must be based on the recognition and

implementation of the inherent right to self-determination including the right to self-government.

And:

Whereas the protection of aboriginal and treaty rights – recognized and affirmed by s. 35 of the Constitution Act 1982 – is an underlying principle and value of the constitution of Canada and Canadian courts have stated that such rights are not frozen and are capable of evolution and growth.

One of the objectives of the act is to amend Canada's laws to bring them into conformity with the UNDRIP. What is not at all clear is whether this will lead Canada to abandon the interpretation of the courts – that the central meaning of s.35 is that Indigenous people must reconcile to the sovereignty of the Crown. If Canada uses that understanding of s.35 to assess whether its laws are in conformity with UNDRIP, very few laws will be changed.

The RCAP, the TRC, and Penner all recommended that Canada – jointly with Indigenous nations – prepare a Royal Proclamation to set out some fundamental principles for a renewed relationship. I propose that any dismantling based on this Royal Proclamation include four concrete actions:

1. Returning land and resources to Indigenous peoples.
2. Phasing out Canada's departments of Crown-Indigenous Relations and Northern Affairs Canada and Indigenous Services Canada, which continue to assert Indian Act-based control over so many aspects of the lives of Indigenous peoples.
3. Implementing the United Nations Declaration on the Rights of Indigenous Peoples.

4. Re-mandating regulatory bodies that make recommendations on proposed projects such as power lines, hydro dams, and pipelines with a requirement that they consider potential Indigenous and environmental impacts as *primary matters* along with technical and financial considerations, rather than as impacts to be minimized to the extent possible in the construction and operation of a project.

1. Land Back: Return of Land and Resources to First Nations

One of the most critical elements of dismantling involves the return of land and resources to First Nations. Reserves are small and often unproductive or flood-prone plots of land that have remained the same size since they were allotted, based on historic (and deliberately misinterpreted) Treaties. While the geographic size of reserves has stayed the same, the geographic footprint of cities, towns, and villages across Canada continue to grow. As their populations increase, these communities receive additional land from what is considered to be provincial Crown land, when in fact it is traditional Indigenous land. Many of these municipal boundaries are now very large, and it is unconscionable that their boundaries continue to expand while First Nation reserve boundaries stay static. Access to a land and resource base that keeps pace with population growth is crucial for all governments, including Indigenous governments. The fact that the size of reserves is frozen means that, as their own populations grow, many First Nations people, predominantly young people, are forced to leave and go to nearby cities or towns where they are ill equipped to live and often end up destitute and homeless.

The Land Back movement, led by Indigenous people and nations in North America, continues to advocate for the return of traditional land to the peoples who inhabited and stewarded it before colonization. Political and economic control of land is central to Indigenous self-determination. In Canada, it is important to understand that the land to be returned is now considered Crown land. Most of it is held by the provinces, based on the constitutional division of powers, which gives them control over land and resources within their borders. The colonial Crown ostensibly came to control that land through historic Treaties, many of which are demonstrably fraudulent. As noted elsewhere, an agenda for reconciliation with First Nations must include a process in which the Treaties are renovated to reflect their original spirit and intent.

In addition to Land Back being the right thing to do, it is becoming more urgent because of Indigenous population growth. In 1996, Indigenous people comprised 2.8 per cent of the Canadian population,[6] whereas according to the 2021 census, the total Indigenous population amounts to 5 per cent. (First Nations comprise 1,048,405; the Métis number 624,220, and the Inuit are 70,540. Of those registered under the Indian Act, who number 750,110, 41 per cent live on reserve and 59 per cent off-reserve.)[7] In fact, the Indigenous population is growing at almost twice the rate of any other Canadian group, yet many of them remain on tiny reserves without real economic opportunities or face a difficult life in unwelcoming cities or towns.

RCAP recommendations 2.4.2 and 2.4.3 affirm Land Back and access to resources. They say federal, provincial, and territorial governments *must provide Aboriginal nations with lands that are sufficient in size* to foster self-reliance and cultural and political autonomy.

Recommendation 2.4.3 says that the goal of negotiations is to ensure that Aboriginal nations within their traditional territories have exclusive or preferential access to certain renewable or non-renewable resources, or a guaranteed share of them, including water; a guaranteed share of the revenues flowing from resource developments; and preferential guarantees or priorities to the economic benefits and opportunities flowing from development projects.

Land and Resource Back Negotiations

Land and resource back negotiations must be offered to Treaty organizations across the country, and the organizations themselves should be given the option of whether discussions take place on a Treaty-wide basis, or fully or partially by individual First Nations. A good model is the current modern Treaty process, under which significant amounts of land and resources are being recognized. As I've described, the Innu modern Treaty AIP provides them with 5,000 square miles that they will own outright, where development can occur with Innu consent as set out in an IBA, and additional large areas where IBAs are required based on negotiations that are subject to arbitration in the event of disagreements.

Crown Land in the Provinces

The good news with respect to the negotiation of the return of land and resources is that a huge percentage of land in Canada, as I said, is deemed provincial Crown land. Land Back proposals do not demand that a portion of privately held real estate or resources be returned. Private landowners came to own their land titles in good faith, based on the premise that the Crown had good title. So, titles to private land are not in jeopardy.

In British Columbia, 94 per cent of land is considered provincial Crown land. In Alberta, it's 60 per cent. In Saskatchewan 58, in Manitoba 90, in Ontario 87 (10 per cent of which is parks and conservation areas). In Nova Scotia, one third. PEI, due to agriculture, is only 12 per cent Crown-held, whereas in NL it's almost *all* in the hands of government: 88 per cent.[8] There is also some federal Crown land in each province, most of which is national parks and conservation areas.[9] Several years ago, Canada devolved much of its northern Crown lands to the territorial governments. In Yukon, only 0.06 per cent of land is held privately. The rest is federal or First Nation land.[10] In Nunavut, the parties are still working on devolution, so for now Inuit own 18 per cent, the government of Nunavut has 1 per cent, and Canada holds over 80 per cent.[11]

Before the northern devolution, 41 per cent of Canada was made up of federal Crown lands, with 48 per cent provincial and 11 per cent held privately.[12] Under the circumstances, if *even 10 per cent* of Crown land and resources were on the table to be returned to Indigenous governments what a huge difference it would make for the First Nations!

Recently, Canada set a goal of conserving 30 per cent of its lands and oceans by 2030 to protect ecosystems. It was determined that Indigenous governments should play the primary role in that protection through the application of Indigenous laws, governance, and knowledge systems. Remarkably, at the UN-sponsored 15th Conference of Parties to the UN Convention on Biological Diversity held in Montreal in December of 2022, 188 countries adopted this target. There is no reason why, in addition to that 30 per cent, we cannot transfer another 10 per cent of Crown land to the jurisdiction of Indigenous governments. What I have stressed several times – but bears repeating – is that returning land and resources to First Nations *does not mean* that there will be no development on those lands. Rather, it means that First Nation governments will set up their own processes for considering and deciding on development proposals, just like they currently do when negotiating IBAs.

Grassy Narrows Land Back

So, what would a Land Back agreement look like? You may recall that Grassy Narrows included a proposal in its mercury pollution settlement negotiations with Ontario and Canada, which can serve as a good example. Considering the destruction of its river-based economy and the reality that, even if the political will was there (which it wasn't and isn't) it would take generations to do the clean up required to restore the river, Grassy proposed that Ontario return 2,000 square miles of traditional land. Leaders detailed the importance of this wilderness for trapping, hunting, fishing, berry-picking, wild rice harvesting, and selective logging. These Grassy-controlled activities would serve as the backbone for the nation to build a new, post-pollution, self-reliant economy. It would also facilitate the social rehabilitation of the community. Grassy also proposed that existing commercial logging, fishing, tourist camps, and sports hunting lodges compatible with traditional activities be licensed and regulated by their nation. So, Grassy not only detailed how it would own and manage the land but also how it would do so in a manner that permitted a number of recreational activities for everyone. Ontario dismissed this proposal out of hand without discussion. The province just loftily – and in the best of colonial postures – announced that it would retain control of the Grassy Narrows traditional land use area for the benefit of all Ontarians. In truth, this meant the benefit of resource extraction companies, like the one responsible for the mercury pollution in the first place, whose Ontario-licensed activities continue to devastate the area.

Why do so many provincial governments across Canada continue to refuse to discuss returning even a portion of the traditional Indigenous land they call Crown land, which they occupy and make decisions about without the consent of the original stewards? Despite Penner and RCAP strongly recommending it, the answer clearly is a mistrust of Indigenous control that is rooted in notions of white supremacy. How else can it be explained when – through IBAs and in so many other ways – First Nations have demonstrated that they, like provincial and territorial governments, will set reasonable criteria for making decisions on the land they manage?

Here are three examples (from several around the country) of how First Nations are successfully exerting a degree of control over their traditional lands and resources, in addition to the IBAs they continue to sign.

Squamish Nation

When a proposed liquefied natural gas project in their territory came to their attention, the Squamish Nation (Sḵwx̱wú7mesh Úxwumixw) in BC successfully asserted jurisdiction over its lands and resources to control if, and how, a development would occur. The community created its own impact assessment process based on its own laws. This hadn't been recognized as valid or enforceable under Canadian or British Columbia law, so there was a risk that it would be seen as symbolic only. However, the Squamish Nation was able to leverage the threat of legal challenge and the uncertainty, costs, and delays associated with that to convince Woodfibre LNG to abide by their assessment. The federal and provincial governments were reluctant to recognize that the Squamish Nation had such authority. But Woodfibre LNG and the Squamish Nation entered into an agreement whereby the company would fund the assessment and provide all necessary information. They also agreed to consider any mitigation measures proposed through the confidential process and respect the outcome.

In the end, Woodfibre LNG accepted all twenty-five conditions and mitigation measures that arose after the assessment process, and the Squamish Nation formally consented to the project, signing an IBA. They also received back nine parcels of traditional territory as part of their deal in 2019 with BC Hydro, including sections of Murrin Provincial Park. (Ironically, Canadian rock-climbing enthusiasts who adore the Murrin geography told CBC News they were "astounded" that they hadn't been consulted about the returned land, which includes one of their favourite climbs.[13] Perhaps now they know how it feels.)

Ktunaxa Nation

The Ktunaxa Nation wanted to protect a sacred area of British Columbia known as Jumbo Valley, which is home to the Qat'muk Grizzly Bear Spirit, whom they revere. The provincial government had approved plans for a new ski resort in the valley, which would drive the Grizzly Bear Spirit away. The Ktunaxa Nation challenged BC's decision in court on lack of accommodation and freedom of religion grounds. In 2017, they lost their appeal to the Supreme Court of Canada. "The S. 35 right to consultation and accommodation is a right to a process, not to a particular outcome,"[14] the justices ruled. (Again, I cannot emphasize enough how the "rights" identified in s.35 have been made up out of whole cloth by the Canadian judicial system.)

But, in this case, the court did not have the last word. The Ktunaxa Nation leveraged public opposition and legal uncertainty (BC was going to require the developer to go through a new environmental assessment) to convince the federal government to support them in creating an Indigenous Protected and Conserved Area for the site.

The Ktunaxa Nation officially unveiled the Qat'muk Indigenous Protected and Conserved Area in 2020. Canada and private donors contributed $21 million to the protection (a chunk of the money going to pay off the developer). It is still to be worked out how the Ktunaxa Nation will be able to exercise control over the lands, but it is an inspiring example of how a First Nation has been able to reclaim a spiritually important site.

Nimkii Aazhibikong

Nimkii Aazhibikong is an example of Indigenous peoples taking back their land in order to reconnect to their culture and language without asking for provincial or federal permission to do so. Nimkii Aazhibikong is a camp north of Elliot Lake, Ontario, which was built by youth and Elders to connect the generations for arts and cultural land-based teachings. It also serves as an Ojibway language revitalization centre. The organizers started this initiative in 2017 and have since added permanent structures such as an art studio, cabins, cook-house, outhouses, and several traditional Anishnaabe lodge structures. The camp has been built within Anishinaabe territory – but on lands that Ontario considers Crown lands. It lacks provincial permits or permissions; the people do not care. They view it as a reoccupation of Anishnaabe land in response to the crisis of culture and language loss. Ontario has not taken any steps to remove them.

2. Dismantling of the CIRNAC and ISC

The return of land and resources is one essential prong in reconciliation with Indigenous peoples. An equally important one is the dismantling of the bloated Ottawa-based bureaucracies that micro-manage their lives: Crown-Indigenous Relations and Northern Affairs Canada (CIRNAC) and Indigenous Services Canada (ISC). CIRNAC and ISC control Indigenous people across the country, as did their predecessor bureaucracies, like Indigenous and Northern Affairs Canada. On a practical service level, we need to close ISC and give individual Indigenous governments the funding and tools they need to administer their own programs. In 2020–1, ISC and CIRNAC had a combined staff of 8,308 full-time equivalent positions, mostly working out of high-rise towers in Gatineau, across the river from Ottawa. As programs and services are transferred directly to Indigenous nations, staff positions can transfer too; not directly, but funding saved from not having all these bureaucrats can flow directly to First Nations to fill the needed positions (such as in-house technical advisors, project managers, administrators, and lawyers).

At issue, of course, is money. As long as Canada holds the purse strings, we cannot decolonize. It's as simple as that. Many Canadians would be shocked to learn that most funding that Indigenous governments receive comes in the form of annual contribution agreements. An inordinate amount of time and money gets spent by both Indigenous governments and Ottawa negotiating these agreements, which number several hundred each year. *Each project and service* may have its own contribution agreement. That means that an Indigenous government has to spend an inordinate amount of staff time preparing work plans and budgets, negotiating, and revising those work plans and budgets to fit Canada's ever-changing requirements, then waiting for funds. Canada operates on a 1 April–31 March fiscal year, and it is not uncommon for an Indigenous government to not receive approval for a given contribution agreement until summer or even fall of the budget year. This creates a highly inefficient system and sadly fuels the non-Indigenous bias that Indigenous governments are somehow wasteful. Indigenous governments either need to spend their own limited funds on projects in the hopes that the requested funding comes through to reimburse them or wait and try to cram work into a few months at the end of the fiscal year, particularly if they lack own source revenue (OSR) and cannot float the projects. They also need to report on each individual contribution agreement, of which there are numerous for even a small First Nation. It takes red tape to a whole new level.

The various reports commissioned and completed through the years have made concrete recommendations for how to change the way funding is administered, including increased access to OSR through lands and resources, and a recognition of Indigenous governments' right to develop their own tax system. RCAP also recommended the creation of a self-government transition centre that can support Indigenous governments in building their internal capacity to develop their institutions and laws. Indeed, it made various recommendations about who ought to exercise self-determination and have the right of self-government. RCAP, and others, have raised concerns about small band councils taking on administration of all programs and services and passing and enforcing all laws necessary. RCAP recommended that self-determination happen at the nation level, but it should not be up to colonial governments to decide. Indigenous peoples are fully capable of making their own decisions about how to organize themselves to administer programs and services effectively and efficiently, as well as to decide based on their own laws the appropriate bodies to pass and enforce their laws. They may choose to work together on matters like healthcare but run their schools independently. Surely, we can all agree that the federal government, with its huge bureaucracy of 8,308 staff devoted to Indigenous issues, should not be the arbiter of what is efficient.

We need to dismantle the paternalistic attitudes of the federal and provincial governments that assumes only *they* can hold Indigenous governments accountable. Indigenous governments must be allowed to create their own strategies for accountability and responsibility, based on their own customs and values. They must be free to make policies and set priorities and be accountable to their own people.

A feeble defence might be made for Canada's ongoing control of the lives of Indigenous people if those lives were actually getting better, but that is not the case at all. Funds for Indigenous programs and services in 2018–19 tallied $12.1 billion. As a percentage of federal spending, Indigenous affairs has increased in the last forty years.[15] According to the Fraser Institute, from the period 1946–47 to 2013–14, federal government spending on Indigenous people increased by 7.1 per cent per year, whereas the per capita spending on all federal programs from 1949–50 to 2013–14 grew by only 2.5 per cent.[16]

Tom Flanagan, who prepared the Fraser Institute reports, notes that while more money is being spent, the majority is not actually going to Indigenous people. He writes, "Taken together, these trends mean that far more money is being spent in the name of Indigenous people than has been seen for 25 years (though, in fact, most of the outlay goes to civil servants and consultants, not to Indigenous persons)."[17] He made this comment in reference to the Trudeau government's increase in spending and has called it the Aboriginal Industry. (I must say that while Flanagan and

I have a diametrically opposed approach to addressing Indigenous issues, he is right about the bloated bureaucracy.)

Statistics Canada's Community Well-Being (CWB) index looks at how people who live in First Nation communities are faring based on four dimensions, equally weighted with a total score out of 100. The dimensions are housing, income, education, and labour force participation. For the year 1981, the index was 45 as opposed to 65.5 for non-Indigenous communities. In 2016, it was 58.4 for First Nation communities and 77.5 for other communities; over the past thirty-five years, the gap has remained more or less constant.[18] (It is also important to note that the CWB misses several factors like security, health, language, culture, environmental integrity, rates of incarceration, and happiness that are so important when measuring the actual well-being of Indigenous communities.)

With respect to housing, in 1977, over a third of houses on reserve were considered overcrowded according to national occupancy standards. That had not improved by 2016. (How could it, when their population has outpaced the frozen allotment of reserve land?) In 2016, 51 per cent of Inuit and 36 per cent of First Nations people on reserves were living in unsuitable housing. The comparable figure for non-Indigenous people is 8.5 per cent. Regarding income, 31.4 per cent of First Nations people on reserve lived in low-income households in 2021. Almost one quarter of Indigenous children aged 0–14 are in low-income households, more than double the national rate. In terms of education, 25.6 per cent of First Nations, Métis, and Inuit youth have not completed high school, compared to 11.5 per cent for all Canadians.

Other factors that should be considered include the health and well-being of children. In 1984, the infant mortality rate (before the age of one) per 1,000 births was 18.4 for registered "Indians."

That rate marked a considerable reduction since 1971, when it was a shocking 41, but was still twice the rate for non-Indigenous babies. In 2004–6, the Inuit infant mortality rate was 279 per cent greater than the non-Indigenous rate, although again down substantially from 560 per cent in 1971. Further, Indigenous children in foster care in 2021 accounted for 53.8 per cent of wards, when they only made up 7.7 per cent of the country's population under fourteen. That unbelievably high rate had not changed since 2016.

Regarding life expectancy, the gains for Indigenous people over the last forty years track the gains for our non-Indigenous population, but the gaps remain. In 2004–6, the life expectancy for non-Indigenous males is 81.4 and for females 87.3. In 2011, the life expectancy for Inuit was 70.0 for males and 76.1 for females. Further, suicide rates per thousand deaths for all ages of First Nations people were 39 in 1980–83 and fell to 24.3 in the period of 2011–16 – except for the Inuit, where it increased to a staggering 72.3, and for First Nation boys on reserve, where the 2016 rate was 78.8. (The non-Indigenous suicide rate went from 14.3 in 1980–3 to 8 by 2016.) These rates are extraordinarily alarming.

And finally, consider incarceration in Indigenous populations. In 2001, 17.1 per cent of inmates in provincial and territorial correction facilities were Indigenous. In 2018–19, the rate had risen to 30.4 per cent. The picture in federal institutions is similar. As of December 2021, almost 50 per cent of all federally sentenced women were Indigenous, whereas it was 9 per cent in the early 1980s. From April 2010 to 2019, the Indigenous inmate population in federal institutions increased by 43.3 per cent. This trend is, of course, deeply disturbing. A significant factor is the number of Indigenous young people who leave the reserves because of lack of opportunities, terrible housing conditions, a freeze on reserve size, and decreasing access to traditional lands. They then have difficulty coping with city life, leading to poverty, homelessness, police carding, racist abuse, criminal charges, and poor access to good legal help.

So, in summary, no: increased federal spending on bureaucracies to service our Indigenous communities has not improved their lives one whit. Why? Because we refuse to give them what they are actually asking for, which is agency.

The Forty Missed Years

Canada has missed at least four decades since the 1982 entrenchment of Aboriginal rights in the Constitution to move towards dismantling its colonial control. This has become, I think, a resounding wake-up call for Canadians. During those same years, the importance of agency for marginalized peoples became almost universally recognized and certainly acknowledged by progressive governments in terms of policies for women, children, and non-Indigenous minority groups. I suppose it could be said that Canada has internalized its approach as a sort of benevolent colonialism based on a charity framework. It provides certain assistance to Indigenous people, but its policy does not derive from what First Nations themselves feel they need, which in so many cases is just fundamental control over their own lives. So, the dismantling of CIRNAC and ISC is really a must; it will be a long road, but it must begin now if – in forty years' time – Indigenous peoples are to thrive.

Dismantling CIRNAC and ISC has to be led by Indigenous peoples and nations. They must decide the pace, as it intrudes on their daily lives. One way it could happen, as mentioned, is by revamping the existing Recognition of Rights tables. According to an analysis done by Hayden King and Shiri Pasternak of the Yellowhead Institute,[19] the tables currently continue to emphasize the supremacy of the Canadian constitutional framework and constrain the possibilities for self-determination among Indigenous peoples. These tables could be re-mandated to focus both on Indigenous-led proposals for land and resources, and the dismantling of CIRNAC and ISC.

Again, it is critical to stress that, unless there is this fundamental shift, the next forty years will see continued entrenchment of colonialism based on Canada's position that reconciliation means subjection to the sovereignty of the Crown. However, if the new path of reconciliation with First Nations is taken, we will see at least a fundamental shift towards the self-determination that is entrenched in UNDRIP.

3. United Nations Declaration on the Rights of Indigenous Peoples

Under Justin Trudeau, as I mentioned, Ottawa passed the United Nations Declaration on the Rights of Indigenous Peoples Act. This act does not actually implement UNDRIP. Instead, it simply says that Canada will take all measures necessary to ensure that the laws of Canada are consistent with UNDRIP and stipulates an action plan. The first step, in consultation and cooperation with Indigenous peoples, is to prepare a plan that achieves the objectives of UNDRIP. Unfortunately, although UNDRIP calls for Indigenous consent to government actions that affect them, Canada has decided that it will consult with Indigenous peoples on the plan, but *their consent is not required*. Hardly an encouraging start!

The second process set out in the act is that Canada "must in consultation and cooperation with Indigenous peoples, take all measures necessary to ensure the laws of Canada are consistent with UNDRIP." But, as with the action plan, Indigenous consent will not be required. Another key weakness is that the act seems to be restricted to looking at laws, but almost all of the ways that Canada relates to Indigenous peoples are embedded in policies. Further, it is essential to understand that this act only addresses federal laws. That is, of course, a big gap because, as we have seen, the provinces control the land and resources that must be on the table if colonialism is actually to be dismantled. British Columbia has enacted its own version of interpreting UNDRIP into provincial laws, but no other province has done so.

Canada's initial objection to signing UNDRIP in 2007 was that the declaration had to be consistent with our understanding of our Constitution rather than the other way around. While Canada is no longer saying that, I don't see a substantive indication that it will seriously employ UNDRIP to re-examine its current interpretation of s.35 (that Indigenous people must reconcile to the sovereignty of the Crown). The lens through which Canada looks at UNDRIP is critical for the approach that we take. Once Canada begins to dismantle colonial laws by reinterpreting our Constitution, all of our laws – and hopefully policies – can be replaced with ones that contribute to reconciliation with Indigenous peoples. The hopes of so many Canadians for meaningful change are invested in the implementation of this UNDRIP Act.

4. Re-mandating Decision-Making Bodies

In the Dene chapter, we discussed the problem of decision-making frameworks for major projects, which relegate Indigenous rights and environmental considerations to afterthoughts. The climate crisis and the ever-growing demands of Indigenous peoples that their rights be respected are raising awareness of the need to re-mandate those institutions, requiring them to consider environmental and Indigenous concerns as key elements. This should, of course, be part of the dismantling of laws that we discussed above, as those bodies are established by federal and provincial law.

A Word in Closing

In reflecting on my fifty years of walking with First Nations and, in particular, with the Dene, Grassy Narrows, Teme-Augama, and the Innu of Labrador, I often fantasize about what life for those First Nations and hundreds of others would be like if Canada and the provinces had embraced *reconciliation with* rather than *reconciliation to*. In my heart and mind, I have no doubt that Canada would be at least a happier and certainly a more just country, where Indigenous and non-Indigenous people were committed to living in harmony and mutual respect.

But as my mind and heart pondered that thought on a December morning in 2022, I read a column in the *Toronto Star* by Brandi Morin (a French/Cree/Iroquois journalist from Treaty 6 in Alberta) and realized how much work we need to do and how much commitment we need to get there. Morin writes, "Canada is a killing field of colonial genocide against Indigenous, women, girls and two-spirit peoples who continue to die and disappear at horrifying rates." A serial killer who had posted racist material to social media has been accused of slaughtering four Indigenous women in Winnipeg.

> These fatalities are a symptom of an out-of-control extermination of Indigenous women and girls ... The evil agenda against our women and girls has existed for over 500 years. Since the colonization of

Indigenous territories in North America our Life Givers have been increasingly targeted with misogyny, disrespect, and violence. Due to racist and unjustified theologies that declared Indigenous lands were for the taking and that Indigenous Nations were not human beings as defined by the Doctrine of Discovery ... The Holocaust of colonial ideology continues.

Then, she laments, "this injustice in a democratic nation is met with apathy."[20]

Morin speaks heartbreaking truths that all Canadians must face and all governments must address if we are worthy of even suggesting that we are actually engaged in reconciliation with Indigenous peoples. In October 2024, Georges Erasmus contacted me about hosting the Toronto launch of his book *Hot'A! Enough!* at our OKT offices in Toronto. In our discussion, I reminded him of our mid-1970s discussion, how he told me that my job was to dismantle the oppressive colonial institutions that made life so difficult for his people. He chuckled when I explained that *dismantle! dismantle! dismantle!!!* had become my mantra in the years since, during which I have tried to walk with First Nation people and nations. It's a mantra that I urge (at least in my mind it's only urging) young lawyers and others to consider adopting – so that all Canadians can live in harmony with respect.

I am truly grateful that you have joined me on this journey. I encourage everyone to continue to work for reconciliation and, in doing so, please ask whether the action you are considering taking will be an authentic step. We have the blueprints. I hope you agree that all non-Indigenous Canadians are called to join in the dismantling of those laws, policies, and institutions that continue to make self-determination so difficult for Indigenous peoples and nations.

Notes

Preface

1 *Toronto Star*, 19 September, A11.

1 The Dene Nation and the Mackenzie Valley Pipeline

1 "Landmark Pipeline Inquiry Sparks Interest 40 Years Later," CBC News, 21 May 2014, www.cbc.ca/news/Indigenous/landmark-pipeline-inquiry-sparks-interest-40-years-later-1.2647366.
2 See, for example: www.encyclopedie-energie.org/en/world-energy-consumption-1800-2000-results/.
3 Thomas A. Berger, *Northern Frontier/Northern Homeland: The Report of the Mackenzie Valley Pipeline Inquiry, Volume One* Minister of Supply and Services Canada, 1977.
4 *Indian Act*, SC 1951, c 29.
5 Peter W. Hogg, *Constitutional Law of Canada*, 5th Edition (Scarborough: Thomson Carswell, 2007), 618.
6 Joshua Ben David Nichols, *A Reconciliation without Recollection?: An Investigation of the Foundations of Aboriginal Law in Canada* (Toronto: University of Toronto Press, 2020), 283.
7 *Indian Act*, RSC 1927, c 98.
8 *Amodu Tijani v. Secretary, Southern Nigeria*, [1921] 2 A.C. 399 at 409–10.
9 H.B. Hawthorn, *A Survey of the Contemporary Indians of Canada – Economic, Political, Educational Needs and Policies* (Ottawa: Indian and Northern Affairs, 1966).
10 The complete text of the "Statement of the Government of Canada on Indian Policy 1969" can be viewed online: http://epe.lac-bac.gc.ca/100/200/301/inac-ainc/indian_policy-e/cp1969_e.pdf.

11 Kelly McParland, "Turning a Blind Eye to Pierre Trudeau's Unseemly Indigenous Assimilation Plan," *National Post*, 7 June 2021, https://nationalpost.com/opinion/kelly-mcparland-turning-a-blind-eye-to-pierre-trudeaus-unseemly-Indigenous-assimilation-plan.
12 Harold Cardinal, *The Unjust Society: The Tragedy of Canada's Indians* (Vancouver: Douglas & McIntyre, 1969/1999), 1.
13 Ibid.
14 Ibid., 2.
15 Paulette (Re), (1973) 39 DLR (3d) 45 (NWTSC), upheld on appeal, *Paulette v. The Queen* [1977] 2 S.C.R. 628 (1976).
16 The complete text of the "Dene Declaration (1975)" can be viewed online: https://publicautonomy.org/2018/08/23/the-dene-declaration/.
17 The Dene Declaration (1975), General Assembly, Indian Brotherhood of NWT (Dene Nation), Ft Simpson, 19 July 1975.
18 *Edmonton Journal*, 27 April 1976, 21.
19 As cited by the author in Hugh McCullum, Karmel Taylor McCullum, and John Olthuis, *Moratorium: Justice, Energy, the North, and the Native People* (Toronto: Anglican Book Centre, 1977), 196.
20 Thomas. A. Berger, *Northern Frontier/Northern Homeland: The Report of the Mackenzie Valley Pipeline Inquiry, Volume One* (Ottawa: Minister of Supply and Services Canada, 1977).
21 *Edmonton Journal*, 21.
22 Testimony in the author's personal files.
23 Testimony in the author's personal files.
24 Testimony in the author's personal files.
25 Testimony in the author's personal files.
26 Testimony in the author's personal files.
27 Testimony in the author's personal files.
28 Testimony in the author's personal files.
29 *Committee for Justice & Liberty Foundation v. Interprovincial Pipe Line (NW) Ltd.*, [1982] 1 FC 619.
30 "Dene Government Past and Future." Recorded by Lesley Malloch from a meeting of Elders held in Behchoko. Sòmbak'è, Denendeh: WCF for Dene Nation, 1984.
31 Ibid.

2 Mercury Pollution and the Grassy Narrows Fight for Justice

1 In conversation with the author.
2 Anastasia Shkilnyk, *A Poison Stronger than Love: the Destruction of an Ojibwa Community* (New Haven: Yale University Press, 1985).
3 W. Eugene Smith and Alison M. Smith, *Minamata* (New York: Holt, Rinehart, Winston, 1975), 33.
4 Julian Cribb citing the report of journalist Eugene Smith in *Earth Detox: How and Why We Must Clean Up Our Planet* (Cambridge: Cambridge University Press, 2021), 2.
5 Araki McAlpine, "Minamata Disease: An Unusual Neurological Disorder Caused by Contaminated Fish," *Lancet* 2, no. 7047 (20 September 1958): 629–31, doi: 10.1016/s0140-6736(58)90348-9.
6 Hansard debates, 26 May 1965.

7 See, for example, comments of Hon. FS Miller in Ontario, Legislative Assembly, *Hansard*, 31st Leg, 3rd Sess (8 November 1979).
8 Letter from Ontario negotiator Robert Burgar to Chief Arnold Pelly dated 14 July 1981.
9 "Fishing for Fun and Death at Grassy Narrows," CBC's *The Fifth Estate*, air date 23 March 1976.
10 "Grassy Narrows First Nations Chief Hails More Funding for Mercury Treatment Centre," Canadian Press, 6 December 2020, www.theglobeandmail.com/canada /article-grassy-narrows-first-nations-chief-hails-more-funding-for-mercury-2/.
11 Robert J. Sharpe, *Islington and Grassy Narrows Bands PreLitigation Study: Final Report* (Toronto: July 1984).
12 "Indecent Delay," *Globe & Mail* editorial, 31 December 1984.
13 Letters in the author's personal files.

3 The Aboriginal Peoples Constitutional Conferences

1 *Dancing Around the Table*, National Film Board of Canada, Dir. Maurice Bulbalian, 1987.
2 *Dancing Around the Table*.
3 Anne Bonds and Joshua Inwood, "Beyond White Privilege: Geographies of White Supremacy and Settler Colonialism," *Progress in Human Geography* 40, no. 6 (2016).
4 Devin Shaw, "We Settlers Face a Choice: Decolonization or White Supremacy," *AnthroDendum*, 28 February 2019. https://anthrodendum.org/2019/02/28 /we-settlers-face-a-choice-decolonization-or-white-supremacy/.
5 *Dancing Around the Table*.
6 Ibid.
7 *R. v. Sparrow*, [1990] 1 S.C.R. 1075 at 1103.
8 April Youpee-Roll, "Just Making It Up: On Justice Scalia, Indian Law, and the Supreme Court's Future," *The Missoula News*, 18 February 2016, http:// missoulanews.bigskypress.com/missoula/just-making-it-up/Content?oid=2688497.
9 Ibid.

4 Paradise Threatened: The Innu of Labrador Fight for Their Homeland – Nitassinan

1 José Mailhot, *The People of Sheshatshit: In the Land of the Innu* (Newfoundland: ISER Books, 1997), 166.
2 Nympha Byrne and Camille Foulliard, eds., *It's Like the Legend: Innu Women's Voices* (Toronto: Women's Press, 2000).
3 Georg Henriksen, *I Dreamed the Animals: Kaniuekutat, the Life of an Innu Hunter* (New York: Berghahn Books, 2009), 17.
4 Testimony of Gregory Andrew, Royal Commission on Aboriginal Peoples (18 June 1992), Transcript at 167, https://data2.archives.ca/rcap/pdf/rcap -260.pdf.
5 Byrne and Foulliard, eds., *It's Like the Legend*.
6 Ibid.
7 From the author's personal files.
8 Copy of testimony in the author's personal files.

9 Copy of testimony in the author's personal files.
10 Copy of testimony in the author's personal files.
11 *Regina v. Ashini* (1989) C.N.L.R., 119.
12 Copy of the statement in the author's personal files.
13 From the author's personal files.
14 *The Labradorian*, 11 October 1988, 2.
15 *Evening Telegram*, 29 April 1989, 34.
16 *Globe & Mail* editorial, 25 April 1989, A5.
17 Peter Armitage, *Homeland or Wasteland? Contemporary Land Use and Occupancy Among the Innu of Utshimassit and Sheshatshit and the Impact of Military Expansion*. Submission to the Federal Environmental Assessment Panel Reviewing Military Flying Activities in Nitassinan. Sheshatshit: Naskapi Montagnais Innu Association, 1990.
18 From the author's personal files.
19 From the author's personal files.
20 Daniel Ashini, "Between a Rock and a Hard Place: Aboriginal Communities and Mining." Keynote speech delivered on behalf of Innu Nation and Mining Watch Canada. Ottawa, 10 September 1999.
21 *Labrador Inuit Association v. Newfoundland (Minister of Environment and Labour)* (1997) 155 Nfld & PEIR 93 at paras. 6–7 (NLCA).
22 Presentation is in the author's personal files.
23 Norah Kielland, *Supporting Aboriginal Participation in Resource Development: The Role of Impact and Benefit Agreements (In Brief)* (Ottawa: Library of Parliament, 2015), https://publications.gc.ca/collections/collection_2016/bdp-lop/eb/YM32-5-2015-29-eng.pdf.
24 Kyle Bakx, "First Nation Can Veto Proposed BC Coal Mine as Part of Unique Deal with Developer," CBC News, 18 January 2023. www.cbc.ca/news/canada/calgary/bakx-first-nation-coal-veto-developer-1.6717396.
25 Amanda Stephenson, "Indigenous Communities Leading Canada's Clean Energy Boom" *Toronto Star*, 19 March 2023.
26 Tom Flanagan, "Gaining Ground, Losing Ground: First Nations' Community Well-Being in the 21st Century," Fraser Institute, December 2019, www.fraserinstitute.org/sites/default/files/first-nations-community-well-being.pdf.
27 Ibid., 3.

5 The Struggle of the Teme-Augama Anishnabai for Old-Growth Trees and Their Land

1 "Temagami: A Living Title to the Land," episode in documentary series *My Partners, My People* by Great Plains Productions. Global Television, 1992.
2 For a full discussion on the history of logging, see John Vaillant, *The Golden Spruce: A True Story of Myth, Madness and Greed* (Toronto: Random House Canada, 2006).
3 "Temagami: A Living Title to the Land," ibid.
4 Race Corelli, "The 112 Year War," *Maclean's*, 20 November 1989.
5 Vaillant, ibid., 41.
6 From the author's personal files.
7 *Bear Island Foundation v. Ontario* (1989) 70 O.R. (2d) 574 (HCJ).
8 Copy of the evidence in the author's personal files.

9 Karin Larsen, "Fairy Creek Protest on Vancouver Island Now Considered Largest Act of Civil Disobedience in Canadian History," CBC (British Columbia), 9 September 2021, www.cbc.ca/news/canada/british-columbia/fairy-creek-protest-largest-act-of-civil-disobedience-1.6168210.
10 "Temagami Logging Road Halted as Ontario Awaits Court Ruling," *Toronto Star*, 20 October 1989, A15.
11 *Ontario (Attorney-General) v. Bear Island Foundation* (1989) 70 O.R. (2d) 758 (HCJ).
12 Ibid.
13 *R v. Potts* (28 November 1990) (ON CJ Prov Div) unreported, copy in the author's personal files.
14 Copy of the evidence in the author's personal files.
15 *R v. Potts*, ibid.
16 Ibid.
17 Ibid.
18 *R v. Drainville* (1990) 5 CR (4th) 38 at 60 (ON CJ Prov Div).
19 Ibid.
20 *Ontario (Attorney General) v. Bear Island Foundation* [1991] 2 SCR 570.
21 Gary Potts in "Temagami: A Living Title to the Land," ibid.

6 The Struggle for Healing Among Mushuau Innu of Labrador

1 Walter Rockwood quoted by Elisabeth Thorring Dalsbo, *We Were Told We Were Going to Live in Houses: Relocation and Housing of the Mushuau Innu of Natuashsish from 1948 to 2002*, master's thesis, University of Tromso, 2010.
2 Author's personal files.
3 *Gathering Voices* Inquiry Report by the Innu Nation, 1995.
4 Michael Valpy, "How About a Cooling-off Period for Davis Inlet?" *Globe and Mail*, 7 September 1994.
5 *Gathering Voices*.
6 Constance Backhouse and Donald McRae, "Report to the Canadian Human Rights Commission on the Treatment of the Innu of Labrador by the Government of Canada," (26 March 2002), Faculty of Law, U of T, 33, https://caid.ca/InnuRepHRC2002.pdf.
7 Thorring Dalsbo, *We Were Told We Were Going to Live in Houses*, 43.
8 From the author's personal files.
9 www.inniuna.ca/.

7 The Road Home: The Innu of Labrador and Modern Treaty Negotiations

1 Copy of the presentation in the author's personal files.
2 Ibid.
3 Ibid.
4 Testimony of Ben Andrew, Royal Commission on Aboriginal Peoples (18 June 1992), https://data2.archives.ca/rcap/pdf/rcap-260.pdf.
5 Canada Royal Commission on Aboriginal Peoples, *Report of the Royal Commission on Aboriginal Peoples. Vol. 3: Gathering Strength* (Montreal: RCAP, 1996), 622–3.

6 Donald W. McRae, "Report of the Complaints of the Innu of Labrador to the Canadian Human Rights Commission," 18 August 1993, copy in the author's personal files.
7 Constance Backhouse and Donald McRae, "Report to the Canadian Human Rights Commission on the Treatment of the Innu of Labrador by the Government of Canada" (26 March 2002), Faculty of Law, U of T, 19, https://caid.ca/InnuRepHRC2002.pdf.
8 "Young Innu Addicts Start Difficult Detox Programs," CBC, 23 November 2000, www.cbc.ca/news/canada/young-innu-addicts-start-difficult-detox-programs-1.223161. "Innu Children Use Solvents to Escape Their Reality in 2000" is a CBC investigative documentary on the topic. It can be viewed online at: www.cbc.ca/player/play/1769538608.
9 Backhouse and McRae, "Report to the Canadian Human Rights Commission," 32.
10 Celeste McKay and David McRae, "Follow-up Report to the Canadian Human Rights Commission on the Human Rights of the Innu of Labrador" (9 August 2021), Ottawa, CHRC, www.chrc-ccdp.gc.ca/sites/default/files/2021-08/2766704-CHRC%20Innu%20Follow-up%20Report%202020-21.pdf.
11 The BC Treaty Commission makes information pertaining to modern Treaties available on its website: https://bctreaty.ca/treaties-and-agreements/modern-treaties/.
12 Royal Commission on Aboriginal Peoples, session held in Sheshatshiu, Labrador, 18 June 1992.

8 Groundbreaking Blueprints for Reconciliation with Indigenous Peoples and Nations

1 Canada Royal Commission on Aboriginal Peoples, *Report of the Royal Commission on Aboriginal Peoples*. Vol. 2: *Restructuring the Relationship* (Montreal: RCAP, 1996), 995.
2 Royal Commission on Aboriginal Peoples, ibid., 214.
3 Royal Commission on Aboriginal Peoples, ibid., 304.
4 The full Royal Commission on Aboriginal Peoples Report is available online in five volumes: www.bac-lac.gc.ca/eng/discover/aboriginal-heritage/royal-commission-aboriginal-peoples/Pages/final-report.aspx. Library and Archives Canada also manages a database with all of the testimony, submissions, research papers, and reports prepared and submitted to RCAP during the commission, which can be searched online: www.bac-lac.gc.ca/eng/discover/aboriginal-heritage/royal-commission-aboriginal-peoples/Pages/introduction.aspx.
5 Yellowhead Institute, "Calls to Action Accountability: A 2022 Status Update on Reconciliation," https://yellowheadinstitute.org/trc/.
6 *Reclaiming Power and Place: The Final Report of the National Inquiry into Missing and Murdered Indigenous Women and Girls*, Volume 1a, 7.
7 *Reclaiming Power and Place*, 231.

9 Doing Our Part for Reconciliation with HEART

1 Eve Tuck and K. Wayne Wang, "Decolonization Is Not a Metaphor," *Decolonization: Indigeneity, Education and Society* 1, no. 1 (2012): 1–40.

2 Ibid.
3 Nicole Winfield, "Indigenous Leaders Hope Vatican's Repudiation of Oppressive Colonial Concepts Leads to Real Change," CBC, 30 March 2023, www.cbc.ca/news/canada/vatican-reject-discovery-doctrine-indigenous-demands-1.6795728.
4 *United Nations Declaration on the Rights of Indigenous Peoples Act*, SC 2021, c.
5 UN General Assembly, *United Nations Declaration on the Rights of Indigenous Peoples*: resolution adopted by the General Assembly, 13 September 2007, A/RES/61/295, www.ohchr.org/en/indigenous-peoples/un-declaration-rights-indigenous-peoples.
6 Statistics Canada, "Aboriginal Peoples in Canada: Key Results from the 2016 Census," *The Daily*, 25 October 2017, https://www150.statcan.gc.ca/n1/en/daily-quotidien/171025/dq171025a-eng.pdf?st=JjrqNDr9.
7 Statistics Canada, "First Nations People, Métis, and Inuit in Canada," 21 September 2022, https://www150.statcan.gc.ca/n1/pub/11-627-m/11-627-m2022057-eng.htm. Though note that census statistics are notoriously inaccurate for Indigenous peoples living in Canada; see James Saku, "Aboriginal Census Data in Canada: A Research Note," *Canadian Journal of Native Studies* 14, no. 2 (1999): 365–79.
8 See Ministry of Forests, Lands & Natural Resources, *Crown Land: Indicators and Statistics Report*, Victoria, 2011, https://www2.gov.bc.ca/assets/gov/farming-natural-resources-and-industry/natural-resource-use/land-water-use/crown-land/crown_land_indicators__statistics_report.pdf; Alberta, *Alberta's Crown Land Vision: Our Rich, Natural Heritage*, Edmonton, 2020, www.alberta.ca/alberta-crown-land-vision.aspx; "Public Lands," Manitoba Wildlands, 30 May 2014, http://manitobawildlands.org/lands.htm; "Crown Land," Government of Ontario, 8 December 2023, www.ontario.ca/page/crown-land.; "Crown Land Management," Government of Ontario, 3 March 2023, www.ontario.ca/page/crown-land-management; "Crown Land in Nova Scotia," Nova Scotia, https://novascotia.ca/natr/land/; "Public Lands," Prince Edward Island, 10 December 2019, www.princeedwardisland.ca/en/information/environment-water-and-climate-change/public-lands; Department of Fisheries and Land Resources, "Crown Lands Information, Resources and Tips," Newfoundland Labrador, June 2019, www.gov.nl.ca/ffa/files/lands-forms-pdf-crown-lands-information-resources-tips.pdf.
9 VP Neimans, *Crown Land*, Canadian Encyclopedia, 2011, www.thecanadianencyclopedia.ca/en/article/crown-land#:~:text=Crown%20land%20is%20the%20term,48%25%20is%20provincial%20crown%20land.
10 "Engagement for a New Public Lands Act Has Begun," Yukon Government, 2 March 2022, https://yukon.ca/en/news/engagement-new-public-lands-act-has-begun.
11 Eva Aariak, "The Next Step in Nunavut's Journey," *Nunatsiaq News*, 8 November 2010, https://nunatsiaq.com/stories/article/98789_the_next_step_in_nunavuts_journey/.
12 Neimans, *Crown Land*, ibid.
13 Claire Hennig, "Crown Land to be Returned to Squamish Nation, Including World-Class Rock Climbing Area," CBC News, 28 October 2019, www.cbc.ca/news/canada/british-columbia/land-transfer-murrin-park-climbing-1.5337627.
14 *Ktunaxa Nation v. British Columbia (Forests, Lands and Natural Resource Operations)* (2017) SCC 54 at para. 114.

15 Total spending from Indigenous Services Canada for 2018–19 is from Indigenous Services Canada, *Departmental Results Report 2018–19*, Ottawa, 2019, https://sac-isc.gc.ca/eng/1562156065850/1562156080548, with expenses for health removed for comparison as health spending up until 2018–19 had been housed in other departments (e.g. Health Canada); total spending from Crown-Indigenous Relations and Northern Affairs Canada of 2018–19 is from Crown-Indigenous Relations and Northern Affairs Canada, *Departmental Results Report 2018–19*, Ottawa, 2019, www.rcaanc-cirnac.gc.ca/eng/1562152041744/1562152062785; total program spending for Government of Canada is from Department of Finance Canada, *Annual Financial Report of the Government of Canada Fiscal Year 2018–2019*, www.canada.ca/en/department-finance/services/publications/annual-financial-report/2019/report.html.
16 Tom Flanagan, "Promise and Performance: Recent Trends in Government Expenditures on Indigenous Peoples," Fraser Institute, 2021, 2, www.fraserinstitute.org/sites/default/files/recent-trends-in-government-expenditures-on-indigenous-peoples.pdf.
17 Flanagan, ibid., i.
18 Flanagan, "Gaining Ground, Losing Ground."
19 Hayden King and Shiri Pasternak, "Canada's Emerging Indigenous Rights Framework: A Critical Analysis," Yellowhead Institute, 2018, https://yellowheadinstitute.org/wp-content/uploads/2018/06/yi-rights-report-june-2018-final-5.4.pdf.
20 Brandi Morin, "It's Time to End the Genocide of Indigenous Women," *Toronto Star*, 8 December 2022.

Index

Aboriginal rights, 14; as barriers to profit, 3, 68–9, 117–18; Canada's insistence on denying/infringing, 34, 84, 86–7, 137–8, 148–9; demands to consider, 4, 25, 126, 174, 197; as inherent/pre-existing colonization, 9, 68, 71, 86, 126, 171–2; section 35 and, 70, 73, 76–8, 84–6, 222; self-government and, 28–9, 32, 62, 83, 174; settler support for, 17, 27, 62, 126, 185; Treaty negotiations and, 12, 171–2, 177, 182; viewed as afterthoughts, 34, 224

Aboriginal title, 122–3; Canada's extinguishing of, 33, 81, 171–2, 177; court cases on, 8–9, 111, 134–43, 147; living, 89, 92, 105, 108–11, 129, 171–2; section 35 and, 73, 84–6; settler colonial recognizing of, 21, 54, 109–13, 144–8, 195, 214; unceded, 13–14, 71, 134–6, 171–2

Agreements in Principle (AIPs), concept of, 91; Dene-Métis, 21–2, 30, 32–3; Innu, 91, 128–9, 175, 181–2, 211; Teme-Augama, 149

Alberta, 212, 225; author's early life in, xx–xxii; Indian Chiefs of, 11, 65; pipelines through, 24, 27; provincial government representatives, 74, 76; Treaties covering, 6

alcohol, abuse, 95, 158–9, 163; community regulation of, 161, 175–6

Allmand, Warren, 22, 185

Andrew, Apetet (Ben), 93, 98–9, 115, 170

Andrew, Gregory, 95

Andrew, Maniaten, 107–10

Anglican church, 17–18, 22, 148, 200

Anishinaabe, 8, 216; *see also* Teme-Augama Anishnabai

Arctic Gas consortium, bid to build pipeline, 1, 18, 22; NEB hearings on, 4, 16, 19, 22–3

Armitage, Peter, 103, 113, 171

Asch, Michael, 25–6

Ashini, Jodie, 88–9, 98, 129

Ashini, Jolene, 88–9, 98, 129

Ashini, Tanien (Daniel), 112, 117–20, 168; arrest and trial, 103–4, 106,

109–11; author friendship/ visits with, 88–9, 105, 129, 151; leadership/negotiation involvement, 98, 117–20
Assembly of First Nations, 130, 168; author's work with, 71, 82–3, 205–6; First Ministers conference involvement, 71–4, 76; NIB history and leadership of, 11, 15, 67, 83, 185
assimilation, Indigenous, 78, 112, 123; constitutional Aboriginal rights versus, 65, 71, 73–4; government policies of, 7–12, 49, 68, 80, 204; impacts of attempted, 50, 87, 108, 205; overall institutional goals of, xix, xxv, 13, 39, 74, 76, 85; via reconciliation/ self-government, xix–xx 169–70, 203–5
Audette, Michele, 196
Australia, xix 79, 122

Backhouse, Constance, 163, 166
Ball Lake Lodge, 37, 40
Baines, Dave, 122–3
Beatty, Perrin, 100
Becker, Walter, 131
Bella Coola Nation, 191
Bennett, Bill, 73–4
Berger Inquiry, xiv, 11, 28; Dene participation in, 2–3, 17, 21; report/recommendations of, 16, 23–4, 191
Bonds, Anne ("Beyond White Privilege"), 79
Bourque, Jim, 28–9
Britain, 69, 139; assumptions of power over Indigenous land, 8–9, 77–8, 93, 168; imperialism of, 12–13, 129; protests against, 67–8, 100; Treaty obligations to Indigenous peoples, 67–8; trespassing on Indigenous land and, 68, 95, 104, 108, 112, 168
British Columbia, 160, 212, 224; anti-logging protests in, 133, 138; Indigenous historical presence in, 72, 81, 181; Indigenous rights mobilizing in, 65–8, 84–6, 133; legislation to disregard Indigenous consent, xxiv, 81, 215–16; premiers, 73, 75–6; resource extraction in, 81, 122–3, 132–3, 214–15; Treaties covering, 6, 13, 180; *see also Calder* case
British North America Act, section 91.24, *see* section 91.24
Brownstone, Mayer, 25–6
Buchanan, Judd, 15, 21–2
Building Canada Act, xxiv, 129

Calder case, x, 13, 33, 52, 172
Campbell, Alexander, 20–1
Canada, assimilationist policies, 7–12, 49, 68, 80, 204; energy consumption of, 1, 3, 20; Impact Benefit Agreements across, 122–3, 213–15; infringement on Indigenous rights, 34, 84, 86–7, 137–8, 148–9; NATO, experimental flight offers to, 97–8, 107, 112, 117; paternalism in, *see* paternalism; reconciliation, notions of, 35, 60, 85–7, 138, 199–203; settler colonialism in, xix, 75–9, 203–4, 217–19, 225; Supreme Court of, *see* Supreme Court of Canada; in Treaty negotiations, *see* modern Treaty negotiations
Canadian Arctic Resources Committee (CARC), 24–5
Canadian Human Rights Commission, Innu appeals to, 158, 177, 179; report findings/ recommendations, 163, 166, 174, 178–80, 182
Cardinal, Harold (*The Unjust Society*), 11–12, 186, 202
caribou hunting, 5; experiences with, 93, 105–6, 151–3; Innu loss of, 94, 98, 164; sacredness/deep knowledge of, 7, 93, 154, 199; settler interference with, 154, 157

Index | 237

Carney, Mark, xxv, 129
Charlottetown Accord, 82–3, 190, 205
Charter of Rights and Freedoms, 69–70, 174, 197
children, Indigenous, xvii, 38, 98; community care of, 6–7, 31, 40, 164–6, 181; demographics, 220–1; harm to, 118, 158, 162, 166, 176–7; memories of, 92, 107–9, 130; mercury poisoning of, 41–4; recognizing rights of, 177, 205, 220, 222; in residential schools, 7, 35, 94–5
child welfare/foster care system, xxviv 166, 221
Chisso Corporation, 41–2
Chrétien, Jean, 1–2, 10
Christians, activism of, 17–18
churches, Anglican, 17–18, 22, 148, 200; apologies from, 34–5, 200, 206; Catholic, 16–17, 22, 93–4, 155–7, 164, 172; Dene/Indigenous support from, 16–17, 22, 34–5, 198; participation in hearings, 26–7; Project North, 17–18, 23, 102; task force on, *see* Task Force on Churches and Corporate Responsibility; United, xiv, 17–18, 200
Citizens for Public Justice (CPJ), xxii–xxiii
Clark, Joe, 66, 170
clean energy, *see* renewable resources
Cockburn, Bruce, 103, 133
colour of right defence, in Innu trial, 105, 108, 110, 113; moral right versus, 144, 147–8; in Teme-Augama trial, 143–7
Committee for Justice and Liberty (CJL) Foundation, author involvement with, xxii, 3, 18; calls for (respecting) pipeline moratorium, 4, 16–17, 19, 23–7; Just Energy Policy proposal, 4, 16, 18–20; NEB pipeline hearing participation, 4, 24–7; *see also* Citizens for Public Justice
Commoner, Barry (*Poverty of Power*), 3
Community Well-Being (CWB) index 124–5, 220
comprehensive claims policy (Canada), 33, 171–2
conservation, environmental, 62, 133, 212; lack of, 1, 132; policies to aid in, 4, 16, 26, 84, 150
Constitution Act, Aboriginal rights negotiations for, 28–9, 51, 84–5; Charlottetown/Meech Lake amendments to, 82–3, 191, 205; entrenching Indigenous rights and Treaties in, 10, 12, 40, 65–9, 83, 190; federal failure of responsibilities under, 172, 175, 182, 196–7; (re)patriation of, 28, 51, 65–70, 172, 185, 204; section 35, *see* section 35; section 91.24, *see* section 91.24
Constitutional Conferences: author involvement in, 67, 69–71, 77, 83; development of, 66–71; differing Indigenous/provincial viewpoints in, 71–6, 81, 86, 224; Indigenous discussions on entrenching rights amid, 67–9, 71, 75, 78, 185; premier/provincial dismissiveness/racism during, 15, 69, 72–8, 86–7, 190; watered-down Indigenous rights proposed in, 68–71, 77–8, 81, 222–3; *see also* harmonization
Constitution Express, 65–7
Cree Nation, 109, 134, 225; author experiences with, xix, xxvi, 106; leadership of, 11, 82
Crombie, David, 52, 55
Crowe, Marshall, 18–19, 22, 34
Crown-Indigenous Relations and Northern Affairs Canada (CIRNAC), 52, 218; need to dismantle, 197, 208, 217, 222–3
Crown land, provincial percentages of, 212, 214; return to Indigenous nations, 60, 201, 209–14, 216

Daschuk, James (*Clearing the Plains*), 79
Da Silva, Judy, 43, 48, 57
Davis, Bill, 45, 73
Davis Inlet, author experiences in, 90–1, 93; gas sniffing children in, 158, 162, 176; forced Innu relocation/poor living conditions in, 156–9, 161–5; Innu experiences/memories of, 92–3, 154–7, 165; mining/colonial settlement near, 117–18, 155–7; mobilizing against colonial/industrial encroachment, 99, 159–62; status benefit negotiations for Innu of, 175–6
decolonization, 217; Indigenous versus settler understandings of, 16, 201–4; Penner/RCAP reports as guides to, 184, 189, 204; steps toward reconciliation and, 34, 77, 202–3
Delgamuukw v. British Columbia, 81, 86
Dene Declaration, 14–16, 21–2, 32–3
Dene Nation, xvii, 224; Agreements in Principle (AIPs), 21–2, 30, 32–3; author experiences with, 4, 16, 27–8, 35, 45, 198, 225; Elders, 2, 21, 30–1; European encroachment on, 5–7, 184; lands, relations with, 1, 5–7, 21, 25–6, 29–31, 96; leadership/Elders, 2, 5, 14–16, 21, 31; mobilizing against pipelines, 1–5, 16–18, 24–8, 204; public government proposal, 28–33; self-determination of, 6–7, 14–16, 26, 191; Treaty negotiations with, 14, 21, 24, 33; *see also* Dene Declaration; Denendeh
Denendeh, author experiences in, 5–6, 14; Indigenous mobilizing against colonial laws, 13–14, 16; proposed pipeline through, 1, 6; public government proposal for, 28–30, 33
Department of Indian and Northern Affairs, *see* Indian Affairs

Department of National Defence (DND), illegal CFB/NATO activity on/over Innu land, 96–8, 102, 112, 115–17; Innu mobilizing/requesting injunction against, 99–101, 103, 108–15
Diamond Fields, 117–18
Diefenbaker, John, 3, 53
dismantling settler colonialism, concept/elements of, xix–xx, 201, 208, 217–26; discussing strategies for, 16, 86, 197–8, 205; settler resistance to, 75–6, 203–4, 217–19; *see also* Crown-Indigenous Relations and Northern Affairs Canada; Indigenous Services Canada; Land Back
Doctrine of Discovery, xxv, 193, 226; renouncing versus repudiation of, 206–7
Douglas, Tommy, 23
Drainville, Dennis, 142, 144, 147–8

Earth, the, xxvi, 11, 82; Indigenous versus European views of, xx, 30, 49, 63
Earthroots (formerly Temagami Wilderness Society), 133–4, 150
economic growth, focus on, 4, 17, 20, 138
ecosystems, 131; destruction for profit, 3, 43, 135, 138; protecting, 3–4, 122, 212
education, colonial approach to, 165–6, 173–4; funding for Indigenous, 57, 186; Indigenous-led, 6, 165, 175, 181; settler systems of, 13, 53, 94–6; studies/reports on, 9, 53, 59, 124–5, 220; *see also* residential schools
Elders, 178–9; councils of, 161, 188; Dene, 2, 21, 30–1; Grassy Narrows, 38, 47, 51–2; Innu, 92–3, 96–8, 105–8, 126, 153; residential school experiences, xxi; teachings of, xxiv, 21, 31, 38, 165, 216; Teme-Augama, 131, 141–3; on

Treaty signing/governance, 14, 21, 30–1, 66, 171
energy industry, 4, 26; renewable, 20, 25, 123; government policy influence of, 1–3, 18–20; impacts of, 17, 23–4, 127; natural gas, 19–20, 23, 214; *see also* Just Energy Policy; National Energy Board
environmental assessments, 216; contravening process of, 113, 133; economic interests prioritized in, 115–17, 120; Innu negotiations for, 113, 118–20, 181
Erasmus, Georges (*Hot'A! Enough!*), xvii, 193; AFN leadership, 67, 76, 81; author experiences with, xvii, 4–5, 67, 198, 226; Dene Declaration/public governance work, 15, 28–9, 81; facing government dismissiveness, 15, 22, 24; as NIB president, 7, 15, 67
Erikson, Kai, 47–50
Extractive Sector Transparency Measures Act, 125
Exxon, 1, 37

Federal Court of Appeal, 8, 19, 28
Federal Environmental Assessment Review Office (FEARO), 115–16; *see also* environmental assessments
fee simple title, 10, 33
First Ministers conferences, 20, 69–74; *see also* Constitutional Conferences
First Nations Financial Transparency Act, 123–4
fish as relations, 21
Fisher, Douglas Mason, 42–3
fishing, author experiences of, 89–90, 93; commercial exploitation of, 39, 95, 119–20; Indigenous significance of, 43, 46–7, 50, 59, 93, 213; mercury/industrial impacts on, 40–3, 137; resorts, 37, 40; traditional rights to, 40, 83–6; Treaties covering, 121, 180–1
Flanagan, Tom, 123–5, 219

Fobister, Philip, 40
Fobister, Simon, 44–5, 48, 63
Fobister, Steve, 62–3
fossil fuel industry, *see* energy industry
foster care, children in, 166, 221
Fournier, Robert, 142; Chief Potts judgment, 143–7; Reverend Drainville judgment, 142, 144, 147–8
Fowler, Robert, 112, 114

Gathering Voices session/report, 92–3, 158, 164
Goose Bay, xvii, 117–18; DND/NATO activity on/over unceded Innu land, 96–8, 107–9, 111–14; Innu runway protests at, 99–106, 108
Grassy Narrows, 184, 225; compensation package for, 36–7, 50–2, 54, 56–7; forced relocation of, 39–40, 45, 49, 154; government refusal to discuss land base, 45–8, 50–55, 57–9, 195, 213; Great Lakes/Reed Paper litigation/settlement, 37, 49, 52–6, 59; mediation/negotiations with province, 44–7, 51–3, 56, 60–4; Ojibway history/lifeways, 36–40, 49–51, 59, 216; provincial lack of responsibility for harm, 42–4, 46–7, 49–51, 57–8; Supreme Court of Ontario lawsuit, 44, 53, 56
Grassy Narrows Traditional Land Use Area (GNTLUA), community mobilizing to control, 51–4, 56–61, 64; government unwillingness to co-manage, 46–7, 59–64, 204; Ojibway importance of land base, 47, 53–6, 58–60, 204; pollution of English-Wabigoon River system, 36–7, 40, 49, 204–5, 213–14; provincial lack of river clean-up/stewardship, 42–4, 57–60, 63–4; Royal Commission on the Northern Environment recommendations, 45–6, 53, 59, 61

Great Lakes Paper, Grassy Narrows negotiations with, 45, 52–4, 59; lack of accountability for harm, 37, 45–6, 54–5, 61; Reed Paper selling plant to, 37, 44
Green, Bonnie, 26–7
Gull Island, 126, 128–9
Gwich'in people, 2, 33
Gzowski, Peter (CBC *Morningside*), 106–7

Hall, Emmett (*Living and Learning*), 13, 52–5
harmonization, of constitutional powers, 82, 182–3, 189, 205, 210; of laws/jurisdiction, 75, 77, 175, 180, 190; of rights, 73–7, 84–6, 177
Harper, Elijah, 82, 170
Harper, Stephen, 98–9
Hart, Eugene, 178
Hawthorn Report, 9–10
Henriksen, Georg (*I Dreamed the Animals*), 94
Hogg, Peter, 8
Honour of the Crown, 55, 86, 177, 197
housing, Indigenous, xvi, 6, 174; failure to provide adequate, xxiii, 40, 91, 124–5, 156–7, 220–1; fire deaths in, 158, 160; proposals/ recommendations for, xxiii, 46, 163, 166; non-Indigenous versus, 10, 107, 157
Hudson's Bay Company, 39, 154–5
hunting, importance of, 46–7, 51, 93–6, 153–4, 213; industrial/ colonial impacts on, 112, 131, 137, 155–7; memories/experiences of, 105–8, 151, 153–4; Treaties/ agreements covering, 40, 121, 153–4, 195; *see also* fishing; trapping
Hydro Quebec (HQ), Churchill River projects, 97, 126–9, 173

Igloliorte, James, 103–4, 142, 146–7, 166; on colour of right defence, 110–11, 113

Impact Benefit Agreements (IBAs), xxvii, 192, 211; across Canada, 122–3, 213–15; community demand for, 125–6, 213–15; for Lower Churchill/Nalcor, 124, 127–8; Innu negotiations with Inco on, 118–22, 124; state clawbacks on, 124–5, 178, 180, 183
Indian Act, xxii, 110, 210; amendments to, 8–9, 185, 189; control over Indigenous people/land, 8, 54, 208; denial of provisions for Innu under, 96, 182; discriminatory provisions in, 12–13, 185; federal powers under, 8, 77–8, 193; Indigenous poverty requests to register, 134, 174, 176–7, 182; prohibiting Indigenous legal/political mobilizing, xxii, 8–9; revocation of, 10–12, 68; White Paper versus, 10
Indian Affairs (Department of), 99; control of communities via, 10, 189; dismissiveness/racism of, 15, 21–2; Indigenous criticisms of, 12, 134; involvement in land/ governance negotiations, 52, 55, 162, 175–6
Indian Brotherhood, leadership of, 15, 22, 67; mobilizing/protesting by, 13–14, 22, 68; National, 11, 67–8; NWT, 7, 15, 22, 67
Indigenous peoples, attempts to assimilate, *see* assimilation, Indigenous; breaching/failing fiduciary obligations to, 68, 95–6, 111, 149, 156, 159, 177–82; children, *see* children, Indigenous; as "Citizens Plus," 9–12; as co-partners, xxviv–xxv 59–62; demographics, 124–5, 210, 212, 220–1; Elders, *see* Elders; laws of, *see* law, Indigenous; nation-to-nation relationships with, xxviv–xxv, xxvii, 71, 73, 174, 195; nature/the land, relationality

with, 2–3, 17, 30, 37–8, 60; paternalism toward, 12–13, 174, 186, 194, 219; reconciliation *with* versus *to*, 35, 63–4, 85, 167, 203, 225–6; self-governance, *see* self-governance, Indigenous; stereotypes/assumptions about, xxvi, 6, 69, 78–9, 84, 95, 187

Indigenous Services Canada (ISC), 124; need to dismantle, 197, 208, 217, 222–3

infant mortality rates, Indigenous, 163–4, 220–1

Innes, Larry, xxviii 151, 173

Innu of Labrador, Agreements in Principle (AIPs), 91, 128–9; author experiences with, xvii–xix, xxviii 88–91, 99–102, 110, 126–7; colonial government/industrial impacts on, 91, 94–8, 100–1, 106, 115–18; denial of services to, 95–6, 104; displacement/relocation of, 91, 96–7; Goose Bay protests/mobilizing, 89, 96–7, 99–110, 113–15; history/origin story of, 89–93; government dismissal/criminalization of, 101–4, 112–17; impoverishment/suicide/substance use, 95; Mushuau, *see* Mushuau Innu; show trial against, 103–10; traditional/unceded territory, living title of, 91–7, 103–11, 171–2; women, 88–9, 99–102, 105–6, 113; *see also* Natuashish; Nitassinan; Sheshatshiu; Tshash Petapan; Upper Churchill hydro project

Innu Nation, 66, 158; Agreements in Principle (AIPs), 91, 128–9, 175, 181–2, 211; archaeological work, 89; Elders, 92–3, 96–8, 105–8, 126, 153; healing strategy round table work, 164–6; IBA negotiations, 118–24, 126–9, 172–3; land claims, 112–13, 126, 171–2, 175; land use and occupancy study, 113, 171; leadership of, 88–9, 93–4, 97–9, 161, 175; modern Treaties of, 91, 94, 97, 126–8, 172–3; *see also* Upper Churchill hydro project

institutions, settler colonial, aim of Indigenous assimilation, xix, xxv, 80, 82; anti-Indigenous discrimination in, 158, 160, 201, 221; capitalist basis of, 17, 22, 200; historical establishment of, xvii, 80, 187; Indigenous governance versus, 27, 75, 78, 137, 191, 218; need to dismantle, 16, 75–6, 86, 197–8, 203–4, 225–6

Interprovincial Pipe Line Company, 24, 26–7

Inuit, asserting inherent constitutional rights, 30, 68–70, 72–3, 78, 83; demographics, 210, 212, 220–1; modern Treaty signing, 91; resource extractions, struggles against, 2, 118–20; settler colonial relocation/violence facing, 91, 155, 196; territorial occupation/safeguarding, 5, 89, 91, 212

invaders, *see* settlers

Inwood, Joshua ("Beyond White Privilege"), 79

Just Energy Policy, 4, 16, 18, 20

Kaniuekutat, 93–4
King, Hayden, 222–3
Kleer, Nancy, xxvii, xxviii, 173
Ktunaxa Nation, 215–16

Labrador, 153; European/colonial control over, 91–5, 104–5, 109, 161, 212; historical geography/settlement of, 89–91, 107, 129, 156; Happy Valley-Goose Bay, *see* Goose Bay; hunting/trapping in, 151–3, 156, 164; Innu, *see* Innu of Labrador; military activity on/over, 96–8, 102, 107, 112, 115–17; modern Treaty negotiations in, 13, 91, 172–5, 178–81; northern, 90,

96, 151, 155; resource extraction in, 97, 126–9
land, 202, 224; Aboriginal right to, 85–6, 135–7, 153–7; claims, *see* land claims; as commodity/property, xxii, 7, 111, 134–6, 146, 133; Crown, *see* Crown land; Dene conceptions/use of, 5, 7, 21, 30–1; Innu conceptions/use of, 96, 106–11, 119, 153–7, 165; Ojibway conceptions/use of, 38, 45–7, 58–9; return, *see* Land Back; sacredness of, 7, 23, 47, 92, 96, 210; sharing of, xxii, 50, 60–1, 96, 136, 213–14; stewardship of, *see* stewardship, land; studies, 58–9; Teme-Augama conceptions/use of, 130–2, 135–7, 144–5; unceded, 13–14, 96, 106, 171–2
Land Back, agreement examples, 213–16; movement, 210–11; as part of Royal Proclamation/RCAP recommendations, 208–11, 214; reconciliation and, 63, 197, 200–1, 210; return of Crown, 211–14, 216
land claims, 2, 14; comprehensive agreements, 4, 33, 171–2; Dene-Métis, 27–8, 32, 204; Innu, 111–13, 126, 171, 175; Teme-Augama, 140, 142, 144; Wet'suwet'en/Gitxsan, 81, 86
law, Indigenous, 88, 214; calls to deepen understanding of, 193, 196–7; historical passage of, 31, 187–8; sacredness of nature/the Earth in, 30–1, 147–8, 212; as separate from settler law, 77, 142, 145, 159, 166, 191; settler infringement on, 161–2, 166, 168, 175–80; supporting right to create/follow, 68, 75–6, 198, 218–29
law, settler-colonial, amendments to conform with UNDRIP, 208, 223–5; colour of right in, *see* colour of right defence; Indigenous rights/title recognition in, 21, 54, 109–13, 144–8, 214; oppressiveness of, 75–6, 80–1, 140–2, 161, 175, 225–6; as separate from Indigenous law, 77, 103–4, 142, 168, 191
Lévesque, René, 72
liberation, concepts of, 4, 201, 203; Indigenous struggles towards, 76, 99, 109–11
"living tree" Treaty relationship, 73, 177, 180
logging, clear-cut, 51, 59, 131–2; disputes over, 8, 47, 58–9, 133–6; harm/displacement from, 39, 58–9, 130–2, 135, 137; old-growth forest, *see* old-growth forests; provincial authorization of, 46–7, 131–3, 137, 141–2, 205; road blockades/protests, 51, 133–4, 138–40; selective, 47, 52, 130–1, 213
Lower Churchill/Nalcor project, 124, 127–8; *see also* Upper Churchill hydro project

Mackenzie (Dehcho) Delta region, 1, 5, 16, 191; Inuvialuit of, 29–30, 33
Mackenzie Valley Pipeline, Dene efforts to halt, 13, 16, 26, 45, 204; hearings on, 4, 11, 19, 22–3; inquiry into, *see* Berger Inquiry
Mailhot, José, 92, 96
Manuel, George, 65, 67
McCullum, Hugh and Carmel (*This Land Is Not For Sale*), 18
McKay, Celeste, 178, 182
McKnight, Bill, 101–2
McMillan, Tom, 115–16
McRae, Donald, CHRC report/follow-up findings, 163, 166, 178; criticism of government (in)actions, 158–9, 174, 182
Mennonites, 18, 104
mercury, minimization of harm and compensation, 42–4, 49–51, 57–8; Ojibway mobilizing against, 44–5, 51–3, 56, 62–4, 213; poisoning/

Minamata disease, 36, 40–3, 56, 62–3; pollution of English-Wabigoon River system, 36–7, 40, 49, 213–14
Mercury Disability Board, 56, 62
Métis Association of the NWT, 24, 29
Métis people, 196; calls for pipeline moratorium, 24–5, 28; constitutional provisions for, 68–70; demographics, 210, 220; First Ministers conferences, 72–3, 78, 83; modern Treaty negotiations, 24, 27; public government proposal, 28–32
Michel, Penote (Ben), 98–9, 103, 106, 110
Miller, Marc, 52, 58
Minamata disease, 40–3, 48, 51, 54
mining, government support for, 20, 95; Impact Benefit Agreement negotiations, 117–20, 122; Indigenous community impacts, 25–6, 137; industry interests, 58–9
Missing and Murdered Indigenous Women and Girls (MMIWG), 172, 203, 225–6; Inquiry report/action plan, xxvii, 184, 196–7, 199–200
Mistenapeo, Mary Georgette, 92–3
modern Treaty negotiations, calls for pipeline moratorium until after, 4, 16–17, 24; Canada's push for unceded land, 13, 33, 70, 180; Dene-Métis, 4, 16, 24, 33; federal policy of only six, 112, 171; Innu, 89–94, 118–21, 161–5, 178, 182–3, 211; lack of honouring Indigenous rights in, 12, 70, 124–5, 168, 203–5; suspended, 33, 149, 161, 173
Moratorium Justice: Energy, the North, and the Native People (McCullum, McCullum, and Olthuis), 18, 23
moratoriums, 100, 124, 140; disregard for, 27–8, 204; pipeline, 2, 4, 16–17, 19, 23–5
Morin, Brandi, 225–6
Mulroney, Brian, 74–6, 82, 86, 115, 192, 204

Munro, John, 189
Mushuau Innu, 164; author experiences with, 90; community policing work versus RCMP, 161–2; healing strategy, 163–5; mining near, 117, 155; modern Treaty negotiations, 175, 178–9; repeated relocation of, 154–7, 163
Musqueam Nation, 84

Naskapi Montagnais Association (NMIA), 170–1
National Energy Board (NEB), Dene/CJL challenging of, 4, 16–20, 24–7, 34; establishment and functioning of, 3, 20, 115, 200; pipeline hearings, 3–4, 18–20, 22–5, 27; support/economic bias for pipelines, 20, 26–8, 34
nation-to-nation relationships, lack of honouring, xxvii, 73; need for affirming, xxviv–xxv 71, 174, 195
NATO governments, Canadian federal/provincial offer to, 97–8, 107, 112, 117; harm from low-level flying experiments, 98, 106, 113; protests against, 97, 100–3, 112–15, 121
Natuashish, 91, 128, 163, 173–4, 181
natural gas, 19–20, 214
natural resources, calls to ensure Indigenous royalties/benefits from, 25, 31, 61, 121–2, 126–7, 218; Constitutional Conference discussions of, 71, 76, 81; returning/reparations for stolen, 200, 204, 208–14; settler focus on exploiting, 4, 33, 50, 119–20; settler stealing of, 81, 106, 133, 206; tensions over co-management of, 19–21, 46–7, 59–64, 120–1, 224; Treaties/agreements sharing entitlements to, 12, 171–2, 178–9, 182–3, 186, 192; *see also* renewable resources
nature, 92; awakening to fragility of, 2, 50; Indigenous living with, 2–3, 17, 30, 37–8, 60

Nault, Robert, 175–6
N'Daki Menan (Teme-Augama territory), 130; Bear Island, 133–5, 143; *nastawgan* (traditional paths), 131, 133–4; old-growth forest defence, 130–1, 133–9, 141–3, 150, 205; Shis-kong-abikong, 131–2; as unceded, 134–6
NDP, xi, 185; Grassy Narrows negotiations with provincial, 61–2; House of Commons fair tax advocacy by, xxiii; support for Indigenous struggles, 23, 42, 70, 140, 142
Nerysoo, Richard, 21
New Democratic Party, *see* NDP
Newfoundland Court of Appeal, 119–20
Nichols, Joshua, 8
nickel mining, struggle against, 117–21, 155
Nimkii Aazhibikong, 216
Nisga'a Nation, 13, 73; *see also* Calder case
Nishnawbe Aski Nation, xxvi, 46, 55
Nitassinan, colonial encroachment on/over, 98, 100, 104; Innu living title to homeland of, 89, 92, 105, 108–11, 129; nickel mining, struggle against, 117–21, 155
Norman Wells pipeline, 24–6, 204
Northwest Territories (NWT), 2, 67; modern Treaties in, 13, 22; NEB hearings in, 24–5, 35; public government proposal for, 28–30, 33; *see also* Denendeh
Nui, John, 178–9
Nui, Mary Ann, 178–9
Nuna, Philomena, 101–2
Nunatsiavut, 91
Nunavut, 30, 32–3, 212
Nunavut Constitutional Forum (NCF), 30, 32

oil and gas industry, 37, 12s5; Berger Inquiry into, 2, 16, 23–4; consortium, 1–2, 16–19;
Indigenous consent versus, 2, 6, 25–6, 214; Just Energy Policy versus, 4, 16, 18–20; NEB hearings/support for, 3, 19, 23–6; Project North versus, 17–18, 23
Ojibway, 44, 58, 134; history/lifeways of Grassy Narrows, 36–40, 49–51, 59, 216
Oka Crisis, 192–3
old-growth forests, destruction of, 132, 135, 137–8, 141–2; Grassy Narrows defence of, 51; logging incursion into, 133; Teme-Augama defence of, 130–1, 133–9, 141–3, 150, 205
Ontario, conservation efforts in, 62, 132–4, 150, 212; Crown land in, 212, 216; English-Wabigoon River system, 36, 40, 48, 57, 205; Indigenous territories in northern, xxvi, 8, 36, 130, 134
Ontario Court of Appeal, 53–4, 134–6
Ontario government, 83; denial of/delayed responsibility for harm, 42–4, 46–7, 57, 136–7; disregard for Indigenous consent, xxv, 47, 59–62, 195; Grassy Narrows mediation/negotiations with, 44–7, 51–3, 56, 60–4; injunction against, 134–41; lack of regulatory oversight, 42–4, 48; logging, licensing/moratorium, 51, 132–7, 140; protection of company interests, 36–7, 44, 48, 61–3, 141, 214; racist attitudes of, 50, 73, 170; refusal to discuss Grassy Narrows land base, 45–8, 50–55, 57–9, 213; Royal Commission on the Northern Environment recommendations, 45–6, 53, 59, 61; Teme-Augama logging resistance versus, 133–6, 142–7, 149–50
Ontario Hydro, 45, 57
own source revenue (OSR), 123, 218; clawbacks, 124–5, 178, 183
Oxfam, 25–6, 110

Pasternak, Shiri, 222–3
paternalism, in government policies, xxvi, 12, 174; institutionalized attitudes of, 186, 194, 219
Paulette Caveat Case, 14
Pelly, Arnold, 36, 48, 63
Peckford, Brian, 76, 107
Penashue, Carolyn, 102
Penashue, Elizabeth/Tshaukuesh (*Nitinikiau Innusi*), 97, 99–101, 103, 110, 153
Penashue, Greg, xvii, 88, 99, 103
Penashue, Mary Ann, 38, 66, 152, 169, 199
Penashue, Matthew, 108–10
Penashue, Peter, 114, 177; author's friendship with, 89, 98; author's legal defence of, 110; protest involvement, 103, 106–7, 162; Tshash Petapen negotiation, 89, 128, 173, 175
Penner Report, 182, 184; guidance for rights harmonization/reconciliation, xxvii, 77, 186; on Indigenous governance, 187–92, 203; lack of implementation of recommendations, 189, 192, 194, 204, 214; process and findings of, 185–7, 189, 196, 206–8
Peters, Frank, 156–7
Peterson, David, 55, 134, 139
Philip, Justice, 136–7, 140
Poker, Thomas, 94, 173
police/policing, Aboriginal community, 160–2, 165, 175, 181–2; monitoring/surveillance/carding, 6, 176, 222; political suppression by, 103–6, 145, 192–3; *see also* RCMP
Potts, Gary, arrest and trial of, 141, 143–7, 150–1; author friendship with, 130, 133–4; chieftaincy, 130, 132–4, 139; clear-cutting protest involvement, 130–1, 133, 136–41, 149–50; Constitutional Conference leadership, 74–5

power, 148; before people, 35, 82, 97; demand for transfer of jurisdictional, 29–30, 120–1, 170, 186; devolution of, 73–5, 165, 189; European versus Ojibway concepts of, 49–50, 76–8, 82, 111, 190–1, 197–203; Indigenous struggles for, 84–5, 125–6, 164, 173, 178–9; unwillingness to share, 58, 69, 72–3, 76–7, 204–5, 210
Privy Council, 8–9, 93
Project North, 17–18, 23, 102
"public convenience and necessity," disputing notions of, 4, 16, 25; granting certificate of, 3, 27

Quebec, 148; focus on constitutional revisions for, 9, 82; Inuit/Innu separation/living conditions in, 91, 93–5; military low-level flying over, 115–16; modern Treaties in, 13, 170; politician racism, 72, 170, 192–3; *see also* Hydro Quebec

racism, settler colonial, in Constitutional Conferences, 15, 73, 82; institutional, xxi, 12, 82, 104, 194; policy-based, xxvi, 207, 222; systemic/societal, 50, 79, 98–9, 201, 205, 225–6
Rae, Bob, 62, 83, 133, 140
Raymond, Clark, 26
RCMP (Royal Canadian Mounted Police), 39, 118; Indigenous standoffs against, 81, 121; Innu risking arrest by, 103–6, 112, 118, 159; *see also* police/policing
reconciliation, 128, 180; authentic, xxvi–xxvii 34, 60, 63–4, 86, 139; decolonization at root of, 34, 77, 202–3; dismantling settler colonialism and, xix–xx, 194–7, 205–9; Indigenous visions of, 58, 64, 91, 167; Penner/RCAP Reports on, 186–8, 192–3, 203; settler notions of, xxv–xxviii 35, 60, 85–7, 138, 199–203; UNDRIP

adoption and, 195, 207–9, 223–4; *with* versus *to*, 35, 63–4, 85, 167, 203, 225–6; *see also* Land Back; Truth and Reconciliation Commission

Red Paper, 11–12, 65

Reed Paper, government protection of, 36–7, 44–5, 48, 54–6, 61; harm to environment and communities, 36–7, 40–3, 46; legal action against, 44–5, 52–4

renewable resources, 211; calls to develop, 20, 25, 58–9, 123

reparations, 126, 182, 200; lack of state offering, xxv, 96

reserves, accountability for pollution impacts on/off, 43, 51, 54, 204–5; concepts of, 40, 169–70, 209; conditions on, 40, 133, 209–10, 220–1; need to leave, 210, 220–1; relocation of, 45, 50, 148–9; requests to create, 134, 176–7; service provision on/off, 10, 96, 166, 175; White Paper/Indian Act on, 10, 76–7, 84–5

residential schools, establishment and aims of, 13, 94, 193; forced attendance at, 7, 39; harm at, xx–xxi, 16, 87, 137, 196, 200; settlement agreement, xxv, 194; survivors, xx, 87, 194, 196

Rich, Charlotte, 96

Rich, Ettienne, 178

Rich, George, 173

Rich, Katie, 158, 160–1

rights, Indigenous, *see* Aboriginal rights

Roberts, Ed, 160–1

Robinson-Huron Treaty, 134, 148

Roche, Jim, 104–6, 172

Rockwood, Walter, 155

Rompkey, Bill, 112–13

Royal Commission on Aboriginal Peoples (RCAP), establishment and recommendations, 164, 166, 172–3, 192–6, 214, 218; guidance for rights harmonization/ reconciliation, xxvii, 170, 184, 203, 206–10; Indigenous leadership testimony/involvement, 15, 88, 95, 115, 170, 181; on settler colonial history/domination, 80, 193, 214

Royal Proclamation of 1763: 80, 187, 195

Royal Proclamation of Reconciliation, proposal of, 195, 208–9

Russell, Peter H., 16, 22

Russell Tribunal, 67–8

Schumacher, E.F. (*Small Is Beautiful*), 3

section 35 (Constitution Act), affirming inherent Aboriginal and Treaty rights, 70–1, 185, 208; court interpretations of, 82–6, 205, 208; harmonization of laws with, 183, 189–90, 215; Indigenous versus settler interpretations of, 71–8; right to self-government and, 62, 72–3, 165, 170, 193; refusal to acknowledge/implement, 32, 74–5, 77–8, 165, 204–5, 224

section 91.24 (Constitution Act), federal powers under, 8, 77, 84–5, 165, 189; Indian Act passage under, 8, 77–8; section 35 rights versus, 77–8, 84–6, 189

self-determination, demand for settler understanding of, xix 72, 99, 190–1, 226; Dene struggles for, xvii, 6, 14–16, 26; Innu struggles for, 89, 91–2, 165, 167–8; reconciliation and, xxvi, 207, 210, 218; settler denial of, 79, 82, 91–2, 223, 226

self-governance, Indigenous, Constitutional Conference discussions of, 71–4, 76, 205–6; Dene-Métis proposal for, 28–32; harmonizing colonial laws toward, 62, 77, 173–4, 207–8; Haudenosaunee, 187–8; as inherent/pre-existing colonization, 71, 83, 142, 170;

Innu struggles for, 126, 165–70, 173–5, 178, 183; Penner/RCAP Reports on, 185–6, 190, 192–4, 218; reconciliation as creating, xx; section 35 and, 62, 72–3, 165; settler denial of, 21, 32, 75, 80, 82–3
settler-colonial countries, 71; concept of, xix; dispossession in, 80–1, 99, 153–4
settler colonialism, assumptions/ paradigms of, 84–6, 95, 133, 137; colonialism versus, 79; cumulative impacts of, 59, 94, 137–8; dehumanization via, xix, 75, 78–9; dismantling, *see* dismantling settler colonialism; Indigenous struggles against, 103, 125, 153–4, 184
Seven Sisters (oil companies), 1, 3–4
Sharpe, Robert J., 53–4
Shaw, Devin, 81
Sheshatshiu, 152; author trips to, xix, 88–9, 171; forced Innu resettlement in, 91, 108, 117–18, 156, 163, 174; mobilizing against military flying, 91, 99, 101–5, 113; Treaty negotiations in, 171–5, 178, 181
Shkilnyk, Anastasia (*A Poison Stronger than Love*), 39
Sinclair, Murray, 194
Sittichinli, Jim, 2–3
Smith, Aileen and W. Eugene (*Minamata*), 42
social justice, xxii, 16; commitment to, 2, 26, 203
South Africa, 6, 110
sovereignty, Indigenous, colonial Crown versus, 35, 84–6, 92, 138, 206–8, 223–4; concept of, 201; as pre-existing (colonization), 8, 81, 191
Sparrow, Ronald, 84–5
Squamish Nation, 86, 214–15
status, Indian, 149; Innu negotiations on, 175–7; loss of, 7–8, 52

St. Catherine's Milling case, 8
stewardship, land, xvii; Dene rights of, xvii, 21, 25; Grassy Narrows, 46–7, 59–64; honouring of Indigenous, xx, 201, 210, 214; settler dismissiveness of, 47–8, 58, 71, 132, 214; Teme-Augama struggle for, 132–4, 140, 143, 149
sub-surface rights, 25, 61
suicide, 95; Indigenous rates of, 125, 158, 163, 221; policies to address, 205
Supreme Court of Canada, 69, 81, 215; on Aboriginal fishing rights, 83–6
apprehension of bias case, 19, 22, 24, 34; *Calder* case, 13, 33, 52, 172; Teme-Augama appeal, 135–6, 140–2, 148
Supreme Court of Ontario, Grassy Narrows lawsuit, 44, 53, 56

Task Force on Churches and Corporate Responsibility, 55
Temagami Wilderness Society; *see* Earthroots
Teme-Augama Anishnabai, Agreement in Principle (AIP), 149; Canada infringing on rights of, 137–8, 148–9; colour of right defence in trial, 143–8; Elders, 131, 141–3; forest/land stewardship struggles, 132–4, 140, 143, 149; land claims, 140, 142, 144; Ontario government versus, 133–6, 142–7, 149–50; Supreme Court of Canada appeal, 135–6, 140–2, 148
Teme-Augama territory, *see* N'Dai Menan
terra nullius, xxv, 193
Tobin, Brian, 126, 175
trapping, Indigenous, 43; constitutional/Treaty right to, 40, 46, 121; importance of land for, 47, 50, 94, 137, 213; memories of, 107–8; settler regulation/suppression of, xxviii, 39–40, 94, 154

Treaties, Aboriginal rights negotiations in, 12, 171–2, 177, 182; constitutional entrenchment of, 10, 40, 65–71, 83, 185, 190, 208; fishing/hunting/trapping rights in, 40, 46, 121, 153–4, 180–1, 195; "living tree" relationship, 73, 171, 177, 180, 182; modern, *see* modern Treaties; resource sharing/entitlements in, 12, 171–2, 178–9, 182–3, 186, 192

Treaty 3 (territory/agreement): 8, 40, 55, 60

Trudeau, Justin, xxviv, 74, 219, 223

Trudeau, Pierre, xxviv, 179; arrogance at Constitutional Conferences, 15, 67, 69, 71–6, 204; government pipeline promotion, 1–2, 23; White Paper, 9–12, 186

Truth and Reconciliation Commission, government failure to respond to recommendations, xvi, 172, 184, 199–200; report as guide for reconciliation, xxvii 194–7, 199, 203, 206–8

Tshash Petapan (New Dawn Agreement), 126–8, 172–3

Tuck, Eve, 201–3

United Nations, 212; Aboriginal rights assertions to, 67–8, 99, 177

United Nations Declaration on the Rights of Indigenous Peoples (UNDRIP), Canada's adoption/implementation of, 195, 205, 207–8, 223–4; right to free, prior, informed consent in, 126, 223

United States, energy consumption of, 1, 3, 20; low-level NATO flying experiments, 97, 103–4, 112, 114; as settler colonial country, xix, 85, 187

Upper Churchill hydro project, 97, 126–9, 173; *see also* Lower Churchill/Nalcor project

Van der Peet, Dorothy, 85–6
Vander Zalm, Bill, 75–6
Vecsey, Christopher, 47–50
Voisey's Bay, mining, 117, 126, 155; Innu IBA for, 118, 121–2, 124

Watkins, Mel, 16, 25–8
Western Constitutional Forum (WCF), 30–2
Wet'suwet'en, 81, 86
White Dog, community harm from mercury poisoning, 37, 44, 56; legal action/settlement by, 44–4, 52–4, 56, 58–9
White Paper, assimilationism beyond, 13, 76; tabling and Indigenous rejection of, 9–12, 69, 186, 204
white supremacy, politicians', 73, 82, 181; settler colonial, 6, 79, 81, 214
Wilson, Bill, 72–4, 76, 185
Wilson-Raybould, Jody, 74
Wolfe, Patrick, 196–7
Woodfibre LNG, 214–15
World Wars, Indigenous participation in, 7–8, 139–40

Yang, K. Wayne, 201–3
Yellowhead Institute, 195–6, 222
Yellowknife, author travel to, xvii, 4–5, 14, 35; National Indian Brotherhood in, 15; NEB hearings in, 24–6; OKT offices in, xxviv, 151
Yukon, 6, 18, 212; modern Treaty negotiations in, 13, 33; pipeline proposal, 1

UTP insights

Books in the Series

- John Olthuis, *On Dismantling Settler Colonialism: An Insider's Perspective on Reconciliation with Indigenous Peoples*
- Ninette Kelley, Jeffrey G. Reitz, and Michael J. Trebilcock, *Reshaping the Mosaic: Canadian Immigration Policy in the 21st Century*
- Peter MacKinnon, *Confronting Illiberalism: A Canadian Perspective*
- Aisha Ahmad (ed.), *Securing Canada's Future: Vital Insights from Women Experts*
- Ingrid Leman Stefanovic (ed.), *Conversations on Ethical Leadership: Lessons Learned from University Governance*
- Sue Winton, *Unequal Benefits: Privatization and Public Education in Canada*
- David A. Detomasi, *Profits and Power: Navigating the Politics and Geopolitics of Oil*
- Michael J. Trebilcock, *Public Inquiries: A Scholar's Engagement with the Policy-making Process*
- Andrew Green, *Picking up the Slack: Law, Institutions, and Canadian Climate Policy*
- Peter MacKinnon, *Canada in Question: Exploring Our Citizenship in the Twenty-First Century*
- Harvey P. Weingarten, *Nothing Less than Great: Reforming Canada's Universities*
- Allan C. Hutchinson, *Democracy and Constitutions: Putting Citizens First*
- Paul Nelson, *Global Development and Human Rights: The Sustainable Development Goals and Beyond*
- Peter H. Russell, *Sovereignty: The Biography of a Claim*
- Alistair Edgar, Rupinder Mangat, and Bessma Momani (eds.), *Strengthening the Canadian Armed Forces through Diversity and Inclusion*
- David B. MacDonald, *The Sleeping Giant Awakens: Genocide, Indian Residential Schools, and the Challenge of Conciliation*
- Paul W. Gooch, *Course Correction: A Map for the Distracted University*

- Paul T. Phillips, *Truth, Morality, and Meaning in History*
- Stanley R. Barrett, *The Lamb and the Tiger: From Peacekeepers to Peacewarriors in Canada*
- Peter MacKinnon, *University Commons Divided: Exploring Debate and Dissent on Campus*
- Raisa B. Deber, *Treating Health Care: How the System Works and How It Could Work Better*
- Jim Freedman, *A Conviction in Question: The First Trial at the International Criminal Court*
- Christina D. Rosan and Hamil Pearsall, *Growing a Sustainable City? The Question of Urban Agriculture*
- John Joe Schlichtman, Jason Patch, and Marc Lamont Hill, *Gentrifier*
- Robert Chernomas and Ian Hudson, *Economics in the Twenty-First Century: A Critical Perspective*
- Stephen M. Saideman, *Adapting in the Dust: Lessons Learned from Canada's War in Afghanistan*
- Michael R. Marrus, *Lessons of the Holocaust*
- Roland Paris and Taylor Owen (eds.), *The World Won't Wait: Why Canada Needs to Rethink Its International Policies*
- Bessma Momani, *Arab Dawn: Arab Youth and the Demographic Dividend They Will Bring*
- William Watson, *The Inequality Trap: Fighting Capitalism Instead of Poverty*
- Phil Ryan, *After the New Atheist Debate*
- Paul Evans, *Engaging China: Myth, Aspiration, and Strategy in Canadian Policy from Trudeau to Harper*

Printed and bound by CPI Group (UK) Ltd, Croydon, CR0 4YY
18/12/2025

14796186-0001